ARIZONA

OFF THE BEATEN PATH®

OFF THE BEATEN PATH® SERIES

EIGHTH EDITION

ARIZONA

OFF THE BEATEN PATH ®

DISCOVER YOUR FUN

REVISED AND UPDATED
BY ROGER NAYLOR

Globe
Pequot
Guilford, Connecticut

All the information in this guidebook is subject to change. We recommend that you call ahead to obtain current information before traveling.

Globe Pequot

An imprint of The Rowman & Littlefield Publishing Group, Inc.
4501 Forbes Blvd., Ste. 200
Lanham, MD 20706
www.rowman.com

Off the Beaten Path is a registered trademark of The Rowman & Littlefield Publishing Group, Inc.
Distributed by NATIONAL BOOK NETWORK

Copyright © 2010 The Rowman & Littlefield Publishing Group, Inc.
This Globe Pequot edition 2019.

Maps by Equator Graphics

All rights reserved. No part of this book may be reproduced in any form or by any electronic or mechanical means, including information storage and retrieval systems, without written permission from the publisher, except by a reviewer who may quote passages in a review.

British Library Cataloguing in Publication Information available

Library of Congress Cataloging-in-Publication Data available

ISBN 978-1-4930-4284-5 (paperback)
ISBN 978-1-4930-4285-2 (e-book)

∞™ The paper used in this publication meets the minimum requirements of American National Standard for Information Sciences—Permanence of Paper for Printed Library Materials, ANSI/NISO Z39.48-1992

This book is dedicated to those adventurers in life who seek out new experiences by taking the road less traveled.

Contents

About the Reviser

Roger Naylor spends his days rambling around the backroads of his beloved Arizona and writes about what he finds. He is the author of several books and is a member of the Arizona Tourism Hall of Fame. He lives in Cottonwood, AZ. For more information, visit www.rogernaylor.com.

Introduction

While the Grand Canyon may be the defining feature of Arizona, it only begins to hint at the scenic diversity of the state. From the red rocks of Sedona to the snow-capped peaks rising above Flagstaff, from the green farm fields of Yuma to the tall saguaros of the Sonoran Desert, from the sparkling lakes of the White Mountains to the lonely monoliths spread across the Navajo Nation, prepare to be surprised and delighted at every turn.

Veer off the interstates and you'll find hidden treasures that the Sunday travel sections often overlook. From secluded inlets on massive Lake Powell and stunning swimming holes in little-traveled regions of the Grand Canyon to an annual jousting fest in the desert and a folklore preserve tucked into a wildlife-rich canyon, Arizona holds more curiosities than any weeklong vacation itinerary could even begin to include.

Arizona is the sixth largest state so there's a lot of ground to cover. This is where you'll find the first International Dark Sky Community. Ancient archeological wonders are scattered across the landscape. Some rodeos here date back to the Old West era. Arizona is known for world-renowned birding hotspots, some of the best Mexican food this side of the border, and hiking trails galore. Bountiful sunshine is another inducement. This is where you go to revel in 70 degree winter days—unless you're skiing the snowy slopes. Feel free to take advantage of both. Arizona is where you go to ski and swim on the same day.

Far from a cultural desert, Arizona has just about any arts-related diversion visitors might wish to enjoy, including Broadway-style shows; resident symphony, ballet, and theatrical companies; and venues for rock concerts and jazz jams. Add to this a generous supply of top-notch museums—showcasing Native American heritage, contemporary fine art, lifestyles of long-gone civilizations, and the flora and fauna of the enigmatic Sonoran Desert—and you'll quickly discover that there is infinitely more here than is often believed.

Sports fans will find their nirvana in Phoenix, the nation's fifth largest city, with professional teams wearing the uniforms of nearly every league imaginable—from the NBA's Phoenix Suns and the major league's Arizona Diamondbacks to the NHL's Arizona Coyotes and the NFL's Arizona Cardinals. Fans can even root for their own home teams during spring-training exhibition games that bring the boys of summer to intimate ballparks throughout the Valley of the Sun. Longtime local favorites include the Arizona State University Sun Devils and their rivals to the south, the University of Arizona Wildcats. For an even wilder sport, visitors should check out one of the many rodeos that are staged each year, demonstrating the best skills that area cowboys have to offer!

At the end of the day, relax and unwind in some of Arizona's unique lodgings. Nowhere will you find your accommodations as diverse or—in many cases—luxurious. City slickers can relive their childhood fantasies at one of the many authentic guest ranches, and those in search of the ultimate in service and style can choose from dozens of top-rated resort hotels that offer activities ranging from their own water parks and European-style spas to horseback riding and championship golf. And if a day on the links is your idea of heaven, Arizona has a course for nearly every day of the year.

Even film buffs will find a fascinating array of locations that include working movie sets to scenic vistas that have served as studio "back lots" for decades. Wander among the landscapes that John Wayne galloped through. This is also where Princess Leia garroted Jabba the Hutt, where Curly McLain sang about the surrey with the fringe on top, where the planet was ruled by apes, where Mars launched not one but two invasions, and where swarms of piranhas munched a bunch of spring break partiers–in gory 3D no less.

Some of the destinations in this book will have you traveling on the main drag into the heart of cities and towns; others will send you down winding back roads where you'll encounter startling beauty, wide-open spaces, and a treasure trove of memory-making sights and attractions. And oh yeah—the sunsets are often lavish extravaganzas of fiery sky and dazzling light.

Elevations and Temperatures

One of the most surprising facts about Arizona is the variety of climates and landscapes. It's not all desert; it's not all lowland. In fact, the terrain ranges from 70 feet above sea level at the Colorado River south of Yuma to 12,633 feet and alpine tundra atop the San Francisco Peaks. Arizona has 27 peaks that tower above 10,000 feet. Even Phoenix is at a higher elevation than you might imagine at 1,117 feet. The ride through the center of the state is a nice surprise as it climbs from the lower deserts, up the Mogollon Rim to 7,000 feet at Flagstaff where the great plateau of the Grand Canyon and the Navajo-Hopi Reservations begins.

ARIZONA CLIMATE AT A GLANCE

Greater Phoenix Average Temperatures

Month	Highs	Lows	Month	Highs	Lows
January	67	46	July	106	83
February	71	49	August	104	83
March	77	53	September	100	77
April	85	60	October	89	65
May	95	69	November	76	53
June	104	78	December	66	45

Average annual days of sunshine: 299

Note: Temperatures in degrees Fahrenheit.

Tucson Average Temperatures

Month	Highs	Lows	Month	Highs	Lows
January	66	42	July	101	76
February	70	45	August	99	75
March	75	49	September	95	71
April	82	54	October	85	60
May	91	63	November	74	48
June	100	72	December	66	42

Average annual days of sunshine: 286

Flagstaff Average Temperatures

Month	Highs	Lows	Month	Highs	Lows
January	43	11	July	81	46
February	45	14	August	78	46
March	50	20	September	73	37
April	58	25	October	63	27
May	67	30	November	52	18
June	77	36	December	43	11

Average annual days of sunshine: 264

Average annual precipitation: 23.14 inches

Average annual snowfall: 77 inches

The Four Corners: Arizona as Part of a Southwest Itinerary

In so many ways Arizona is the heart of the Southwest. It is home to more Indian tribes than any other state in the union, and it is bordered by several major national parks, monuments, and recreation areas. Traveling from New Mexico in the east, you can develop an itinerary that might include several national monuments and national historic parks (El Morro and El Malpais between Albuquerque and Gallup, Gila Cliff Dwellings west of Truth or Consequences, White Sands near Las Cruces, or Aztec Ruins and Chaco Culture near Farmington in the northwest corner). In western Colorado you can visit Curacanti National Recreation Area and Black Canyon of the Gunnison National Park between Montrose and Gunnison, then continue through the western Colorado ski country to Durango and visit Mesa Verde National Park and Canyons of the Ancients National Monument near Four Corners. In southern Utah you'll find the beginning of the extensive chain of national parks, monuments, and recreation areas that stretches

FOR MORE INFORMATION ABOUT ARIZONA

**Arizona Office of Tourism
(Administration Office)**
100 N. 7th Ave., Ste. 400
Phoenix, AZ 85007
(602) 364-3700
or (866) 275-5816
visitarizona.com

Phoenix Visitor Information Center
125 N. 2nd St., Ste. 120
Phoenix, AZ 85004
(602) 254-6500
or (877) 225-5749
visitphoenix.com

**Flagstaff Convention and Visitors
Bureau**
One E. Rte. 66
Flagstaff, AZ 86001
(928) 213-2951
or (800) 379-0065
flagstaffarizona.org

**Tucson Visitor Center and
Administration Offices**
811 N. Euclid Ave.
Tucson, AZ 85719
(800) 638-8350
visittucson.org

WEBSITES
**Official site of the Arizona Office of
Tourism:** visitarizona.com

Arizona Bureau of Land Management:
blm.gov/arizona

Arizona Game & Fish: azgfd.com

Arizona Department of Commerce:
azcommerce.com

Arizona Department of Transportation:
azdot.gov

Arizona Highways **magazine:**
arizonahighways.com

Arizona Republic **newspaper:**
azcentral.com

Arizona State Parks and Trails:
azstateparks.com

US Fish and Wildlife Services: fws
.gov/southwest

from Utah through northern Arizona to southern Nevada and includes Arches, Canyonlands, Capitol Reef, Glen Canyon/Lake Powell, Grand Canyon National Park, and Lake Mead/Hoover Dam; also in southern Utah are Zion and Bryce Canyon national parks. In southern Nevada, adjacent to Lake Mead, you'll find the popular Red Rock Canyon and Valley of Fire State Park. Finally, to the west in California are the Joshua Tree and Death Valley National Parks, and the Mohave National Preserve and Imperial Sand Dunes Recreation Area.

NEW MEXICO

Navajo and Zuni Reservations (both are partly in New Mexico and partly in Arizona)
Bisti/De-Na-Zin Wilderness Area

El Morro National Monument
El Malpais National Monument
Gila Cliff Dwellings National Monument
Chaco Culture National Historic Park
Aztec Ruins National Monument
White Sands National Monument

COLORADO

Curecanti National Recreation Area
Black Canyon of the Gunnison National Park
Canyons of the Ancients National Monument
Mesa Verde National Park

UTAH

Arches National Park
Canyonlands National Park
Capitol Reef National Park
Natural Bridges National Monument
Glen Canyon National Recreation Area
Bryce Canyon National Park
Zion National Park

NEVADA

Red Rock Canyon National Conservation Area
Valley of Fire State Park
Lake Mead National Recreation Area

CALIFORNIA

Joshua Tree National Park
Mojave National Preserve
Death Valley National Park
Imperial Sand Dunes Recreation Area

Fast Facts About the Grand Canyon State

State gem: Turquoise
State fossil: Petrified wood
State mammal: Ringtail
State reptile: Arizona ridge-nosed rattlesnake
State fish: Apache trout

State amphibian: Arizona tree frog
State butterfly: Two-tailed swallowtail
State song: The "Arizona March Song"
State colors: Blue and gold
State tree: Paloverde
State bird: Cactus wren
State flower: Saguaro cactus blossom
State motto: *Ditat Deus* (God Enriches)
Official state neckwear (yes, there really is one): Bolo tie
Arizona's largest newspaper: *The Arizona Republic*, Phoenix

Dining and Lodging Pricing Key

Arizona dining and lodging vary greatly throughout the state and change seasonally.

PLACES TO EAT

The price code reflects the average price of a dinner entrée (excluding cocktails, wine, appetizers, desserts, tax and tip). You can usually expect to pay less for lunch and/or breakfast, when applicable.

Up to $12 $

$13 to $25 $$

$26 and up $$$

PLACES TO STAY

The price code reflects the average cost of a double-occupancy room during the high season (not including tax or extras). Always ask if any special discounts are available.

Up to $100 $

$101 to $200 $$

$201 and up $$$

Northern Arizona

Flagstaff Area

Those who consider Arizona as nothing but a desert state have never ventured to the northlands. In just a short drive, travelers leave the lower deserts behind, climbing in elevation to high green meadows and expansive forests. Sitting at 7,000 feet above sea level, along the base of the towering San Francisco Peaks is the alpine community of *Flagstaff.* This is the anchor of Northern Arizona, a cool escape during summer heat and a snowy wonderland in winter months. The community acquired its name following a flag-raising ceremony marking the nation's centennial. Settlers chose a tall pine, trimmed its branches, and attached a flag to the top.

The city of 72,000 is located in Coconino County, the second largest county in the United States. Over the years "Flag" (as it's known to Arizonans) has been a logging and ranching community and an important railroad stop. Check out the historic, redbrick Santa Fe train depot on Historic Route 66 in the middle of town, where the *Flagstaff Visitor Center* (928-213-2951 or 800-379-0065; flagstaffarizona.org) provides a great starting point for exploration in the area.

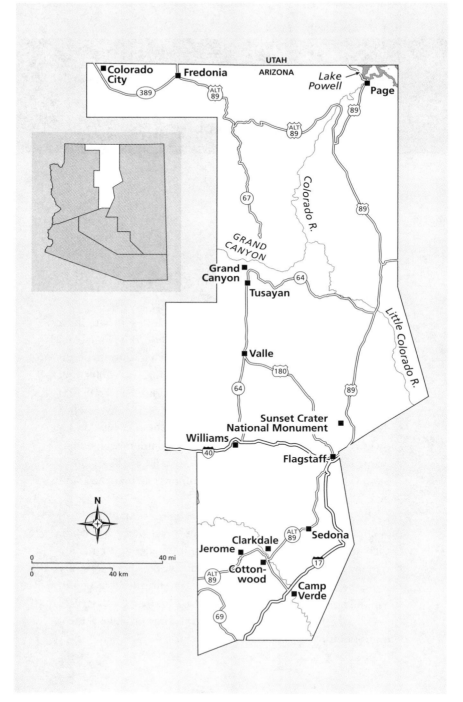

Colorado City
Fredonia
UTAH
ARIZONA
Lake Powell
Page
389
ALT 89
89
ALT 89
67
89
Colorado R.
GRAND CANYON
Grand Canyon
Tusayan
64
Little Colorado R.
Valle
180
64
89
Sunset Crater National Monument
Williams
40
Flagstaff
N
Clarkdale
ALT 89
Sedona
Jerome
0   40 mi
0   40 km
Cotton-wood
ALT 89
17
Camp Verde
69

AUTHOR'S FAVORITES IN NORTHERN ARIZONA

Antelope Canyon

El Tovar Lodge

Glen Canyon National Recreation Area

Grand Canyon National Park— North Rim

Jerome Art Walk

Museum of Northern Arizona

Oak Creek Canyon

Pink Jeep Tours

Verde Canyon Railroad

Wupatki National Monument

Because of the elevation, the forests around Flagstaff are lush with ponderosa pine (the largest spread of ponderosa pine in the world, in fact, sprouts in this area), aspen, and brilliantly colored wildflowers. Surrounded by gorgeous scenery, including the volcanic remains of the 12,000-foot San Francisco Peaks, it has preserved many of its historic sites and much of its architecture and thus retains a small-town feel. Still, it has modern amenities that make it comfortable and convenient for residents and visitors alike. The main street, Milton Road, is lined with restaurants (both national chains and local mom-and-pop places), motels, hotels, and shopping centers; it also passes right by Northern Arizona University (NAU).

If you came to Flag for the mountains, take a fast route into the high country. US 180 bears north from downtown toward all sorts of recreational opportunities, with a couple of educational stops along the way. Look for the ***Pioneer Museum*** (928-774-6272; arizonahistoricalsociety.org), and the Museum of Northern Arizona. The Pioneer Museum, which is run by the Arizona Historical Society and located in the former 1908 Coconino County Hospital, has an impressive collection of photographs from Flagstaff's early days. This collection includes early twentieth-century photos and equipment from the Kolb brothers, who became famous for capturing the splendor of the Grand Canyon. Also located on the grounds are antique farming machines, an early motorized fire engine, and an original 1880s cabin. Hours vary seasonally. Admission.

arizonatrivia

Flagstaff garnered the honor as the world's first "International Dark Sky City" by the International Dark Sky Association.

FEBRUARY

Sedona International Film Festival
Sedona
(928) 282-1177
sedonafilmfestival.com
International independent cinema, documentary, and animation, panel discussions featuring leading film professionals.

Chocolate Lovers' Special
Clarkdale
(800) 582-7245
verdecanyonrr.com
A romantic Valentine celebration aboard a vintage excursion train with wines and beverages, gourmet chocolate, and flowing chocolate fountains along with plated fruit slices and marshmallows.

MARCH

Verde River Runoff
Camp Verde
(928) 641-6013
verderiver.org
This kayak, canoe, and standup boarder race draws novices and seasoned paddlers alike as it helps raise funds to protect the endangered Verde River.

APRIL

Verde Valley Birding & Nature Festival
Cottonwood
(928) 641-6013
verderiver.org
Celebrate nature with workshops and field trips to birding hot spots in the Verde Valley and at Dead Horse Ranch State Park. Other activities include geology trips, butterfly and plant walks, and nature photography exhibits.

MAY

Jerome Home and Building Tour
Jerome
(928) 634-2900
jeromechamber.com
Take a tour of historic homes and public buildings from Victorians to renovated miner's shacks.

Zuni Festival of Arts and Culture
Flagstaff
(928) 774-5213
musnaz.org
Zuni artists, dancers, and flute players perform at this festival at the Museum of Northern Arizona in partnership with the A:shiwi A:wan Museum and Heritage Center.

JUNE

Flag Wool and Fiber Festival
Flagstaff
flagwool.com
Sheep shearing, spinning and weaving demonstrations, and livestock competition at the Pioneer Museum.

Flagstaff Pro Rodeo
Flagstaff
(928) 707-1119
flagstaffrodeo.com
PRCA approved rodeo featuring bull riding, bareback riding, team roping, steer wrestling, barrel racing, and tie-down roping.

JULY

Arizona Highland Celtic Festival
Flagstaff
(928) 556-3161
nachs.info
Celtic celebration honoring the people of Brittany, Cornwall, Scotland, and Wales.

Hopi Festival of Arts and Culture
Flagstaff
(928) 774-5213musnaz.orgHopi artists, demonstrations, tribal dances, storytelling, and children's activities at the Museum of Northern Arizona.

AUGUST

Cool Country Cruise-In
Williams
(928) 635-4061
experiencewilliams.com
1950s-style fun with a classic car show lining Historic Route 66, live music, and more.

Navajo Festival of Arts and Culture
Flagstaff
(928) 774-5213
musnaz.org
Navajo artists, demonstrations, storytellers, hoop dancing, and music at the Museum of Northern Arizona.

Grand Canyon Music Festival
Grand Canyon National Park South Rim
(928) 638-9215
grandcanyonmusicfest.org
A series of concerts, jazz to classical, performed at Shrine of the Ages Auditorium, by musicians from all over the country.

SEPTEMBER

Slide Rock Fall Festival
Oak Creek
(928) 282-3034
azstateparks.com
Pick apples from an orchard planted in 1912, birding, history tours, arts and crafts, and kids' games at Slide Rock State Park.

Coconino County Fair
Flagstaff
(928) 679-8000
coconinocountyfair.com
Northern Arizona's largest county fair features educational exhibits, livestock, live entertainment, a demolition derby, and carnival at the Fort Tuthill Coconino County Fairgrounds.

Festival of Science
Flagstaff
scifest.org
Promotes science awareness and enthusiasm through field trips, exhibits, and lectures.

Fiesta del Tlaquepaque
Sedona
(928) 282-4838
tlaq.com
Mexican-style celebration: piñatas, mariachi bands, folklorico dance groups, and flamenco/classical guitarists.

Verde River Day
Cottonwood
(928) 634-5283
verderiverday.com
This environmental event showcases the importance of the Verde River with environmental exhibits, hands-on activities, fishing, canoeing, nature walks, and live entertainment at Dead Horse Ranch State Park.

OCTOBER

Celebraciónes de la Gente
Flagstaff
(928) 774-5213
musnaz.org
Diá de los Muertos (Day of the Dead) celebration at the Museum of Northern Arizona. Hispanic artists, Latin music, Aztec fire dancing, storytelling, mariachis, and ballet folklorico performances.

Fort Verde Days
Camp Verde
(928) 567-3275
azstateparks.com
March to the beat of a different drum and learn about Arizona's military history with flag ceremonies, living history presentations, cavalry drills, and a vintage baseball game.

TOP ANNUAL EVENTS IN NORTHERN ARIZONA (CONT.)

NOVEMBER

Page Lake Powell Balloon Regatta
Page
(928) 645-2741
lakepowellballoonregatta.com
Enjoy the spectacle of 60 hot air balloons wafting above the azure waters of the lake, above the sandstone cliffs. There's also a street fair, beer garden, and Saturday night balloon glow.

Polar Express
Williams
(800) THE-TRAIN thetrain.com
Take a journey to the "North Pole" on this special evening train ride held through Dec. The magical adventure takes its cue from the classic children's book *The Polar Express* by Chris Van Allsburg and includes hot chocolate, cookies, caroling, storytelling, and a visit from Santa Claus.

Parade of Lights
Williams
(928) 635-4061
experiencewilliams.com
Carolers, luminaries, fine-arts show, shopping, and hot chocolate.

DECEMBER

Great Pinecone Drop
Flagstaff
(928) 779-1919
weatherfordhotel.com
A giant lighted pinecone drops from the top of the Weatherford Hotel in downtown Flagstaff rings in the New Year. It drops first at 10 p.m. on New Year's Eve to coordinate with the Times Square festivities, then again at midnight.

Just up the road, the **Museum of Northern Arizona** (928-774-5213; musnaz.org) first opened in 1928. The exhibits at the museum encompass the biology, geology, anthropology, and fine arts of both northern Arizona and the Four Corners region. The museum has displays ranging from a life-size statue of a Dilophosaurus (a carnivorous dinosaur whose remains are found only in this region), an anthropology exhibit that traces the region's history back 12,000 years, and fine arts made by Zuni, Hopi, and Navajo Indians. Open Mon through Sat 10 a.m. to 5 p.m., and Sun noon to 5 p.m.

Just beyond the Museum of Northern Arizona you can take **Schultz Pass Road,** also known as Forest Road 420. The scenic drive winds through the national forest offering lovely mountain views. Also popular with bikers, the gravel road is suitable for sedans in dry weather. It is located 2 miles north of Flagstaff off US 180 and is open from Apr through Nov.

US 180 also takes you to the turnoff for the **Arizona Snowbowl** (928-779-1951; snowbowl.ski.com), 7 miles from downtown. The ski resort offers 55 trails for skiers and snowboarders of all abilities, and includes the longest vertical drop in Arizona. Snowbowl receives an average of 260 inches of snow per year, and supplemental snow making equipment makes for a long season. Ski rentals and repairs are available, and you can sign up for beginner or intermediate lessons (also a children's ski school, beginning at age four, runs throughout the season). There are two places where you can park yourself at the end of a long day of schussing—***Hart Prairie Lodge*** and ***Agassiz Lodge,*** both of which offer ski and snowboard rentals, restaurants, and retail shops.

In the summer Flagstaff's moderate temperature (the average high is eighty degrees) draws many Arizonans who want to escape the heat. The surrounding forest area offers premier hiking and camping opportunities. The city even has an urban trails system that allows visitors and residents to access forest areas, canyons, and national monuments. The Flagstaff Visitor Center has specific maps of these trails, which include treks to the summit of Humphreys Peak (the tallest mountain in Arizona at 12,633 feet) and to many scenic aspen groves and alpine meadows in the Coconino National Forest.

Nature buffs will especially enjoy exploring the wide-open spaces at the ***Hart Prairie Preserve*** (928-779-6129; nature.org). Located 14 miles north of Flagstaff, this 245-acre preserve protects such endangered plants as the delicate bloomer stock and the rare Bebb's willow trees. The preserve is open by appointment only May through Sept.

Nearby, a mile-long lava tube cave offers an opportunity to explore a volcanic vent that was created from a lava flow more than 700,000 years ago. Notice the stone icicles hanging from the ceiling and the ripples in the rock from the path of the molten lava. The temperature stays cool year-round, so be sure to wear warm clothes and sturdy shoes. Also, bring several light sources to explore the mile-long ***Lava River Cave.*** The cave is located about 14 miles north of Flagstaff. Take US 180 to FR 245 at milepost 230. Turn west and drive 3 miles to FR 171. Turn south and drive 1 mile to where FR 171B ends at Lava River Cave. For more information contact the Flagstaff Ranger Station (928-526-0866; fs.usda.gov/coconino).

The ***Lowell Observatory,*** located at the top of Mars Hill, was built by astronomer Percival Lowell, a Mars buff who published a book about that planet's canals. Lowell erroneously believed there was life on the Angry Red Planet. He was right on the mark, however, when he predicted that a ninth planet—Planet X—would be discovered. In 1930, fourteen years after Lowell's death, astronomy assistant Clyde Tombaugh found the heavenly body, now known as Pluto, while studying photographic plates. Visitors to the observatory can hear the full story at the visitor center (928-774-3358; lowell.edu). The observatory is open Mon through Sat from 10 a.m. to 10 p.m., and Sun from 10 a.m. to 5 p.m. Guided tours are given during the day and evening programs are conducted except for Sundays. Admission.

All year round, downtown Flagstaff bustles with activity. It supports an eclectic mix of college students, ski bums, cowboys, hikers, mountain bikers, international travelers, and desert refugees. Much of the Phoenix population heads to Flag to cool off in the summer and to zip down snowy slopes in winter. Shops, eateries and bars are packed into historic buildings spread across a few walkable blocks. The adjacent campus of NAU adds an artistic free-spirited vibe to the scene. You'll find everything from outdoor outfitters to galleries selling exquisite Native American artwork. Heritage Square serves as a town center and is the site of concerts, events and even summertime movies.

Downtown also nourishes a thriving craft brewing scene. The ***Beaver Street Brewery*** (11 S. Beaver St.; 928-779-0079; beaverstreetbrewery.com) features an extensive menu that includes everything from salads and sandwiches to wood-fired gourmet pizzas. Killer desserts include a chocolate bread pudding and a huge fruit cobbler. $$. ***Flagstaff Brewing Company*** (16 E. Rte. 66; 928-773-1442; flagbrew.com) offers a casual pub atmosphere that spills onto a nice patio, where diners enjoy burgers and sandwiches paired with their handcrafted beers. $$.

As Flag's main drag, ***Historic Route 66*** cuts through downtown, running parallel to the railroad tracks that still rattle with trains throughout the day. While the visitor center occupies one half of the 1926 depot, a Tudor Revival brick building with cross-gabled roof, the other end still serves as the Amtrak station. The Southside District stretches south from the railroad tracks and was once known for a handful of dive bars but has undergone a renaissance. It's now packed with boutiques, galleries and great restaurants.

Numerous motels, ski lodges, and bed-and-breakfast inns provide accommodations in and around Flagstaff. Just about every moderately priced national chain has a presence in Flagstaff, but ***The Inn at 410*** (410 N. Leroux St.; 928-774-0088 or 800-774-2008; inn410.com) is one of the best lodging choices in town. Close to the visitor center, this 1907 Craftsman-style home has 10 guest rooms and suites. Many have fireplaces and some offer Jacuzzi tubs. Rates include a homemade breakfast in the dining room. $$$.

For another historic Craftsman-style home, stop by the ***Riordan Mansion State Historic Park*** (409 Riordan Rd.; 928-779-4395; azstateparks.com). Tucked away behind the Target store on Milton Road, this massive, multistory log cabin was built in 1904 for Timothy and Michael Riordan, owners of the Arizona Lumber & Timber Company. The building's architect was none other than Charles Whittlesey, designer of the El Tovar Hotel at the South Rim of the Grand Canyon as well as Old Faithful Lodge at Yellowstone. State Park rangers give guided tours of the mansion. Hours vary seasonally. Guided tours are offered on the hour, and can be concluded with self-guided tours of the grounds. During December the mansion is decked out in all of its Victorian holiday finery. Admission. Reservations are recommended.

Before leaving the Flagstaff area, make sure to stop by **Walnut Canyon National Monument** (928-526-3367; nps.gov/waca), which comprises more than 300 rooms built into limestone cliffs as part of a prehistoric Sinaguan pueblo. The visitor center has displays of pottery and artifacts recovered from the area. The monument can be reached by traveling east on I-40 about 7 miles. Admission is good for seven days.

South of Flagstaff, Plateau Country extends from the San Francisco Peaks to the rolling highlands, filled with scattered prairies and lakes including **Mormon Lake.** Recreational activities include boating, fishing, camping, wildlife watching, hiking, and cross-country skiing. **Plateau Lakes Scenic Drive,** open Apr through Oct, follows Forest Hwy. 3 (Lake Mary Road) about 33 miles to FR 213. Turn west and drive 15 miles on FR 213 to I-17. For more information contact the Flagstaff Ranger Station (5075 N. US 89; 928-526-0866; fs.usda.gov/coconino) in Flagstaff.

During the winter months, the **Mormon Lake Ski Touring Center** offers groomed cross-country skiing trails along the lower slopes of Mormon Mountain. To reach the Mormon Lake Ski Touring Center, drive south from Flagstaff 20 miles on Forest Hwy. 3 (Lake Mary Road) to the FR 90 intersection. Turn west on FR 90 and drive 8 miles to the Mormon Lake Village. The nearby **Mormon Lake Lodge** (928-354-2227; mormonlakelodge.com) has a restaurant, and offers cabin rentals, ski rentals, and ski school.

Many visitors to Flagstaff make Grand Canyon's South Rim their next stop. An excellent way to see this natural wonder is to take I-40 west and drive about 30 miles to the town of **Williams** (928-635-4061; experiencewilliams.com), which is named for William Sherley "Old Bill" Williams, a famous trapper and Arizona mountain man. One of the first sights you'll encounter is **Bearizona** (928-635-2289; bearizona.com), just off I-40 at exit 165. The drive-through wildlife park gives visitors a chance to see black bears, bison, wolves and a host of other critters relaxing in the pine shade. Pilot your own vehicle or hop aboard the Wild Ride Bus Tour that runs several times each day. The Fort Bearizona section can be explored on foot. Admission.

This tiny Main Street locale was the last Historic Route 66 town to be bypassed by the completion of I-40 in 1984, and with its old-fashioned street lamps and century-old brick storefronts, it offers visitors a trip back in time. For a bite to eat, drop by **Rod's Steakhouse** (928-635-2671; rods-steakhouse .com), a Historic Route 66 landmark with a steer-shaped sign on the roof. Rod's has steaks, prime rib, and seafood. $$.

For a blast to the past, travel a few more blocks west on Historic Route 66 to **Twisters** (928-635-0266; route66place.com). The 1950s soda fountain serves up hamburgers and hot dogs as well as good old-fashioned sundaes, floats, and phosphates. $. An adjoining gift shop adds to the experience with a wide selection of Historic Route 66 merchandise, classic Coca-Cola memorabilia, and fanciful items celebrating the careers of such celluloid characters as Betty Boop, James Dean, and Marilyn Monroe.

For outdoor adventure, head out of town and check out one of the four nearby lakes—**Dogtown, White Horse, Cataract,** and **Kaibab Lakes.** The small lakes have some fine fishing and make a great backdrop for camping, hiking, and wildlife watching in **Kaibab National Forest.** For more information stop by the Williams Ranger District (200 W. Railroad Ave.; 928-635-1418; fs.usda .gov/kaibab). This is also the same building housing the Williams Visitor Center.

If camping isn't your style, you can't go wrong with a stay at the **Sheridan House Inn** (460 E. Sheridan Ave.; 928-635-8991; grandcanyonbedandbreakfast .com). This cozy inn is nestled among two acres of pines on a hillside overlooking town. The romantic bed-and-breakfast offers nice-size bedrooms, and a child-free environment. A complementary bottle of wine awaits guests who book at least a two-night stay. Breakfast is always a grand affair and the owners enjoy helping guests plan their Grand Canyon getaways. $$$.

Williams is also the home of the **Grand Canyon Railway** (800-843-8724; thetrain.com). Initially built both for passengers and to serve area mines, the railway carried its first passengers to the Grand Canyon in 1901. Over time it transported US presidents as well as other dignitaries and celebrities to see one of the world's most famous attractions.

Unfortunately the train couldn't compete with America's love affair with the automobile, and in 1968 it carried its last passengers. The defunct railroad was purchased in 1989 by Max Biegert, who restored not only the tracks, the engines, and the cars, but also the **Grand Canyon Railway Hotel** (800-843-8724; thetrain.com), which now serves as the railway's depot as well as a museum and gift shop.

Using historic diesel (and on special days, steam) engines, the train not only takes passengers through 65 miles of glorious Arizona territory (which is especially spectacular when it's wearing a snowy winter mantle), but it also takes them back in time. There are six classes of service, including an observation dome. The end car, which has an observation platform, actually uses upholstered chairs and sofas. Entertainers perform traditional and original music about life and love on the frontier. If you take this route to the canyon, be prepared for some excitement—it's not unusual for a "train robbery" to take place, staged by bandits on horseback.

Beverages and snacks are served during the trip, which begins in Williams at 9:30 a.m. (be at the depot between 8:30 and 9 a.m.) and arrives at the Grand

Canyon's South Rim at 11:45 a.m. Passengers debark at the canyon's historic depot and can tour the area's numerous attractions before the train pulls out at 3:30 p.m. for the trek back to Williams. You will return by 5:45 p.m. Admission.

Besides being an easy and entertaining way to see the canyon, the train helps to cut down on pollution from the nearly 100,000 cars yearly that—without the railroad—would otherwise all be driven to the scenic wonder.

The approximately three-hour layover at the canyon gives you plenty of time to see El Tovar Hotel, Lookout Studio, Bright Angel Lodge, Hopi House, and the other attractions in the immediate area. If you wish to stay longer—especially if you want to hike or take a mule ride in the canyon—you can book a return at a different date and stay at one of the lodges within the park.

Grand Canyon National Park: South Rim

Named a national park by President Woodrow Wilson in 1919, **Grand Canyon National Park** (928-638-7888; nps.gov/grca) remains the crown jewel of Arizona's tourism offerings. Drawing 6 million visitors a year, this natural wonder is a jaw-dropper no matter how many times you peer over its edge. Each time of day and each season brings a distinct palette of hues to the canyon, providing its own unique panorama. A word of caution though: There is often no barrier between visitors and the abyss. Unfortunately, it's not at all unusual for a hapless tourist to discover the laws of gravity a little too late. Enjoy the view, but respect the potential danger that exists—particularly for the careless. The entrance fee to the national park is good for 7 days.

Approximately 90 percent of the visitors heading to **Grand Canyon** come to the **South Rim.** It's more accessible and open all year, which can also lead

Grand Canyon Fun Facts

Age: 6-7 million years old

Depth: North Rim inner canyon—5,700 feet; South Rim inner canyon—4,500 feet

Width: 10 miles average

Length: 277 miles

Area: 1,904 square miles

Elevation: North Rim—8,200 feet; South Rim—7,000 feet

Visitors: 6 million per year

to lines at the entrance station, especially during the busy spring and summer season. If it will fit your itinerary, try to plan your trip during the slower fall and winter months. Approaching from the south, the town of **Tusayan** (844-638-2901; grandcanyoncvb.org) sits just outside the park entrance. Along with the hotels, restaurants, shops and service stations, Tusayan also operates a free shuttle from March through September. You can purchase a park entrance pass at several businesses in town and glide past some of the traffic.

Another option is to skip the main entrance on AZ 64/US 180 approached from Williams or Flagstaff. You can travel an off-the-beaten-path route by entering the east entrance. It means driving north from Flag on US 89 to Cameron, then turning west on AZ 64 toward the park. While in **Cameron,** stop at the **Cameron Trading Post** (928-679-2231 or 800-338-7385; camerontradingpost .com), where you can shop for everything from Native American artifacts and artwork to more run-of-the-mill souvenirs.

Entering the east entrance of the Grand Canyon at **Desert View,** visitors will find an array of services including general store, deli, gift shop, ice cream parlor, and campground. Of course, the most eye-catching structure is perched on the rim, a sharp vertical note of weathered stone. The **Watchtower** was designed by Mary Jane Colter (who also was the architect for the Hopi House, Bright Angel Lodge and several other Grand Canyon buildings). Built in 1932, the Watchtower is done in the style of ancient people and is the highest viewpoint on the South Rim. Hopi artist Fred Kabotie painted the wall murals inside. Visitors can climb several flights of stairs to the top of the 70-foot tower, where you will find fabulous views of Painted Desert and the Vermilion Cliffs in the distance and an imposing stretch of the Colorado River far below. When you're finally done savoring the remarkable vistas, continue traveling on the 25-mile **Desert View Drive** as it snakes its way along the rim. Don't plan on making especially good time. Several designated overlooks entice you to pull over. Each viewpoint provides a different perspective of the terraced cliffs and colorful strata of the inner canyon. From **Lipan Point,** you may be able to watch rafts plunge through rowdy Hance Rapid on the Colorado River.

arizonatrivia

Explorer John Wesley Powell was a brave soul, becoming the first man to successfully navigate the Colorado River through the Grand Canyon in 1869—despite the fact he lost an arm in the Civil War.

Other highlights along the Desert View Drive are the remains of an Ancestral Puebloan dwelling at the **Tusayan Ruin and Museum,** the lovely **Buggeln** picnic area, and **Moran Point,** where three main rock groups are clearly visible.

The Desert View Drive ends at **Grand Canyon Visitor Center,** an expansive hub for information, bike rentals, coffee, snacks, exhibits, gift shop, and bookstore. Whether you're approaching from the main or east entrance, plan on stopping here. If you'd prefer to let someone else do the driving, park here and board one of the free shuttle buses that loops through **Grand Canyon Village** and to a variety of scenic overlooks.

There are several lodging options available at the South Rim in Grand Canyon Village. **El Tovar** (928-638-2631 or 888-297-2757; grandcanyonlodges .com) is the hotel of choice here. This 1905 hotel, named for a Spanish explorer who personally never laid eyes on the canyon, is elegant yet has an undeniable frontier simplicity and ruggedness that might make you remember the Scout lodges of your childhood. $$$. The lobby and common areas are open to sightseeing tourists, and the hotel's dining room serves southwestern cuisine, fresh seafood, and specialty desserts. The restaurant is often booked solid, so reservations are recommended and can be made 90 days in advance. $$.

Another favorite is the **Bright Angel Lodge** (928-638-2631 or 888-297-2757; grandcanyonlodges.com), designed by famed architect Mary Colter. The 1935 log-and-stone structure, which sits within a few yards of the canyon rim, offers both motel-style rooms or cabins. $$. The **Harvey House Café** serves family-style meals all day whereas the **Arizona Room** serves lunch and dinner with a menu focused on local and sustainable dishes. Dinner reservations can be made up to 30 days in advance. $$.

When you're ready to walk off your meal, check out **Lookout Studio,** which sells everything from fossil specimens (not from the park, which is protected) to books and videos about the area. At the rear of the studio, visitors can step out onto a balcony that offers a great view and a good photo opportunity. Another popular gift shop is the **Hopi House** (928-638-2631), a National Historic Landmark constructed in 1904 to look like an adobe-block Hopi village.

Don't miss the **Kolb Studio,** a sprawling structure clinging to the canyon wall near the head of the Bright Angel Trail. It served as home and studio to Ellsworth and Emery Kolb, pioneering photographers of Grand Canyon. The brothers got their start photographing mule riders as they would descend into the canyon. After snapping the photo, one of the Kolbs would then sprint down the trail past the mule string, down the switchbacks, traveling 4.6 miles to the oasis of Indian Garden, where a small stream of fresh water flowed. They had a darkroom there and would develop the photo, then turn around and climb the 4.6 miles out of the canyon—9.2 miles total—and be standing at the trailhead with the souvenir photograph for sale when the mule riders emerged. The brothers later became the 26th and 27th men to successfully raft the Colorado River through Grand Canyon. And they shot a motion picture of the journey, which they began showing at the studio in 1915. Although Ellsworth left in the 1920s to chase other adventures, Emery stayed put and continued to photograph mule riders (although he did stop his canyon sprints after a few years), and dignitaries, and even raised a family. He died in 1976, the last of the Grand Canyon pioneers. Today, the studio has been restored and serves as a retail shop and art gallery. Tours of the private residence are occasionally conducted.

If you'd rather hike than shop, you'll have several options. The Rim Trail serves as the main artery through the Village and beyond. The 13-mile route is level and mostly paved as it stretches along the rim from the South Kaibab Trail all the way to Hermits Rest. The views never stop, and away from the hubbub of the commercial district it becomes easy to form a personal connection to this big hole in the ground. To dip your toes into the abyss, the **_Bright Angel Trail_** is one of the most popular hiking trails in the world. You should consider yourself warned: It's a lot easier hiking down the steep switchbacks than climbing back up! This hike should only be attempted if you're wearing appropriate hiking shoes and carrying enough water and snacks. The park rangers like to remind folks that hiking into the canyon is optional, but hiking out is mandatory. For a slightly less crowded and even more scenic experience, take a saunter down the **_South Kaibab Trail_**, east of the Village. Most trails into the canyon follow a natural fault formed in the rock layers. But the south Kaibab chases a ridgeline, so after a few cliff-hugging switchbacks it bursts into the open with views up and down the gorge. There is a broad plateau and vault toilet at Cedar Ridge, 1.5 miles from the trailhead. This 3-mile round-trip hike makes a good outing for reasonably fit and prepared visitors.

For the adventure of a lifetime, you might consider spending the night at the bottom. Nestled along the banks of Bright Angel Creek on the north side of the Colorado River, **_Phantom Ranch_** (888-297-2757; grandcanyonlodges.com) is a shady oasis. Designed by Mary Colter in the 1920s, this collection of rustic cabins is spread among the trees. The cabins vary in size and can sleep 2 to 10 people, and are equipped with bedding and a cold-water sink. There are also dormitories for men and women.

arizonatrivia

Summertime temperatures on the South Rim range from fifty to eighty degrees Fahrenheit; in the canyon on the Colorado River 5,000 feet below, they can climb higher than one hundred degrees Fahrenheit.

Each dorm has 5 bunk beds, a shower and shared bath. Breakfast and dinner are served up family-style in the mess hall–style restaurant. All Phantom Ranch

A Scenic Jaunt

You can take a scenic horseback trail ride up to the East Rim from **Apache Stables** in Tusayan (928-638-2891; apachestables.com). Sign up for a one-hour or two-hour ride taking you through Kaibab National Forest. One of the best times to make this trek is in the morning when the sun is rising over the canyon and the colors are deep and vibrant.

reservations, for meals and bed space must be made in advance by entering a lottery system.

There are established backcountry campgrounds in the canyon and numerous backcountry campsites. Call 928-638-7875 for information. Permit requests can be downloaded from the park website nps.gov/grca. By the way, you can actually post mail from down here—it will be stamped with the postmark "Delivered by Mule from the Bottom of the Canyon."

Another rim drive extends west from Grand Canyon Village. **Hermit Road** is closed to private auto traffic from Mar through Nov and is accessed only by a free shuttle bus. If you go off-season, you can drive the historic roadway, which features nine overlooks along the 7-mile drive. Some of the

arizonatrivia

Only one Indian tribe occupies the bottom of the Grand Canyon—the Havasupai tribe.

best scenery can be seen at **The Abyss,** which reveals a 3,000-foot cliff to the Tonto Platform and a few isolated sandstone columns. Another favorite on Hermit Road is **Hopi Point,** with its wide vistas making it a popular sunrise and sunset viewing spot. The road ends at Hermits Rest, built by Mary Colter in 1914 to resemble an old miner's cabin. This is the westernmost viewpoint on the South Rim and the trailhead for **Hermit Trail**—a wickedly steep and rugged trail leading into the inner canyon.

The mules of Grand Canyon are almost as iconic as the rocky formations. The canyon is well known for its mule trips, which take riders along the canyon trails. The **World Famous Mule Rides** (888-297-2757; grandcanyonlodges .com) are offered daily and range from a three-hour rimside ride to strenuous overnight trips to Phantom Ranch. All riders must weigh less than 200 lbs. or 225 lbs. fully dressed (depending on the ride—and, yes, they do weigh everyone!), must be at least 4 feet, 9 inches in height, and, for safety's sake, must be able to speak and understand English. Long pants, long-sleeved shirts and closed-toed shoes are also required. These beasts do walk right along the trail's

Lolita's Lepidopterist

During Russian author Vladimir Nabokov's first visit to Arizona in 1941, he and his party stopped at the Grand Canyon. Nabokov—who was a serious lepidopterist as well as the author of the controversial classic novel *Lolita*—discovered an unnamed butterfly at the canyon. He called the diminutive brown butterfly *Neonympha dorothea*, after Dorothy Leuthold, the student doing the driving on the trip.

edge, so the faint of heart may want to find another activity. The treks are popular, so reservations should be made as far in advance as possible.

Travelers who plan ahead may want to consider scheduling one of the excursions offered by the **Grand Canyon Conservancy Field Institute** (928-638-2481 or 800-858-2808; grandcanyon.org). Guides from the institute take small groups of people on hiking, backpacking, and educational tours throughout the park. Special courses are planned for people interested in geology, human history, ecosystems, wilderness skills (including classes just for women), and photography. Fees and lengths of classes vary, as does the difficulty level of the hikes.

There are so many ways to see the canyon. You can fly over by helicopter on **Papillon Grand Canyon Helicopters** (888-635-7272; papillon.com) or take a longer airplane tour. The airport is located in the town of Tusayan.

Some visitors prefer rafting down the Colorado River to clambering around on the cliffs. About a dozen companies are licensed for canyon river trips. These are the full-out, go-for-the-gusto, *The River Wild*–style, three-day to three-week white-water expeditions in a variety of watercraft. You have to book your tour at least six months to one year in advance, or there's a good chance you won't get a slot. Call the park (928-638-7888; nps.gov/grca) to find out about trips and companies and for reservations.

Grand Canyon National Park: North Rim

Though many tourists choose to limit their exploration of the canyon to the views from the South Rim, there is another, very different side to this spectacular locale. The **North Rim** of the canyon is about 1,200 feet higher than the South Rim, and during the winter it gets snowed in. All lodging and restaurants at North Rim are closed every year from mid-Oct to mid-May. It has far fewer amenities than the South Rim has, and requires a long but scenic drive. Admission fee is good for seven days at both the North and South Rims.

Located on the Kaibab Plateau, the North Rim is significantly lusher than the South Rim. It also has spectacular views without the crowds found on the more popular South Rim. Only 10 percent of the total number of visitors to the canyon travel to the North Rim, so solitude is easy to find. If you want to stay in the park on the North Rim, your only choice is the *Grand Canyon Lodge* (877-386-4383; grandcanyonforever.com) or at the *North Rim Campground* (877-444-6777; recreation.gov). Fortunately, the Grand Canyon Lodge is a nice place to stay, and the main building (constructed of native pine logs and limestone slabs) is built right at the edge of the canyon not far from *Bright Angel Point.* The view out the windows of the dining room of this 1937 National Historic Landmark is unparalleled. In addition to the dining room (which serves traditional western fare such as prime rib, steaks, and seafood, with some vegetarian items thrown in), the main lodge also has a lobby, sunroom, and gift shop. A saloon, deli, and bookstore are adjacent. The National Park Service offers evening programs on different canyon topics in the lodge's old ballroom.

Accommodations range from historical log cabins to basic motel rooms, which once served as lodgings for on-site personnel. $$. Two miles down the road, near the North Rim campground, you will find a gas station, a general store, and a coin-operated laundry.

After checking in, take the 23-mile paved road to *Cape Royal.* Nearly 3 miles along Cape Royal Road, a spur to the left leads to *Point Imperial* (which, at an elevation of 8,803 feet, is the highest lookout on either rim). This popular viewpoint offers a grand view of the Vermilion Cliffs to the north, the Painted Desert to the east, the Little Colorado River Canyon to the southeast, and Navajo Mountain to the northeast. Picnic tables at the viewpoint make this a convenient place to stop for a picnic lunch. It is also the only viewpoint, other than Cape Royal, that has bathroom facilities. You'll encounter several worthwhile vistas along the drive. The most remote of the viewpoints on Cape Royal Road is *Cape Final,* which can only be accessed by a 2-mile hike along an old jeep trail through a ponderosa pine forest. The viewpoint features panoramic views of the northern canyon, the Palisades of the Desert, and the impressive spectacle of Juno Temple. The road ends at Cape Royal, the North Rim's southernmost viewpoint, filled with dazzling sights. A short paved walk leads to the natural arch of Angels Window.

While the viewpoints along Cape Royal Road are definitely worth visiting, those seeking even more solitude should head out to *Point Sublime.* The 17-mile dirt road winds through gorgeous high country forest and dead-ends at what is arguably the most scenic viewpoint on the either rim. The road is only intended for use by high-clearance vehicles (four-wheel-drive is recommended) and will take at least two hours to travel one way. Camping is allowed at this solitary viewpoint as long as you procure a permit from the Backcountry Information Center (928-638-7875; nps.gov/grca) ahead of time.

There are several trails leading through the forest to remote viewpoints accessible only by foot. The best of the bunch is the 10-mile round-trip *Widforss Trail.* The trailhead is accessed across from the North Kaibab Trail parking lot and leads through meadows and timber to Widforss Point. Although there are several hiking trails in the vicinity, the *North Kaibab Trail* is the only trail on the North Rim leading into the canyon. The long, steep path descends 5,840 feet over 14.5 miles to the Colorado River and Phantom Ranch. Day hikers should attempt to go no further than Roaring Springs (5,020 feet), a strenuous 9.4 mile round-trip journey. For a fee, a shuttle takes hikers to the North Kaibab trailhead twice daily from Grand Canyon Lodge.

If you'd rather have someone else do all the hard work, hitch a ride with *Canyon Trail Rides* (435-679-8665; canyonrides.com). This outfitter, with an information desk in the Grand Canyon Lodge, offers everything from one-hour rides on rim trails to three-hour trips down the North Kaibab Trail to Supai Tunnel.

Die-hard adventurers can find even more solitude by hiking, snowshoeing, or cross-country skiing to the North Rim after AZ 67 closes at Jacob Lake, which is usually in mid-Oct or early Nov after the first heavy snows. Winter visitors must obtain a backcountry permit for overnight use during the winter season (mid-Oct through mid-May).

Keep in mind that the Grand Canyon National Park's North Rim is surrounded by *Kaibab National Forest* (928-643-7395; fs.usda.gov/kaibab). The North District Ranger Office can supply you with maps of hiking trails, scenic drives, and camping sites outside the park boundaries. Cyclists in particular might be glad to learn the route of the Rainbow Rim Trail, an 18-mile, one-way trail that begins at Parissawampitts Point at the end of FR 214 and ends at Timp Point on FR 271. Cycling within park boundaries is limited to the Bridle Trail, making this alternative ride through a ponderosa pine forest and high mountain meadows a real treat. Best of all, the trail stops at three other Grand Canyon viewpoints—Fence, Locust, and North Timp. The trail is also open to hikers.

Although the North Rim of the Grand Canyon is fairly remote, true solitude seekers can exit the park and travel east to the *Grand Canyon-Parashant National Monument.* In January 2000, President Bill Clinton set aside more than one million acres of land along the northern edge of the Grand Canyon in the northwest corner of Arizona. The isolated area is seldom visited and is co-managed by the National Park Service and the US Bureau of Land Management. There are no facilities at the monument. Camping is primitive and hikers should expect wilderness hiking conditions. No paved roads access the monument and cell service is spotty at best. Travel in a high-clearance vehicle, and carry two spare tires, extra food, and water. For maps and information on the national monument, check with the Interagency Information Center (345 E. Riverside Dr.; 435-688-3246 or 435-688-3200; nps.gov/para) in St. George, Utah. You can also gather informational materials at the Pipe Spring National Monument Visitor Center on AZ 389.

Arizona Strip

The Arizona Strip is the very essence of off-the-beaten-path; the section of the state that lies north of the Colorado River. Cut off by the Grand Canyon, this sparsely populated landscape includes sagebrush plains, forested plateaus, and soaring cliffs. The only way to access the North Rim of the Grand Canyon is by crossing the Arizona Strip. The road to the national park is the 43-mile stretch of Arizona 67, heading south from the small community of *Jacob Lake.* Designated as a National Scenic Byway known as the Kaibab Plateau-North Rim Parkway, the winding road passes through mixed conifer forests, aspen groves and long green meadows on the way to the park. Due to winter weather the road is generally closed from Dec 1 through spring. *Jacob Lake Inn* (928-634-7232; jacoblake.com) consists of a lodge, cabins, service station, store, restaurant and bakery.

Even though Grand Canyon National Park's North Rim never experiences very substantial crowds, there's an even more remote corner for those well-prepared people that don't mind long bouncy drives into remote wilderness. *Toroweap Point* (also known as Tuweep) is about 61 miles from the last bit of asphalt on AZ 389 down a lengthy stretch of unpaved road. The primary access point, also known as the Sunshine Route, is on County Road 109, which leaves the highway about 8 miles west of Fredonia. Allow two to three hours to travel to Toroweap and be aware that the routes may be impassable when wet. There is no water, gas, food, lodging, or phone service. Carry everything that you might need, including tire plugs and portable air compressor to repair flat tires. The point juts out over the Colorado River, which lies about 3,000 feet below. Because it's closer to the river than many areas of the Grand Canyon are, you get both a spectacular view and a real sense of the power of the Colorado. There is no charge for day use but reservations are required for the handful of primitive campsites at the rim. A couple of hiking trails can be accessed from the point.

The quaint community of *Fredonia* (928-643-7241), on the Utah border, was founded more than one hundred years ago by Mormon settlers. Some folks say the town's name is a combination of "free" and the Spanish word *doña,* meaning "lady." Accounts collected by the Daughters of the Pioneers claim that Mormons residing in Kanab would send their extra wives over the state line into the Arizona border town in an attempt to evade US Marshals cracking down on polygamy. Don't miss the **Red Pueblo Museum and Heritage Park** (1145 N. Main St.; 928-643-7777), a surprisingly expansive collection of Indian artifacts including pottery, tools, arrowheads, and the much more rare medicine bags, moccasins, and blankets. Admission. While there are few services in Fredonia, you'll find plenty of lodging restaurants, shops, and more just a few miles north in the picturesque town of Kanab, Utah.

It's really the natural beauty of this area and evidence of ancient cultures that draw visitors. Less than a two-hour drive from the city limits are Zion National Park and Bryce Canyon National Park (both in Utah), as well as Lake Powell and the North Rim of Grand Canyon. There are a multitude of solitary trails for hiking in the 75,300-acre **Kanab Creek Wilderness Area** and the 40,610-acre **Saddle Mountain Wilderness Area,** both of which are south of Fredonia and are managed by the North Kaibab Ranger District (928-643-7395; fs.usda.gov/kaibab). Information on the trails and wilderness area conditions can also be found at the Kaibab Plateau Visitor Center (928-643-7298) at the juncture of US 89 and AZ 67 in Jacob Lake.

One of the hidden gems of the Arizona Strip is **Pipe Spring National Monument** (928-643-7105; nps.gov/pisp) on AZ 389, where an original Mormon fort (constructed of brick and wood) sits surrounded by high-desert vegetation and trees fed by underground springs. The fort, known as Winsor Castle, is accessible by ranger-guided tours. During the summer months there are guided walks, talks and re-creations of pioneer life, but year-round you can feed the ducks in the duck pond and enjoy the serenity of this remote area. You will also learn about the little-known Paiute Indians at the **Pipe Spring National Monument–Kaibab Band of Paiute Indians Visitor Center and Museum.** Admission is good for seven days.

Taking US 89A southeast from Fredonia leads you across the broad back of the Kaibab Plateau, dropping to the valley floor where you'll spot the rising line of the **Vermilion Cliffs,** which John Wesley Powell described as "a long bank of purple cliffs plowed from the horizon high into the heavens." Designated as **Vermilion Cliffs National Monument** (435-688-3200; blm.gov/visit/vermilion-cliffs) in 2000, the unspoiled wilderness spreads across 294,000 acres and includes geologic treasures like Paria Canyon, Coyote Buttes, the swirling sandstone beauty of the Wave, and of course, the Vermilion Cliffs, soaring 3,000 feet above the landscape. There are no visitor centers or services within the monument, and roads are rocky and seldom maintained, so once again, be prepared to handle any and all emergencies that might arise. A permit is required for hiking Coyote

Buttes North (the Wave), Coyote Buttes South, and for overnight trips into Paria Canyon and they are hard to come by. Call or visit the website for details.

Branching off to the south is a marked, gravel road that leads to **House Rock Ranch,** a state-managed ranch where buffalo roam free. This road is passable most times of the year in an ordinary vehicle, although it's a bit bumpy in places and has been known to get washed out. Call the North Kaibab Ranger District (928-643-7395; fs.usda.gov/kaibab) for information on road conditions. The ranch, founded in the 1920s as part of a buffalo-raising venture that failed, is now operated by the Arizona Game and Fish Department. There are also antelope, deer, and bighorn sheep in the House Rock Valley area, though they can all be rather elusive. The best wildlife-watching advice from locals is to drive south of the ranch on the 26-mile road until you come to the end. Then get out and walk around a bit.

Continuing east on US 89A, the scenic road flows along the base of the Vermilion Cliffs, beautiful in almost any light and stunning beneath stormy skies. The route leads to **Marble Canyon.** In 1995 the state built a new bridge for car traffic over the Colorado River at Marble Canyon while retaining the older Navajo Bridge, which is about 200 feet away from the new one, as a pedestrian crossing. This gives you the opportunity to actually walk out and stand nearly 500 feet over the river that carved the Grand Canyon.

There are several lodges near Marble Canyon, including the **Marble Canyon Lodge** (928-355-2225 or 800-726-1789; marblecanyoncompany.com) and the **Cliff Dwellers Lodge** (928-355-2261 or 800-962-9755; leesferry.com). Marble Canyon Lodge includes a variety of room styles and has a restaurant, a convenience store, a small trading post, a gas station, a post office, and a coin-operated laundry. $. Besides rooms, Cliff Dwellers Lodge has a small convenience store, a gas station, a fly-fishing guide service and fly-fishing shop, and an excellent restaurant. $.

At Marble Canyon is the turnoff to **Lees Ferry** (928-608-6200; nps.gov/glca), now part of the **Glen Canyon National Recreation Area.** In this rugged canyon country, this is one of the only places that allowed access to the Colorado River in hundreds of miles. John Doyle Lee settled here and established the rickety ferry that still bears his name in 1873. Boat service operated at this crucial river crossing until 1928 when the ferryboat capsized, and took three men to a watery grave. By then, Navajo Bridge was just months from completion so ferry service was not reestablished.

The short paved road to Lees Ferry leads down through the hills, past some curious mushroom shaped rocks all the way to the river. There's a campground and the remains of an old Mormon fort. A short hiking trail traces the shoreline past the crumbling stone buildings and the remains of an old steamboat. A more strenuous trail climbs one of the rocky cliffs affording some sweet views. Visitors can also visit Lee's old homestead, the **Lonely Dell Ranch.** The park service maintains the historic orchards, making this an intriguing little middle of nowhere oasis. Weathered buildings and a pioneer cemetery tell the stories of those who scratched out a living here. Day hiking into Paria Canyon is allowed along the shallow muddy Paria River, but a permit is required for overnight outings. Lees Ferry serves as the put-in place for Grand Canyon rafting trips so don't be startled by the stream of boats and people showing up in the mornings to load up and begin their journeys. Make sure to bring your rod and reel. This stretch of ice-cold, crystal-clear water at Lees Ferry below Glen Canyon Dam provides arguably the best trout fishing in the Southwest. Admission.

Lake Powell to Sunset Crater

It may be difficult to imagine Arizona as an aquatic play park (particularly because the state is more famous for its giant cacti and desert sunsets), but the truth is that this state has a plethora of lakes and rivers that are perfect for any activity from relaxing float trips to shooting the rapids.

On the border with Utah sits **Lake Powell,** in the **Glen Canyon National Recreation Area.** Lake Powell began to flow into life in 1963 with the closing of the gates on **Glen Canyon Dam** on the Colorado River. Nine years later, 186 river miles had filled about one hundred canyons, creating a playground that includes 1,960 miles of shoreline and boating opportunities galore. Admission.

From the Arizona side, Lake Powell can be reached by driving on US 89 to Page, near the southern tip of the lake or at Antelope Point off AZ 98. **Page** started as a construction camp for workers building the dam. It now serves as a base for tourists looking to explore this remarkable area. Most of the motels, restaurants, and other businesses are concentrated along Lake Powell Boulevard, the name given to US 89 as it loops through town.

The Glen Canyon Dam and the **Carl Hayden Visitor Center** (928-608-6200; nps.gov/glca) are located off US 89 about 2 miles north of Page. These attractions provide travelers with the opportunity to learn some of the area's history (even prehistory—dinosaur footprints, taken from the canyon, are on display), as well as tour the massive dam and witness its energy-producing prowess. The second-highest concrete arch dam in the United States, Glen Canyon Dam has a maximum power output of 1,320 megawatts, enough power for a city of more than one million inhabitants. The power is sold to independent companies that utilize it in southern Arizona, Las Vegas, and as far away as Los Angeles.

Less than 5 miles northwest on US 89 is the **Wahweap Marina** (888-896-3829; lakepowell.com). The marina rents houseboats and other watercraft, and the lodge provides comfortable accommodations for travelers. Multiple restaurants offer something for every taste, including the elegant Rainbow Room, with its wall of windows overlooking the water. Located off AZ 98, the newer **Antelope Point Marina** (928-645-5900; antelopepointlakepowell.com) also rents houseboats and personal watercraft. If you want to experience a houseboat for just a night or two, the marina rents them as hotel rooms. Luggage service, a floating restaurant and general store, and charter boats make Antelope Point Marina a welcome addition to Lake Powell's offerings.

If you want to check out the other side of the dam and would prefer not to do your own piloting, guides from **Wilderness River Adventures** (800-992-8022; riveradventures.com) can take you from Lake Powell on a 15-mile float trip aboard a large raft. The journey starts at the base of the Glen Canyon Dam and makes a stop where you can get a close-up view of ancient petroglyphs. The float trip concludes at **Lees Ferry,** where Mormon pioneers used to cross the Colorado River on their way back to Utah to get married.

arizonatrivia

Lake Powell, along the northern Arizona–Utah border, has more miles of shoreline than the entire Pacific coast of the United States.

The beauty of the Glen Canyon area is astounding: clear mountain vistas of sand-sculpted and water-worked stones, high-desert vegetation, and sunsets of breathtaking dimensions. Over the years the region's majesty has attracted many film companies. Notable movies filmed here include *Planet of the Apes, Maverick* and Hong Kong director John Woo's *Broken Arrow.*

One of Glen Canyon's most famous examples of nature's creative power is **Rainbow Bridge,** which the Navajos consider sacred. At 290 feet, it's one of the world's largest natural bridges and is located on the Utah side of the border. Some of the lake excursion packages offered by the marinas include visits to this marvel, via a boat ride across the water followed by short hike.

Another natural landmark not to be missed is **Antelope Canyon,** just southeast of Page. Curving, swerving red sandstone forms a narrow convoluted defile that is pierced in spots by shafts of sunlight streaming in from above. Water-smoothed walls that seem to glow from within comprise the most famous slot canyon in the Southwest. Antelope is actually divided into two scenic segments known as Lower Antelope and Upper Antelope. Upper is an easy flat 100-yard walk reached by a short drive. Lower Antelope is longer and requires some stair climbing. It begins directly across from the Tribal Park Gate on US 98. All areas of Antelope Canyon are only accessible via guided tour. A handful of companies offer sightseeing tours and photography tours. For prices and more information, visit the website navajonationparks.org. If you're looking for something a little more off the beaten path, a couple of other enticing little slot canyons are gouged out of this plateau country. Canyon X and Secret Canyon might be more to your liking. Check with the tour groups that specialize in these out of the way spots.

Turn south on US 89 to head back toward Flagstaff. After skirting along the Echo Cliffs and rambling through the crumpled badlands lining the road near Tuba City, you'll cross the Little Colorado River and soon arrive at the ***Wupatki National Monument*** (928-679-2365; nps.gov/wupa). The monument, about 40 miles north of Flagstaff, is composed of more than 800 ruins of structures built by the ancient Sinagua Indians, who moved into the area around AD 1066. The ruins include a kind of handball court and a cool-air "blowhole" that releases a constant stream from deep underground. Seasonal mini-lectures are offered when visitor numbers are high. During the winter, two-hour ranger-led discovery hikes are scheduled as well.

Just down the road from Wupatki is ***Sunset Crater Volcano National Monument*** (928-526-0502; nps.gov/sucr). Sunset Crater, named by Grand Canyon explorer John Wesley Powell for its orange-colored rim, erupted around 1085, leaving behind a 1,000-foot-high cone and a bizarre landscape of lava flow and ice caves. Several easy-to-follow hiking trails take visitors around the lava flow, and picnic areas are not too far down the road. Admission is good for seven days at both Wupatki and Sunset Crater National Monuments.

To see a volcanic cinder cone and lava flow off the beaten path, head to the 10,141-acre ***Strawberry Crater Wilderness.*** Explore ancient Indian ruins or take a hike up the established trail on the north side of Strawberry Crater. Views of the San Francisco Peaks, Sunset Crater, and the Painted Desert add to the dramatic views. The Strawberry Crater Wilderness is located 20 miles north of Flagstaff with access on Sunset Crater/Wupatki Road (FR 545). This 36-mile scenic drive is called the ***Volcanoes and Ruins Loop*** and exits at US 89. For more information contact the Flagstaff Ranger District (5075 N. US 89; 928-526-0866; fs.usda.gov/coconino) in Flagstaff.

Sedona Area

Travel south from Flagstaff and you'll experience one of the most scenic drives in the country, the winding road through ***Oak Creek Canyon.*** At first AZ 89A meanders south through ponderosa pine forests until it reaches the head of the canyon. Make your first stop here at Oak Creek Vista, along with the commanding views down the defile, you'll find an information stand (manned in summer), restrooms, and picnic tables. Native American vendors are on hand selling handcrafted artwork. From here the road drops in a series of tight switchbacks to the canyon floor. For the next dozen miles or so you'll follow the lazy course of Oak Creek beneath a lush canopy of trees that blaze with a cornucopia of colors during the fall. More than 130 species of birds call the region home, and campgrounds and hiking trails are abundant. There are designated campgrounds and picnic areas, as well as many informal pullouts where you can get out and experience some of the riparian magic beneath towering canyon walls. Numerous resorts and cabins are hidden along the banks of the creek, serving up an interesting array of accommodation choices. ***Orchard Canyon on Oak Creek*** (8067 N. AZ 89A; 928-282-3343; enjoyorchardcanyon .com) features cozy cabins set amid organic gardens and apple orchards. A stay includes breakfast, afternoon tea and an elegant four course dinner. Open Mar through mid-Nov. $$$.

 The Canyon Wren, Cabins for Two (6425 N. AZ 89A; 928-282-6900 or 800-437-9736; canyonwrencabins.com) is a cluster of four cabins located 6 miles from Sedona and is on the hilly side of the highway away from the creek. Nonsmoking inside and out, the Canyon Wren also caters to couples seeking a tranquil retreat. Each unit comes complete with a small kitchen. A two-night minimum stay is required. $$$.

 Oak Creek Terrace Resort (4548 N. AZ 89A; 928-282-3562 or 800-224-2229; oakcreekterrace.com) is 5 miles from uptown Sedona and features a two-story A-frame cabin that sleeps up to five, triplexes, motel-style rooms, and unique bungalows of varying layouts in a creek-side setting. Nearly every unit is complete with fireplace and in-room whirlpool tub; many offer kitchenettes and outdoor barbecues. $$.

 Midway up the canyon is ***Slide Rock State Park*** (928-282-3034; azstate parks.com), a state-run facility that, as its name implies, boasts a natural waterslide created by the waters of Oak Creek as they rush over smooth stone chutes. Historic apple orchards still produce fruit that's sold by the bag, along with delicious cider, in autumn. An original apple-packing barn remains, as well as buildings and equipment from the old homestead. For visitors, shaded picnic areas are available, and snacks and supplies can be purchased inside Slide Rock Market. Admission.

arizonatrivia

Though it is a relatively small community, Sedona is located in both Coconino and Yavapai Counties and is completely surrounded by the Coconino National Forest.

 If you continue south on AZ 89A from Slide Rock, you'll cross Midgely Bridge. There's a small parking area here, with views of the canyon, and hiking trails for those that want to stretch their legs. In about 2 miles you'll reach the red-rock-ringed community of **Sedona** (928-282-7722 or 800-288-7336; visitsedona.com). The town was named in 1902 for Sedona Schnebly, the wife of T. C. Schnebly who began the first mail service. Traveling from Oak Creek Canyon, you'll first arrive in Uptown, where dozens of shops, galleries, restaurants and more line the streets, and sandstone towers and spires define the surrounding skyline. There's never a season where you won't find the sidewalks of Uptown teeming with tourists. Sedona is an international destination, much like Grand Canyon. The Sedona Chamber of Commerce & Tourism Bureau Visitor Center is located here at 331 Forest Rd.

This small town is best known as an arts community, a vacation getaway spot, and a haven for people seeking a different spiritual path. In the 1980s, Sedona acquired the reputation of being a New Age center. Allegedly several electromagnetic energy sources (known as vortexes) were found in the area, and a wide variety of psychics and spiritual healers decided to tap into them by making the town their home. **The Center for the New Age** (341 Hwy. 179; 928-282-2085; sedonanewagestore.com) has been providing services since 1995. You can get psychic readings, healing massages, and aural photographs at the center or you can sign up for a personalized vortex tour. Four primary areas have been identified as possessing unusual electromagnetic forces. They are **Cathedral Rock** (off US 89A and Upper Red Rock Loop Road); **Bell Rock** (north of the Village of Oak Creek, off AZ 179); **Airport Mesa** (near the edge of the small airport); and **Boynton Canyon Vortex** (Boynton Pass Road, west of Sedona off AZ 89A and Dry Creek Road). Some believe these outcroppings of red rock (the first two named after their respective shapes, and the latter two named for their locations) emit a palpable energy. All are worth a visit, even for non-believers because they are places of jaw-dropping scenery. If there is a healing power to beauty, you'll find it here.

Hollywood filmmakers and music video, television, and television commercial producers have long been lured to Sedona, starting in 1923 when the Zane Grey feature *Call of the Canyon* was lensed here. The pilgrimage continues today with films and commercials still being produced here. Glancing around at the intense, vibrant red rocks and the lush vegetation, it's easy to see why so many artists also have been drawn to this setting. Although the **Cowboy Artists of America** (cowboyartistsofamerica.com) was founded here in 1965, artists of every description and from different regions, including the Southwest, have worked here. Two of the most famous were painter/sculptor Max Ernst, whose surrealistic works helped to redefine art in the 1950s, and his wife Dorothea Tanning, a powerful painter, sculptor and poet with a long distinguished career.

Arizona in the Movies

Visit Sedona for the first time and you'll likely feel as though you've been there before—and for good reason. More than 100 movies have used the crimson canyons of Sedona as their backdrop. Some cinematic offerings shot here include *Angel and the Badman* with John Wayne, *Blood on the Moon* with Robert Mitchum, *Stay Away, Joe* with Elvis Presley, *Kingdom of the Spiders* with William Shatner, *Midnight Run* with Robert DeNiro, and *Dead Man* with Johnny Depp.

Many artists have their works on display at **Tlaquepaque Arts and Crafts Village** (928-282-4838; tlaq.com). Pronounced *T-lockey-pockey,* the center's name is a Native American word meaning "the best of everything." Designed to resemble an actual Mexican village near Guadalajara, the center's shops and galleries surround a courtyard. Each September, **Fiesta del Tlaquepaque** is held, and strolling mariachis play while children swing at a piñata and food vendors fill the courtyard with the aroma of southwestern cooking. Tlaquepaque is also the setting for an annual **Festival of Lights,** an evening event usually held on the second Sat in Dec. Thousands of luminarias are placed all around the balconies, walkways, and on the fountain, bathing the village in a golden glow. The luminarias are lighted at dusk, but the festival is open from 3 to 8 p.m.

Located next door to Tlaquepaque is the **Los Abrigados** ("the shelter") **Resort and Spa** (928-282-1777 or 800-438-2929; diamondresortsandhotels .com), a first-class facility is set on twenty acres. The all-suite resort has a health club with workout machines and classes, a tennis court, an outdoor pool and Jacuzzi, and two restaurants. $$$. **The Matterhorn Inn** (928-282-7176 or 800-372-8207; matterhorninn.com) occupies a hillside in Uptown where guests enjoy views from their private balconies or patios. $$.

With more than 300 miles of trails weaving among the red rock formations, Sedona is a paradise for hikers and mountain bikers. It's rare to have such instant access to wild country while never straying far from the comforts of town. Developed trailheads require a Red Rock Pass, that can be purchased for the day, week or annually. Passes are available at the visitor centers in town and from kiosks at the trailheads where they're required. A few easy to moderate trails include Courthouse Butte Loop (4.2 miles), Margs Draw (4 miles), Jim Thompson (6 miles), and Scorpion-Pyramid (4.1 miles). All mileages are round trip totals. Gather more maps and details at the Red Rock Ranger District Visitor Center (8375 AZ 179; 928-203-7500; fs.usda.gov/coconino), a mile south of the Village of Oak Creek.

If you tire of hiking, several companies can give you a lift—literally. *Northern Light Balloon Expeditions* (928-282-2274 or 800-230-6222; northernlightballoons.com) and *Red Rock Balloons* (928-284-0040 or 800-258-3754; redrockballoons.com) are both permitted to fly over the Coconino National Forest. Few things are more stunning than watching the sunrise above the sandstone towers and mesas from the basket of a hot-air balloon. Or take a bouncing, boulder-climbing ride to Broken Arrow with *Pink Jeep Tours* (800-873-3662; pinkadventuretours.com). If you'd like to combine a jeep tour with a horseback ride, *A Day in the West* (928-282-4320; adayinthewest.com) offers exciting combos. By the way, you can take your own jeep tour up Schnebly Hill Road where sensational vistas await if you're driving a high-clearance or all-terrain vehicle.

One Sedona sight you definitely shouldn't miss is the *Chapel of the Holy Cross* (780 Chapel Rd.; 928-282-7545; chapeloftheholycross.com). This small cathedral rising amid the red rocks was built in 1956 by Margurite Brunswig Staude, a sculptor and rancher who had long envisioned building a contemporary monument to God. Originally slated for Budapest, Hungary, the project was cancelled with the outbreak of World War II. Staude decided to build it closer to home. Taize prayer services are held Mon evenings. The chapel is open to anyone of any creed to come in and light a candle (for which there is a small donation), browse in the downstairs gift shop, and marvel at the incredible scenery. The chapel is open daily from 9 a.m. to 5 p.m., except Thanksgiving, Christmas, and Easter.

Besides the wintertime Festival of Lights, annual events in Sedona include the *Sedona Annual International Film Festival* (928-282-1177; sedonafilmfestival.com) in February; *Sedona Mountain Bike Festival* (sedonamtbfestival .com) in March; and *Sedona Arts Festival* (928-204-9456; sedonaartsfestival .org) in October.

It's not hard to find a comfortable place to stay overnight in Sedona: The area is loaded with quaint bed-and-breakfast inns and has several top-notch resorts. At gorgeous *Adobe Grand Villas* (866-900-7616; adobegrandvillas .com) guests enjoy spacious, standalone villas that contain multiple fireplaces, a balcony or garden patio, and bread baked fresh in room. A five-course breakfast is part of the package. $$$.

Despite its small size, Sedona also has a healthy assortment of eateries, from eclectic to European. You'll enjoy some of the best views to accompany excellent food at *Mariposa Latin Inspired Grill* (700 W. AZ 89A; 928-862-4444; mariposasedona.com). Set on a bluff, Mariposa overlooks forest ringed by red rock cliffs. Argentine-style grilled meats and seafood, wood-fired flatbreads and roasted vegetables are prepared in the large exhibition kitchen. $$$.

Tamaliza Café (1155 W. AZ 89A; 928-202-9056; sedonatamaliza.com) serves up a simple menu of delicious tamales made with fresh, healthy ingredients. $.

Those seeking sites off the beaten path can visit two carefully preserved pieces of Sedona's ancient past. The **Palatki Heritage Site** and its sister site **Honanki,** were the largest cliff dwellings of red rock country. The ancient Sinagua Indians lived in both of these cliff dwellings from about AD 1150 to AD 1350. Displays of rock art are visible along with the dwellings. There is a small visitor center at Palatki. Both sites are open to the public seven days a week, but reservations are required since the forest service limits the number of visitors. Call the Palatki Heritage Site at (928) 282-3854 between 9:30 a.m. and 3:30 p.m. to make reservations. Free admission.

Another worthwhile spot is **Red Rock State Park** (928-282-6907; azstate parks.com) with a network of trails carving the hills above Oak Creek. The park is just west of Sedona off AZ 89A and features daily guided hikes with a different focus, such as bird hikes, geology hikes, sunset walks, and the ever-popular moonlight hikes. Numerous exhibits are on display and short films are shown at the visitor center. Admission.

When you're ready to move on from Sedona (and a word of warning: Vortex or not, the town has a very seductive character, so you may be there awhile), visit the other towns of the Verde Valley.

Jerome and the Verde Valley

Nestled between the Verde River and the rising wall of mountains known as the Black Hills lies **Cottonwood** (928-634-7593; visitcottonwoodaz.org). The town has long served as the commercial center of the Verde Valley. While Sedona was primarily a farming town and the copper mines of Jerome were booming, the little community named for the graceful cottonwood trees growing along the river offered folks a chance to sell some goods on their own or open a business. That commercial trend continues today with a strong retail profile that often brings residents from the surrounding towns to do at least some their shopping. Most of the few big box stores in the area can be found in Cottonwood. Yet rather than devolve into a generic stopover, Cottonwood has carved out a strong identity in recent years as a destination for wine lovers.

Several boutique vineyards cover the hillsides outside of town, thriving in the rocky volcanic soil and prime elevations prompting the dramatic temperature swings that bring out the best characteristics of the grapes. **Old Town Cottonwood** (oldtown.org) consists of a few blocks of Prohibition-era buildings fronted by covered sidewalks. It's packed with half a dozen wine tasting rooms, three small hotels, restaurants, shops, and bars. **The Tavern Hotel** (904

Main St.; 928-639-1669; thetavernhotel.com) makes an excellent base of operations. Modern furnishings, plush bedding and walk-in showers are all standard in their 41 rooms. They also offer several packages that include outings like kayak tours and train rides, but their most popular by far is the Sip & Stay Wine Package, where guests can sample some of the best of local wines and food, just footsteps from the room. $$.

You'll have plenty of dining options while exploring Old Town. For an authentic taste of the Italian countryside, try the wood-fired artisan pies from *Pizzeria Bocce* (1060 N. Main St.; 928-202-3597; boccecottonwood.com). Don't worry if there's a wait. It will give you time to sample a specialty cocktail and try your luck on the bocce ball court on the patio. $$. Or step back in time with a visit to *Bing's Burger Station* (794 N. Main St.; 928-852-0109; bingsburgers.com). It may look like a vintage gas station, but inside it's a shiny diner with hand-formed patties sizzling on the flattop. The juicy burgers come topped to your liking. Pair them with a basket of slender fries and a creamy milkshake. $.

At nearby *Dead Horse Ranch State Park* (928-634-5283; azstateparks .com) you will find a multitude of outdoor recreational activities. The 423-acre park includes three shaded lagoons, and is sliced by a long stretch of the Verde River. The rare cottonwood and willow gallery forest is one of less than 20 such riparian zones in the world. The lush corridor makes excellent birding habitat and bald eagles are frequently spotted here. The system of trails climbs into the rolling hills above the river and are popular with hikers and mountain bikers. Some exit the park to traverse the surrounding *Coconino National Forest* (928-527-3600; fs.usda.gov/coconino.com). Two campgrounds are supplemented by cozy camping cabins tucked away in a mesquite grove. Horseback rides are available from a concessionaire. Admission.

Between Cottonwood and Clarkdale lies *Tuzigoot* (an Apache name meaning "crooked water") *National Monument* (928-634-5564; nps.gov/tuzi). This pueblo, built by the long-vanished Sinagua Indians near the Verde River, is more than 800 years old. The Sinaguans, whose culture included farming as well as hunting and gathering, founded settlements throughout northern and central Arizona, often choosing the land near streams and hot springs as sites for building their elaborate dwellings. Besides the ruins, a nearby visitor center displays Sinaguan artifacts and sells books about the area's history. The park is open daily from 8 a.m. to 5 p.m. Admission.

Located north of Cottonwood on AZ 89A, *Clarkdale* is home to the *Verde Canyon Railroad* (800-582-7245; verdecanyonrr.com). Clarkdale was built as a copper smelting company town for workers in the Jerome mines, just up the mountain slope. The tracks for Verde Canyon Railroad were laid in 1911 to haul copper ore from Clarkdale northwest to the town of Drake. Over time it became popular among those who wanted easy access to the wilderness areas of Verde Canyon. Even after the mines closed, the railroad continued hauling freight. It was purchased in 1988 by David Durbano, who turned it into an excursion train in 1990. The railway uses renovated Metro New York Line coach cars, and offers first-class and coach accommodations. There are also open-air cars where passengers from any part of the train can get a good look at the scenery as the trains ramble through the protected Verde Canyon area, a gorgeous stretch that includes a riparian cottonwood forest, desert areas, and towering red rocks.

The trip also is a wildlife lover's delight. Antelope, javelina, black hawks, and blue herons live here. In winter months, bald and golden eagle sightings are common. During the four-hour ride, singer/storytellers dressed in rustic frontier attire keep passengers entertained and help to point out the wildlife.

The railway operates year-round and even has moonlight excursions in the summer, as well as wine and beer tasting trains, chocolate lovers trains, and visits from Santa Claus. The train operation offers cocktails, hors d'oeuvres, and deli treats. Admission.

Due west on AZ 89A, the former mining community of *Jerome* (928-634-2900; jeromechamber.com) is proud to call itself the "largest ghost town in Arizona." The fact is that it isn't a ghost town at all, although it nearly suffered the fate of total abandonment. Built on Cleopatra Hill in the early 1880s, the town thrived with the copper industry. At first the land beneath the town was drilled into and blasted out to form a series of tunnels (almost 90 miles in all) from which rich copper ore was extracted. Fires drove the workers out of the tunnels, however, in 1918, and surface mining became the new standard operating procedure.

The dynamiting necessitated by this strip mining caused a shake, rattle, and roll greater than anything Jerry Lee Lewis ever dreamed of, and the town discovered to its horror that it had created a massive slide zone. The *City Jail,* known as the "traveling jail," in fact, has slid 225 feet across the highway since a 1920s dynamite explosion dislodged it from its original foundation.

In the early 1950s the mines closed altogether, and Jerome languished. But just as hippies discovered the Haight-Ashbury District in San Francisco in the 1960s, so too did they find the Victorian buildings of Jerome to their liking, and many settled in the area permanently. Today Jerome is a thriving arts community, with renowned sculptors, painters, jewelers, and musicians plying their trades and professions here.

From its high perch atop Cleopatra Hill, Jerome makes for one of Arizona's most enticing day trips. The winding mountain drive makes it a popular destination for motorcycle riders, as well as the live music that keeps the legendary **Spirit Room** (928-634-8809; spiritroom.com) jumping on weekend afternoons. But it's a family-friendly town filled with shops, galleries and eateries housed in historic buildings. Views stretch across the Verde Valley past the red cliffs of Sedona to the distinctive outline of the San Francisco Peaks rising above Flagstaff. The narrow angled streets lined with old buildings, plus the occasional hulking ruin, make Jerome a paradise for photographers.

Like many Arizona mining towns, Jerome is easy to navigate on foot, though some of the hills are a bit steep and walking shoes are highly recommended. A few of the fun and funky shops on Jerome's steep streets include **Nellie Bly** (928-634-0255, nellieblyscopes.com), known for its impressive collection of kaleidoscopes, and **Jerome Artists Cooperative** (928-639-4276; jeromecoop.com), featuring the work of about 35 artists in a wide range of mediums. You'll find an excellent selection of paintings, photographs, ceramics, jewelry, clothing and more—everything from gift items to fine art. To delve even deeper into the artistic side of town, visit on the first Saturday of any month to experience the **Jerome Art Walk** (jeromeartwalk.com), from 5 p.m. to 8 p.m. Galleries stay open late, many featuring openings of new work. There's often a spread of food, sometimes live entertainment, and it's a pretty special feeling to stroll the hilly streets (or take the free shuttle) as dusk gently descends on the mile-high town.

Definitely worth seeing (and staying at) is the **Surgeon's House** (928-639-1452; surgeonshouse.com), the restored former residence of the chief surgeon for the town hospital, Arthur Carlson. Furnished with antiques, the Mediterranean-style bed-and-breakfast recalls an earlier time when the pace of life was slower and more elegant. The owner has retained the home's charm while adding modern luxuries. It can be arranged for a professional masseur to attend to your aches and pains. A buffet breakfast is served each morning and homemade snacks are available through the day. $$$.

For another lodging option, check into the **Ghost City Inn Bed and Breakfast** (888-634-4678; ghostcityinn.com), a one-hundred-year-old bed-and-breakfast that has had many incarnations in its time, but mostly operated as a boarding house for miners. This Victorian structure, furnished in original style, has modern amenities like air-conditioning and flat-screen televisions, yet a few spirits from the old days are said to linger. $$.

There are several quaint eateries, including **The Flatiron** (928-634-2733; theflatironjerome.com), a tiny place serving espresso, breakfast and lunch. $. **Bobby D's BBQ** (928-634-6235; bobbydsbbqjerome.com) also proves hard to resist with the aroma of slow-cooked meats from its smoker wafting down the street. $$.

For some of the best views in town as well as great grub, try the ***Haunted Hamburger*** (928-634-0554; thehauntedhamburger.com) where they serve tender burgers, sandwiches, and salads on a beautiful covered deck. $$.

If you travel southeast from Cottonwood on AZ 260 you'll encounter ***Out of Africa Wildlife Park*** (3505 W. AZ 260; 928-567-2840; outofafricapark.com). This park showcases big cats and offers a popular attraction, their daily *Tiger Splash* show that involves staffers swimming with tigers and other ferocious felines. Take the African Bush Safari for an up-close encounter with zebras, antelopes, and smoochy giraffes that will happily accept hand-offered treats. Staff will provide the treats so there's no need for you to smuggle in any acacia branches. The park is open daily from 9:30 a.m. to 5 p.m. Admission.

Just past the intersection of AZ 260 and I-17 is ***Camp Verde*** (928-554-0851; visitcampverde.com), a town with strong ranching and agricultural roots. It's once again supplying fruits, vegetables, pecans, and beef to restaurants emphasizing fresh and local ingredients. Located in the small downtown is ***Fort Verde State Historic Park*** (928-567-3275; azstateparks.com).

Like a number of Arizona communities, Camp Verde is a great example of Old West architecture—and outmoded cultural interface: It sprang up as a military outpost to protect miners, ranchers, and homesteaders against Indian raids. The fort was established in 1865, with final construction beginning in 1871. There were originally 22 buildings arranged around a parade ground for this critical outpost on the Arizona frontier. It was here in 1873 that General George Crook presided over the surrender of Apache Chief Chalipun and 300 warriors. Crook is well known in American history as a tough and savvy commander who used Apache scouts and adapted old-fashioned military tactics to work in the rugged and hostile terrain of Arizona. He also forged a trail connecting Fort Whipple (near Prescott) with Fort Apache in the Apache-Sitgreaves National Forests, a road that is still referred to as the General ***Crook Trail.*** Today the trail passes through Prescott, Coconino, and Apache-Sitgreaves National Forests. Some portions are passable by passenger vehicle, while other portions of the trail are suitable for hiking and equestrian use in summer and cross-country skiing in the winter. For more information contact the Apache-Sitgreaves National Forests (928-333-6280; fs.usda.gov/asnf) or the Prescott National Forest (928-443-8000; fs.usda.gov/prescott).Today, four of the original buildings of Fort Verde are carefully preserved and filled with period furnishings and artifacts. They each serve as a functioning museum. Admission.

The most famous structure in Camp Verde is one of the oldest, a five-story, 20-room dwelling built by the Sinagua early in the 12th century. ***Montezuma Castle National Monument*** (928-567-3322; nps.gov/moca) is perhaps the best-preserved cliff dwelling in the southwest, and certainly one of the most dramatic. Tucked in an alcove of the limestone cliffs high above the floodplain of Beaver Creek, the structure makes an imposing sight. No wonder it was called a castle. When discovered during Arizona's territorial days by white settlers, it was erroneously thought to be the work of the Aztec king, Montezuma. A paved walking path loops beneath a canopy of sycamore and cottonwood trees. The visitor center museum includes exhibits depicting the lifestyle and history of the Sinaguan culture. Located 11 miles to the north, ***Montezuma Well*** acts as a detached unit of the monument. The well, actually a collapsed limestone cavern 1,750 feet in diameter is fed by underground springs flowing with 1.5 million gallons of water per day. Hohokam Indian pithouses dot this area. The Hohokam were an ancient Native American tribe that built elaborate communities based upon agriculture. They populated much of the state until around the late fifteenth century. Later Sinagua dwellings are also found at the well, plus the remains of an ancient irrigation system. Admission is good for both segments of the monument. Each are open daily from 8 a.m. to 5 p.m.

Places to Stay in Northern Arizona

COTTONWOOD

Cottonwood Hotel
930 N. Main St.
(928) 634-9455
cottonwoodhotel.com
Since 1917, the Cottonwood Hotel has been an anchor of Old Town. But despite the historic designation, the rooms are spacious and thoroughly modern. $$.

Iron Horse Inn
1034 N. Main St.
(928) 634-8031
ironhorseoldtown.com
Another old town property, the Iron Horse started as a motor court back in the 1930s but has been exquisitely reimagined as a boutique hotel surrounding a gracious courtyard. Rooms may be on the smallish side but spotlessly clean. $$.

FLAGSTAFF

England House Bed & Breakfast
614 W. Santa Fe Ave.
(928) 214-7350 or
(877) 214-7350
englandhousebandb.com
A 1902 stonecutter's house with four rooms with private baths. Pressed-tin ceilings and French antiques add an air of Old World charm to the inn. Breakfast included. $$.

Weatherford Hotel
23 N. Leroux St.
(928) 779-1919
weatherfordhotel.com
Built in 1887, this historic hotel offers clean, restored rooms decorated in turn-of-the-twentieth-century style. Some rooms have private baths while others have shared baths. $.

GRAND CANYON SOUTH RIM

Kachina Lodge
(928) 638-2631 or
(888) 297-2757
(reservations only)
grandcanyonlodges.com
Perched on the South Rim, this motel-style lodge has basic rooms; some with partial canyon views (slightly more expensive).

Check in at El Tovar Hotel to the east. $$$.

Maswik Lodge
(928) 638-2631 or
(888) 297-2757
(reservations only)
grandcanyonlodges.com
Accommodations, nestled in the ponderosa pine forest a quarter mile from the rim, are comfortable but rustic motel rooms. $$$.

Thunderbird Lodge
(928) 638-2631 or
(888) 297-2757
(reservations only)
grandcanyonlodges.com
Situated on the rim, this motel-style lodge has a slightly more contemporary style with natural touches. Rooms with partial canyon views are more expensive. Check in at Bright Angel Lodge to the west. $$$.

Yavapai Lodge
(877) 404-4611
visitgrandcanyon.com
This large motel-style lodge is located near the eastern end of Grand Canyon Village, a quarter mile from the rim. $$.

JACOB LAKE

Jacob Lake Inn
Junction of N. US 89A and AZ 67
(928) 643-7232
jacoblake.com
A rustic lodge with cabins and rooms, restaurant, bakery, soda fountain, service station, and country store. $$.

JEROME

Connor Hotel
160 Main St.
(928) 634-5006
connorhotel.com
Twelve first-class, Victorian rooms in an 1898 hotel. Note that rooms 1 through 4 are located over the bar and can be noisy on weekend evenings. $$.

Jerome Grand Hotel
200 Hill St.
(928) 634-8200 or
(888) 817-6788
jeromegrandhotel.net
The imposing structure looming above the town was once the hospital, now converted to a lovely mountainside hotel. Ghost-hunting tours are regular events and an excellent restaurant should not be missed. $$$.

PAGE

Lulu's Sleep Ezze Motel
105 8th Ave.
(928) 608-0273
lulussleepezzemotel.com
Located on the Historic Avenue of Hotels, Lulu's offers sweetly simple accommodations with easy access to downtown. $.

SEDONA

Casa Sedona
55 Hozoni Dr.
(928) 282-2938
casasedona.com
A 16-room bed-and-breakfast inn offering luxury accommodations, stunning red rock views, gas

fireplaces, spa tubs, and refrigerators. $$$.

Enchantment Resort
525 Boynton Canyon Rd.
(928) 282-2900 or
(888) 250-1699
(reservations only)
enchantmentresort.com
A gorgeous resort hidden in scenic Boynton Canyon. Amenities include a full-service spa, three restaurants, tennis courts, a pool, and hiking and biking trails. $$$.

The Lodge at Sedona
125 Kallof Pl.
(928) 204-1942 or
(800) 619-4467
lodgeatsedona.com
In West Sedona, this secluded bed-and-breakfast, set on two wooded acres, was formerly a private home and now has 10 rooms and four suites, each with a distinct theme—from the exotic Far East to the rugged Old West. $$$.

TUSAYAN

Best Western Grand Canyon Squire Inn
74 AZ 64
(928) 638-2681 or
(800) 622-6966
grandcanyonsquire.com
Just south of the park's entrance in Tusayan, this hotel offers 318 rooms and suites, along with heated pools, fitness center, bowling center, arcade, restaurants, etc. $$.

The Grand Hotel
149 AZ 64
(928) 638-3333 or
(888) 634-7263
grandcanyongrandhotel
.com
In the Village of Tusayan near the entrance to Grand Canyon National Park, guests will enjoy upscale lodging and additional amenities like an indoor pool, fitness center, restaurant and saloon. $$$.

WILLIAMS

The Canyon Motel and RV Park
1900 E. Rodeo Rd.
(928) 635-9371 or
(800) 482-3955
thecanyonmotel.com
Situated on ten acres, this remodeled 1949 motor lodge offers rooms in flagstone cottages and renovated, historic cabooses and railcars. $.

Red Garter Inn
137 W. Railroad Ave.
(800) 328-1484
redgarter.com
This bed-and-breakfast houses four rooms in a two-story 1897 brick building that once served as a bordello and saloon. The rooms are on the upper floor and a bakery occupies the first floor. $$.

Places to Eat in Northern Arizona

COTTONWOOD

Concho's Mexican Restaurant
206 S. Main St.
(928) 649-9680
Flavorful Mexican cuisine seems even more vibrant thanks to the wonderful service; one of the friendliest staffs you'll find. $.

Cork and Catch
1750 E. Villa Dr.
(928) 649-2675
corkandcatch.com
Definitely off the beaten path but worth the trip, this eatery is tucked down a side street. The seafood specialties can always be paired with an excellent wine. $$.

Crema Craft Kitchen & Bar
917 N. Main St.
(928) 649-5785
cremacottonwood.com
It's all brunch all the time at this small eatery attached to a colorful patio, complete with a bar fashioned from a storage container. Finish off the meal with made-from-scratch gelato. $$.

FLAGSTAFF

Black Bart's Steakhouse and Musical Revue
2760 E. Butler Ave.
(928) 779-3142
blackbartssteakhouse.com
Slightly corny, but a lot of fun, this spot features food servers who double as singers—all students at nearby Northern Arizona University, and these are some seriously talented kids. Dinner only. $$$.

Salsa Brava
2220 Historic Rte. 66
(928) 779-5293
salsabravaflagstaff.com
Spice things up with the fresh selections at this award-winning Mexican restaurant. The cantina and fresh salsa bar add extra seasoning to this local favorite. $$.

JEROME

Grapes Restaurant & Bar
111 Main St.
(928) 639-8477
grapesjerome.com
This Italian eatery specializes in pizzas and pasta bowls you create yourself. $$.

Mile High Grill & Inn
309 Main St.
(928) 634-5094
milehighgrillandinn.com
This casual grill serves up tasty breakfast, lunch and dinner entrees ranging from French toast and cheese steak to blackened salmon and blue cheese burgers. $$.

FOR MORE INFORMATION ABOUT NORTHERN ARIZONA

Arizona Department of Tourism
visitarizona.com

Grand Canyon National Park
nps.gov/grca

Camp Verde Chamber of Commerce
visitcampverde.com

Jerome Chamber of Commerce
jeromechamber.com

Coconino National Forest
fs.usda.gov/coconino

Kaibab National Forest
fs.usda.gov/kaibab

Cottonwood Chamber of Commerce
cottonwoodchamberaz.org

Prescott National Forest
fs.usda.gov/prescott

Flagstaff Convention and Visitors Bureau
flagstaffarizona.org

Sedona–Oak Creek Chamber of Commerce
visitsedona.com

Glen Canyon National Recreation Area
nps.gov/glca

Williams–Grand Canyon Chamber of Commerce
experiencewilliams.com

SEDONA

Coffee Pot Restaurant
2050 W. AZ. 89A
(928) 282-6626
coffeepotsedona.com
Serves a huge selection of omelets and is known by locals for the "Best Breakfast in Sedona." $$.

Oak Creek Brewery & Grill
336 AZ 179
(928) 282-3300
oakcreekbreweryandgrill.com
Watch your wood-fired pizza, cedar-plank salmon, burgers, and steaks being cooked up in the grill's exhibition kitchen. Polish it all off with a mug of one of the brewery's award-winning microbrews. $$.

WILLIAMS

Cruisers Cafe 66
233 W. Rte. 66
(928) 635-2445
cruisers66.com
This 1950s cafe serves up a nice selection of burgers, sandwiches, and salads on the "Mother Road." Homemade malts and microbrews on tap add to the casual atmosphere. $$.

Pine Country Restaurant
107 N. Grand Canyon Blvd.
(928) 635-9718,
pinecountryrestaurant.com
Home-style country cooking in a cozy local restaurant. Open breakfast, lunch, and dinner and known for their artistic homemade pies. $$.

Red Raven Restaurant
135 W. Rte. 66
(928) 635-4980
redravenrestaurant.com
Casual fine dining emphasizing fresh ingredients and innovative menu offerings including fish, steak, and salads. $$.

Western Arizona

Lake Mead and Grand Canyon West

When it was created in the 1930s by the construction of **Boulder Dam** (702-494-2517 or 866-730-9097; usbr.gov/lc/hoover dam), the 110-mile-long Lake Mead was the largest artificial lake in the world. The dam itself was no small achievement either. The massive construction project was undertaken by an army of men desperate for employment during the Great Depression. They worked in punishing heat and dangerous conditions and 112 died before it was complete. Yet they finished under budget and two years ahead of schedule. Built to harness the awesome power of the Colorado River on the mitten tip of the Arizona–Nevada border, the dam is more than 726 feet tall. Enough concrete was used to build a two-lane highway stretching from San Francisco to New York City. Renamed **Hoover Dam** in 1947, it's linked to a power plant with 17 generators producing 4 billion kilowatts of electricity. The guided Powerplant Tour lasts for 30 minutes. The hour-long Dam Tour encompasses the power plant but then takes you deeper into the passageways within the structure. Tickets

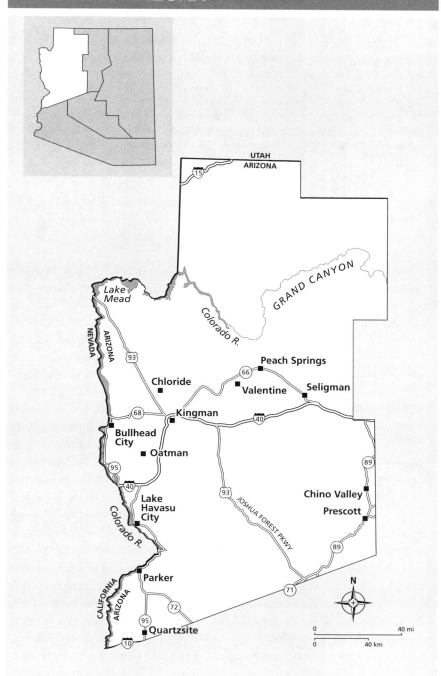

UTAH
ARIZONA

15

Lake
Mead

GRAND CANYON

Colorado R.

NEVADA
ARIZONA

93

Peach Springs

66

Chloride
Valentine
Seligman

68
Kingman
40

Bullhead
City
Oatman

95

89

40
Lake
Havasu
City

93
JOSHUA FOREST PKWY

Chino Valley
Prescott

Colorado R.

89

Parker
71

CALIFORNIA
ARIZONA
95
72

N

10
Quartzsite

0   40 mi
0   40 km

Artistic Leanings

Not only was Hoover Dam considered anengineering marvel when it was built, but it was also lauded as a modern work of art. Architect Gordon B. Kaufmann, designer of the Los Angeles Times Building, used art deco and modernist ideas in the dam's overall look. This style is complemented by Native American geometric designs in the terrazzo floors by artist Allen Tupper True (whose murals are prominent in the Colorado State Capitol in Denver) and the striking 30-foot bronze statues, named the *Winged Figures of the Republic,* sculpted by Oskar J. W. Hansen.

may be purchased online for the Powerplant Tour but must be purchased on site for the Dam Tour, which involves over a mile of walking on concrete or other hard surfaces. Tours begin at 9 a.m. and the last tickets are sold at 3:45 p.m. Admission.

If you are looking for some river running below Hoover Dam in **Black Canyon,** sign up for a rafting trip with **Black Canyon River Adventures** (800-455-3490; blackcanyonadventures.com). For those who don't mind paddling, snag a boat with **Boulder City River Riders** (702-293-1190; bouldercityriver riders.com), which offers guided kayak tours through Black Canyon. They'll even rent you a kayak if you'd like to explore on your own.

arizonatrivia

Though Arizona boasts one of the largest per capita boat ownerships in the country, most of Arizona's lakes are man-made. In fact, Lake Mead is the largest man-made lake in the United States.

Just about anything you can do in a body of water, you can do on **Lake Mead.** Swimming is a leisurely pastime in the summer months; Boulder Beach near the Alan Bible Visitor Center is a favorite for sunbathers. With 225 square miles to explore, boating of all kinds rules at Lake Mead. Anglers can cast a line twenty-four hours a day here, year-round. Just be sure to have fishing license for both Arizona and Nevada (details are on the National Park Service website, nps.gov/lake). Once you have your bait set, be ready to land a big one. This lake is known for its record-size fish. Freshwater diving is also a favored activity here, even though the lowered lake levels have closed some of the marked diving sites. Other activities abound, including jet skiing, water skiing, wakeboarding, sailboarding, and snorkeling. If you'd like to spend more than a day at Lake Mead, consider renting a house-boat. There are 550 miles of shoreline, which include hidden coves and tiny backwater inlets that are perfect for lengthy exploration. There are countless

Reservoir Recreation

The construction of Hoover Dam created the 110-mile-long reservoir of Lake Mead, which was named after US Bureau of Reclamation commissioner Elwood Mead. This enormous reservoir drew thousands of visitors to what became the first National Recreation Area in the United States in 1964. Today, more than six million visitors come to this water-sports wonderland each year.

areas where you can go ashore and have a picnic lunch while gazing at the surrounding mountains.

The **Alan Bible Visitor Center** (702-293-8990; nps.gov/lake), as well as facilities for renting equipment or booking steamboat tours, is on the Nevada side. However, the **Temple Bar Marina** off US 93 in Arizona (928-767-3211; templebarlakemead.com) offers camping and boat rental (including houseboats) and launching facilities, in addition to a cafe, grocery store, motel, and cabins. RV facilities are also available.

About 40 miles south of Lake Mead on US 93, look for the turnoff for **Dolan Springs** (928-767-4473; dolanspringschamber.org). The small community sits at the foot of the Cerbat Mountains. Local volunteers have constructed a network of interconnected trails across 480 acres of BLM land at the edge of town. What makes these trails special is that they are a chance to hike among groves of **Joshua trees** (*Yucca brevifolia*). This is a rare treat in Arizona. Natives of the dry Mojave Desert, Joshua trees are strange, spiky-topped relatives of the lily family that can reach more than 40 feet in height and live up to 300 years. They were allegedly named by Mormon pioneers who believed that the upraised arms resembled Joshua leading the Israelites. Trailheads are on 13th, 14th and 15th Street. And you can download a map at dolansprings trails.com.

Continuing north of Dolan Springs off Pearce Ferry Road on the way to Meadview is one of the largest stands of Joshua trees in the world. (Joshua Tree National Park is actually located in California.) If you arrive between February and March, you may see the trees in bloom with their creamy white flowers. The trees don't branch until after they bloom, and, because they rely on perfect conditions to flower, they don't necessarily bloom every year.

If you continue on Pearce Ferry Road (sometimes erroneously labeled on maps as Pierce Ferry Road) north from Dolan Springs to the unpaved Diamond Bar Road, you will be just a hop, skip, and a jump away from Grand Canyon West. The canyon's western end is 4,800 feet above the river and very different from its better-known northern, southern, and eastern boundaries. Sprinkled

AUTHOR'S FAVORITES IN WESTERN ARIZONA

Cattail Cove State Park	Lake Havasu
Grand Canyon Caverns	Lake Mead National Recreation Area
Havasu Canyon	London Bridge/English Village
Hualapai River Runners	Historic Route 66
Keepers of the Wild	

with high-desert vegetation, the canyon itself seems scaled down, more intimate and peaceful.

Grand Canyon West (928-769-2636; grandcanyonwest.com) is part of the one million acres of tribal land owned by the plateau-dwelling Hualapai ("people of the tall pines"). In recent years the Hualapai have successfully developed a booming tourism business on the West Rim—known for its spectacular *Skywalk,* a glass walkway suspended 70 feet over the edge of the canyon rim. Unhampered by the tight restrictions in place at Grand Canyon National Park, the Hualapai are able to offer everything from helicopter rides into the canyon to Hummer tours along the rim. Admission.

Once you reach the visitor center, you will be required to purchase a tour package from Grand Canyon West. The Hualapai Tribe offers the basic Hualapai Legacy tour package, which includes a Hualapai visitation permit and shuttle transportation. Admission. A free shuttle will take you to Eagle Point, where the Indian Village walking tour visits authentic dwellings; Hualapai Ranch, site of western performances, cookouts, and horseback and wagon rides; and Guano Point, where the "High Point Hike" offers panoramic views of the Colorado River. For an extra cost you can add a helicopter trip into the canyon, a boat trip on the Colorado River, a zip line adventure, a horseback ride to the canyon rim, or a walk on the Skywalk. Local Hualapai guides add a Native American perspective to a canyon trip.

For an overnight stay, the *Hualapai Ranch* (928-769-2636; grandcanyon west.com) offers small cabins with front porches perfect for watching the sun set. The cabins are adjacent to a small "western" town, where visitors can pose for snapshots, sign up for guided horseback tours and wagon rides, shop in a western store and watch gunfight reenactments. There is a dining room open for breakfast, lunch, and dinner. $$.

One hundred and twenty miles away, *Peach Springs,* on Historic Route 66, is the tribal capital and the location of the Hualapai Lodge. The *Hualapai Lodge* (900 Historic Rte. 66; 928-769-2230; grandcanyonwest.com) offers clean and comfortable rooms and the on-site *Diamond Creek Restaurant,* which is open for breakfast, lunch, and dinner. $. The concierge desk arranges river trips with the *Hualapai River Runners.* Admission.

Among the lesser-known, although unquestionably idyllic, settings in the area is an exotic canyon located within the tiny Havasupai Indian Reservation. Secluded and seemingly untouched by time and technology, *Havasu Canyon,* 5 miles wide and 12 miles long, appears to be more Hawaiian than mainland, with its cascading turquoise waterfalls and flowering orchids. No doubt the biggest reason for its enduring tranquility is its remoteness—visitors must either fly, hike, or ride into the canyon.

The Havasupai ("people of the blue-green waters") guard the canyon habitat by limiting the number of visitors allowed access to the village of *Supai* and the renowned canyon waterfalls, reaching as high as 200 feet, cascading over red cliffs into travertine pools below. Over the years, flash floods occasionally alter the turquoise pools, but the Havasupai persevere through their stewardship and commitment to their homeland. As a result, visitors continue to flock to the Havasu Canyon for the stunning views and the remote location. The only way to access the canyon is the 8-mile-long Hualapai Trail, which drops 2,000 feet from the canyon rim to Supai. From there it's another two miles to the campground and Havasu's main waterfalls—Navajo, Havasu, and Mooney Falls. The trail leaves from Hualapai Hilltop, 63 miles north on Indian Route 18 from Historic Route 66. You must obtain a reservation to enter the canyon, and since space is limited they can be extremely hard to come by. No day hiking is allowed. Admission.

Saddle horses and pack mules are also available but be aware that there has been widespread concern about the treatment and health of the animals. Think long and hard before utilizing this option. Admission. Visit the tribal website (theofficialhavasupaitribe.com) for general information and to make reservations. Phone numbers are posted there. Keep in mind that you will need to secure a room or a camping permit if you're hiking or riding.

Minerals and the Mother Road

It doesn't take Bill Nye the Science Guy to figure out how the mining town of *Chloride* (928-565-9777; chloridechamber.com), south of Dolan Springs on US 93, got its name. Silver chloride ore, silver, lead, zinc, and other precious

JANUARY

Great Oatman Bed Race
Oatman
(928) 768-6222
oatmangoldroad.org
This fun festival includes bed races through the streets, a chamber pot parade, burro biscuit toss, a burro braying contest, and a toilet seat toss.

The Main Event
Quartzsite
(928) 927-5200
quartzsitetourism.com
This annual "world famous gemboree" and merchandise sale attracts thousands for its wide selection of gems and minerals, trade show, and arts and crafts.

Tyson Well's Rock and Gem Show
Quartzsite
(928) 927-6364
tysonwells.com
Leading the pack of gem and mineral shows, this large event includes incredible displays of gems and minerals from around the world, lapidary work, and artist demonstrations.

MARCH

Bluegrass on the Beach
Lake Havasu City
(209) 480-4693
bluegrassonthebeach.com
Enjoy some of that high lonesome sound on the shores of Lake Havasu during the first weekend in March. There are jam sessions and workshops as well so bring your axe.

MAY

Route 66 Fun Run
Seligman
(928) 753-5001
historic66az.com
The Mother Road turns into a rolling party on the first weekend in May with more than 800 classic cars leaving from Seligman and traveling to Kingman and finally to Topock. Along the way there is live music, barbecues, dances, car shows and other festivities.

George Phippen Memorial Day Western Art Show and Sale
Prescott
(928) 778-1385
phippenartmuseum.org
This juried outdoor western art show held at the Courthouse Plaza is one of the best in the state. Other activities include a "Quick Draw" competition, gala benefit, and a miniature masterpiece auction.

JUNE

Folk Arts Fair
Prescott
(928) 445-3122
sharlot.org
Enjoy a weekend of living history with demonstrations of traditional arts such as quilting, wood carving, blacksmithing, spinning, weaving, and candle making at the Sharlot Hall Museum. You can also try your hand at churning butter and gold panning before enjoying live music and dancing performances.

Territorial Days
Prescott
(928) 445-2000
prescott.org
This arts and crafts show at Courthouse Plaza always draws a crowd. Other activities include games for kids, old-time photos, and live entertainment.

JULY

Frontier Days and World's Oldest Rodeo
Prescott
(928) 445-3103
worldsoldestrodeo.com
People have been gathering in Prescott since 1888 to watch rodeo games. Enjoy the celebration with rodeo performances, a parade, arts and crafts, fireworks, live entertainment, cowboy church, and a rodeo dance.

Prescott Indian Market
Prescott
(928) 445-3122
sharlot.org
This outdoor market at the Sharlot Hall Museum features traditional and contemporary Indian arts including jewelry, ceramics, sculpture, handwoven baskets, and blankets. Other activities include artist demonstrations, children's activities and Native American song and dance.

Sidewalk Egg Fry
Oatman
(928) 768-6222
oatmangoldroad.org
This yearly Independence Day celebration takes place at high noon when contestants attempt to fry an egg solar-style. Other activities include Old West gunfights, games, and arts and crafts.

AUGUST

Arizona Cowboy Poets Gathering
Prescott
(928) 713-6323
azcowboypoets.org
Working cowboys from all over the West converge at the Yavapai College Campus to sing original songs and to recite poetry about their lives and work.

SEPTEMBER

Andy Devine Days
Kingman
(928) 753-6106
gokingman.com
Honoring Kingman's own film and television actor, the city celebrates with their largest street festival that includes rock climbing walls, water slides, bungee stations, car shows, music and a PRCA Rodeo.

Mohave County Fair
Kingman
(928) 753-2636
mcfafairgrounds.org
This county fair touts a lineup of livestock exhibits, arts and crafts, carnival rides, contests, and children's activities.

OCTOBER

Folk Music Festival
Prescott
(928) 445-3122
sharlot.org
This family-friendly event features folk music from around the world being performed on the grounds of the Sharlot Hall Museum. Get ready for a good time listening to everything from bluegrass to gospel.

Old Miners Day
Chloride
(928) 565-9777
chloridechamber.com
Enjoy this silver mining capital's longest-running event with vaudeville acts, street dance, gunfights, horseshoe-pitching contest, swap meet, parade, live music, and a bake sale.

TOP ANNUAL EVENTS IN WESTERN ARIZONA (CONT.)

NOVEMBER

Festival of Lights
Lake Havasu City
(928) 453-3444
golakehavasu.com
More than one million lights are on display at English Village and London Bridge through New Year's Day.

DECEMBER

Boat Parade of Lights
Lake Havasu City
(928) 453-3444
golakehavasu.com
This colorful floating parade winds its way through the Bridgewater Channel under London Bridge and along Lake Havasu.

Christmas Parade
Prescott
(928) 445-2000
prescott.org
The parade that kicks off the season for "Arizona's Christmas City" culminates in the evening with the lighting of the Courthouse. That's not just a single tree mind you, but a veritable galaxy of twinkling lights that swaddle the plaza grove.

Acker Night
Prescott
(928) 778-5460
ackernight.com
Dozens of musicians perform in the downtown shops to raise money for scholarships, instruments and music lessons for Prescott kids.

minerals such as turquoise have been found in the area. At one time there were as many as seventy-five mines working in the hills. Founded in 1862, Chloride is the oldest continuously inhabited mining town in Arizona. Today, the cluster of historic buildings includes a couple of restaurants, a small motel, a few shops and a curious collection of yard art. Drive through the streets and you'll find metal sculptures, painted bowling balls, bottle trees, stacked mining tools and more. Maybe such a quest for creative expression was inspired by one of the most intriguing art displays in the state. Located 1.3 miles east of town are the *Roy Purcell murals.* Created in 1966 on a cliff in the Cerbats, the paintings are spread across 2,000-square-feet of boulders down a dirt road. "The Journey" depicts images of a snake, an eagle's talon, the phases of the moon, and a princess, all sort of flowing into one another. In 2006 artist Roy Purcell returned to town and repainted the murals for their fortieth anniversary.

Several sights in Chloride, including the *Old Jail* and the *Santa Fe Train Station* are worth a look. The jail may remind you of the dunk tank on the *Andy Griffith Show*. A century-old miner's house is now preserved as the *Jim Fritz Museum,* open on Sat from 10 a.m. to 1 p.m. Free, but donations are gratefully accepted as the Chloride Historical Society continues their work of protecting the weathered buildings. Every first and third Saturday a local group stages shoot-out reenactments at the recreated western village called Cyanide Springs.

The **Mine Shaft Market** (4940 E. Tennessee Ave.; 928-565-4888) sells groceries and goodies like ice cream and soft drinks. In the same building is the visitor center where tourists can get Arizona travel information and make reservations for rooms in several national parks, Laughlin, Nevada, and other destinations.

Yesterday's Restaurant (9827 2nd St.; 928-565-4251; chlorideaz.com) offers everything from burgers to prime rib. They also stock an impressive beer selection. $$. Also part of the property is **Shep's Miners Inn** with a handful of modest but comfortable rooms in an old adobe building that dates back to the early 1870s. $.

A great way to explore the area west of Flagstaff to the border of California is to follow Historic Route 66. **Route 66** was built in 1926 as the nation's first transcontinental highway. Beginning in Chicago and ending 2,448 miles later at the Santa Monica pier, it became known as the "Main Street of America." John Steinbeck immortalized it in 1939 as the "Mother Road" in his classic novel of dustbowl-hardened Okies, *The Grapes of Wrath*. Throughout the 1930s, many an Oklahoma farmer followed the rutted tracks of the Mother Road (which hadn't been completely paved yet) out to what he hoped was a better life in the citrus fields of California.

Traveling a vastly improved Historic Route 66 in 1946, singer/songwriter Bobby Troup wrote a song about this highway—"Get Your Kicks on Route 66"—and different versions (sung by everyone from Depeche Mode to Nat King Cole to the Rolling Stones) were hits in every decade. The early 1960s TV show *Route 66,* about a couple of young guys cruising the Mother Road in a Corvette, introduced the *American Graffiti* generation to Route 66 and created a romanticism about the diners, drive-in theaters, and motels that lined this two-lane road.

But a death knell was in the air. In 1956 President Eisenhower had signed the Interstate Highway Act, which helped to create safer, multilane superhighways like Interstate-40. It also changed forever how Americans traveled. With the completion of I-40 in 1984, the Mother Road became unnecessary. By the very next year, this relic from a bygone era was cast aside. US 66 was decertified in 1985. It was removed from maps and all signs were taken down. The highway that had been a symbol of freedom and the open road, and that had permeated popular culture was no more.

Then Arizona came to the rescue. More specifically, a handful of residents in a small town called Seligman led by the town barber, stepped up to save this paved river of Americana. With the advent of the interstates, traffic ceased to flow through towns (there was a reason Route 66 was called the "Main Street of America") but instead, roared past on the superslab. Businesses shuttered and economies began to crumble. Seligman was one of the communities struggling to hang on. They tried to come up with a way to stay viable. One man, a barber named Angel Delgadillo, had the idea of promoting Route 66. In 1987, he organized a few like-minded folks and they formed the Historic Route 66 Association of Arizona. Then they launched a campaign to have Arizona Department of Transportation designate their section of the old highway as Historic Route 66. By November 1987, they succeeded. It was the first portion of the road granted that designation, thus launching the preservation movement. Today, nearly all remaining segments of the Mother Road in Arizona are certified as Historic Route 66, and likewise, in all the other states that wisely followed our barber's example. Today, millions of people come from all over the world to travel Route 66 to experience a slower, more deliberate adventure. It is wildly popular with international visitors. Tour groups, car clubs, motorcycle riders and bicyclists from virtually every country on earth can be found rambling along this ribbon of pavement across northern Arizona. What has your barber done lately?

arizonatrivia

The Beale Wagon Road, surveyed and constructed between 1857 and 1859 by Lt. Edward F. Beale, stretches through New Mexico and Arizona near the 35th parallel. The road, which was one of the major routes to California, made history as the first federally funded inter-state highway.

Driving west from Williams, **Ash Fork** will be one of the first places you reach. Ash Fork, named for the area's native trees and the spot where three southerly flowing forks of Ash Creek come together. It is known as the "Flagstone Capital of the World," and indeed, these quarries have provided material for countless walls and floors not only all over Arizona, but nationwide via the railroad. The variety of colors and the smooth texture of Arizona flagstone have made it especially popular. The town was founded in 1882 as a stop on the Atlantic and Pacific Railroad. Route 66 kept it vibrant for a while but the loss of the old highway coupled with devastating fires in the 1970s and '80s took a toll. Be sure not to miss the **Ash Fork Route 66 Museum** (901 W. Route 66; 928-637-0204), a surprising gem filled with artifacts, dioramas and photographs. It also serves as the visitor center for the small town.

Ash Fork also boasts the ***first all-steel dam*** ever built. This National Historic Engineering landmark was erected in 1898 in Johnson Canyon. The mammoth steel plates, which make it look like a massive radiator, are designed to expand and contract with the temperature, and it shows few signs of wear after more than century of use. The dam is one of two structures near Ash Fork (the other is a stone dam) that were built to create water reservoirs for steam trains. Today, the small lakes make nice recreational outings. Volunteers have constructed a short hiking trail connecting the two landmarks, called the Stone to Steel Dam Trail. Grab a map and specific directions at the museum.

Just a few miles west of Ash Fork, you can exit I-40 at Crookton Road. This begins the longest intact stretch of Historic Route 66 still in existence. You can drive the Mother Road for the next 158 miles, all the way to California. As you're curving across the high plains dotted with junipers, you'll have some rustic poetry keeping you company. Recreated Burma-Shave signs line the road with their sequential rhymes. The original Burma-Shave campaign dates back to 1926, the same year Route 66 was completed. That was when America began learning the joys of a road trip.

You'll soon pull into the holy city for Route 66ers, **Seligman** (seligmanaz chamber.com), **Birthplace of Historic Route 66.** Don't be surprised to find multiple tour busses parked on the street and vintage vehicles rolling through town. You'll likely hear more languages spoken on the sidewalk of Seligman than at a UN cocktail party. Angel Delgadillo's barber shop has been transformed into an unofficial welcoming center and the **Original Route 66 Gift Shop** (22265 W. Route 66; 928-422-3352; route66giftshop.com). Visitors from all over the world stream through the doors each day to pay their respects to Angel—the Guardian Angel of Route 66—now in his 90s.

Gift shops overflowing with souvenirs line the streets of Seligman, squeezed in among the vintage motor courts and eateries. Treat yourself to a meal at **Delgadillo's Snow Cap** (22235 W. Route 66; 928-422-3291). Juan Delgadillo, Angel's brother, built the little drive-in out of scrap lumber in 1953. And it quickly earned a reputation among travelers, not just for good food, but also for Juan's quirky sense of humor. His antics delighted families for decades. Juan was also one of the co-founders of the Historic Route 66 preservation movement. Sadly, Juan passed away in 2004 but the restaurant and sense of fun are being carried on by his family. Stop by for some laughs and great road food like "cheeseburgers with cheese" and "dead chicken" sandwiches. The Snow Cap closes for part of the winter. $.

If you're looking for restaurants where you can sit inside, you can't go wrong with **Westside Lilo's** (22270 W. Route 66; 928-422-5456; westsidelilos .com). There are some German favorites among the homemade offerings but be sure to save room for dessert. The cream pies and luscious carrot cake at Lilo's are legendary. $.

Driving west from Seligman across the wide Aubrey Valley you'll reach one of the very first Route 66 roadside attractions. **Grand Canyon Caverns**

(928-422-3223; gccaverns.com) at mile marker 115 is the largest dry cave in the United States. In 1927, an underground chamber was accidentally discovered by Walter Peck, who filed a claim expecting to harvest great mineral wealth. When the assay report proved unpromising, Peck decided to mine the pockets of tourists traveling the new highway. For the cost of a quarter, he would lower them by rope into the caverns as they held a kerosene lamp, no doubt praying they didn't drop it. Conditions have since been upgraded and visitors now descend via elevator 210 feet for guided tours. Five different tours are offered and range from gentle strolls to scrambling around in some tight passageways wearing helmets and headlamps. The regular tours depart throughout the day every half-hour from 9:30 a.m. to 4 p.m. specialty tours, including the Ghost Walk, requires reservations. Admission. There's a motel, restaurant, gift shop and mini-golf course on the surface, and you can book horseback and wagon rides. But for a most memorable meal, dine in the **Cavern Grotto** (928-422-3223, Ext 3) deep in the bowels of the earth. Reservations are required. There's even the Underground Cave Suite, billed as the "largest, oldest, deepest, darkest, quietest motel room in the world." It's an amazing experience but quite pricey.

Next up is previously mentioned Peach Springs, headquarters for the Hualapai Indian Nation. Along with the Hualapai Lodge, you'll spot a couple of weathered buildings, including the **Osterman Gas Station.** The tribe floats occasional plans to restore the service station but there's been no progress so far. After continuing past the tiny burg of **Truxton,** Route 66 squeezes through scenic Crozier Canyon, lined with oddly-stacked boulders. As for nearby **Valentine,** it used to be that each year many thousands of Americans sent their Valentine's Day cards here to be canceled with the post office's distinctive stamp. Several years back, however, the community's postal carrier was kidnapped and murdered (a terrible crime anywhere but especially shocking here in this small, peaceful community), and the post office was closed.

In any case, the town is named for a former commissioner for Indian Affairs, not for any romantic notions. Film buffs may be interested to know that Valentine's **Hunt Ranch** (off Buck and Doe Road) is featured prominently in a scene in *Easy Rider*. Peter Fonda's character fixes a flat tire in front of the ranch, while in the background a cowboy shoes a horse.

With such a sweetheart of a name, it may not come as a surprise that Valentine is the heart-warming home for the **Keepers of the Wild Nature Park** (13441 E. Rte. 66; 928-769-1800; keepersofthewild.org). Located at mile marker 87, this wildlife refuge is home to hundreds of exotic animals rescued from neglectful and abusive situations. The 175-acre sanctuary offers educational tours, wildlife viewing opportunities, a gift shop, and a snack shop. The park is open daily (except Tues) from 9 a.m. to 5 p.m. Admission. Guided **Safari**

Tours are offered on a first-come, first-serve basis for an additional fee. Tours leave at 10 a.m., 1 p.m. and 3:30 p.m.

Blink! You just missed it. *Hackberry,* the next stop, is that small. Hackberry, named for a regional native tree, was an 1880s mining community located just off the Santa Fe Railroad tracks. With the development of Historic Route 66, Hackberry had a brief new life as a refueling stop for motorists. The *Hackberry General Store* (928-769-2605), which is about all that remains of the town, was first rescued by acclaimed artist and traveler, *Bob Waldmire.* Even though he passed away in 2009, his whimsical maps and artwork can still be seen along the Mother Road. Hackberry has continued to evolve under the care of subsequent owners and today is a beloved stop for road warriors. The time capsule effect begins at the vintage gas pumps and classic vehicles parked on the grounds. Nearly every square inch of the weather-beaten buildings are covered in old signs. Inside it's a combination gift shop/market that feels like a creaky-floored museum. You'll stop for a peek and spend an hour or more.

Farther down the road, just east of Kingman, you'll come to Hualapai Mountain Road. This 15-mile mountain drive will take you from the desert through a high elevation pine forest perfect for hiking, wildlife viewing, and picnicking at *Hualapai Mountain Park* (928-681-5700, ranger station, or 877-757-0915, cabin reservations; parks .mohavecounty.us). Maps for the 10 miles of hiking trails are available at the park office. Admission. The nearby *Hualapai Mountain Resort* (4525 Hualapai Mountain Rd.; 928-757-3545; hmresort.org) offers eight comfortable rooms. This rustic retreat is light on amenities, but loaded with opportunities to get away from it all. $. The resort restaurant serves salads, steaks, and pastas. $$.

Like many frontier towns, *Kingman* (866-427-7866; gokingman.com), about 25 miles west and south of Hackberry on Historic Route 66, is named after one of its founders. Lewis Kingman was a surveyor whose work helped to establish the Santa Fe Railway. The town is actually much bigger than its Main Street appearance would suggest, with a population of about 25,000. Because it's within a one-hour drive of Lake Mead, Lake Havasu, Lake Mohave, and other recreational areas, it's a major stopping point for camping and boating aficionados.

arizonatrivia

A modified Volkswagen Microbus owned by Bob Waldmire was the inspiration for the character "Fillmore" in the animated motion picture *Cars*. Pixar planned to name the character "Waldmire" but Bob, a dedicated vegetarian, refused to sell marketing rights for a series of toys that would be included in McDonald's Happy Meals.

Kingman is home to the ***Historic Route 66 Association of Arizona*** (928-753-5001; historic66az.com), along with a gift shop, located in the restored ***Powerhouse Visitor Center*** at 120 W. Andy Devine Ave. The Powerhouse was constructed as a generating station between 1907 and 1909. With the completion of Boulder (Hoover) Dam in the 1930s, the plant was put on standby. It sat vacant for many years. Demolition was too costly to be considered, and in 1986 the building was placed on the National Register of Historic Places (in all, sixty Kingman buildings enjoy the same distinction). Following extensive renovation, the building reopened in the fall of 1997. Upstairs is the ***Arizona Route 66 Museum*** with an excellent collection of exhibits detailing the significance of the Mother Road through the decades, along with research archives. An hour-long movie is shown in the small theater. Downstairs is the visitor center, gift shop and ***Route 66 Electric Vehicle Museum,*** which displays everything from micro-cars, the world's first electric street rod and a 1909 baggage tug—one of only two known to exist. Both museums are open from 9 a.m. to 5 p.m. Your admission fee entitles you to both museums and two additional ones.

Make your next stop the ***Mohave Museum of History and Arts*** (400 W. Beale St.; 928-753-3195; mohavemuseum.org). Here you'll discover exhibits on ranching, mining, and pioneer life. Native American artifacts and art (the Mohave, Hualapai, Chemehuevi, Havasupai, and Paiute Indians all had a presence on this corner of the state); displays of military might (there once was an aerial gunnery school in Kingman); and movie memorabilia from actor Andy Devine (Kingman's "favorite son") are all prominently displayed in this often-overlooked, 18,000-square-foot museum. The museum is open Mon through Fri from 9 a.m. to 5 p.m., and

arizonatrivia

Route 66 is also known as Andy Devine Ave. in Kingman.

Sat from 1 to 5 p.m. Then if you're in the mood for more history, head over to the ***Bonelli House*** at 430 E. Spring St. This two-story territorial-style mansion is named for the wealthy Swiss family that built it in 1915. Today it has been restored as a museum, and the interior has been decorated with much of the same furniture it held nearly one hundred years ago. The home is open for guided tours Mon through Fri from 11 a.m. to 3 p.m. Four museums for one admission price is a pretty sweet deal.

You won't find any bed-and-breakfast inns right in downtown Kingman, but there are a number of motels on the Historic Route 66 strip, such as the pre–World War II motor court, the ***El Travatore*** (1440 E. Andy Devine Ave.; 928-753-6520; eltrovatoremotel.com). $. If you're hungry, drop into ***Mr. D'z Route 66 Diner*** (105 E. Route 66; 928-718-0066). $.

Follow Route 66 out of Kingman as the road angles southwest across the desert flats for the next 20 miles to the edge of the Black Mountains. Once you reach the mountains, you'll begin what most aficionados consider the most scenic stretch of the entire Mother Road. But stop first. Just as you begin your climb into the rugged landscape, the lonely outpost of ***Cool Springs*** (928-768-8366; route66coolspringsaz.com) perches at the edge of the road, in the shadow of Thimble Butte. The original Cool Springs opened as a service station and diner in the 1920s and for decades was a crucial stop for early travelers about to cross the unforgiving Mojave Desert. It burned down in 1966 but was brought back to life in 2004 by a Chicago native who wanted to preserve this piece of the past. Now a gift shop and museum, the building is a painstaking recreation built atop the old stone foundation. Free.

The next 8 miles are a steep winding climb. The narrow two-lane road snakes its way up the mountains. Sharp hairpin curves and lack of guardrails make this a harrowing drive for some. It's hard to imagine that this was once the primary road for all commercial traffic but when Route 66 was being designed the mines in this area were still booming. The ore eventually played out and in 1952 Route 66 was realigned through the wide Sacramento Valley, pretty much the same corridor taken by I-40 today. The road climbs through Sitgreaves Pass, where you can gaze into three states (CA, NV and AZ), winds past the Gold Road Mine, which reopened a few years ago on into ***Oatman*** (928-768-6222; oatmangoldroad.org). Located only a few miles from the Nevada border, a visitor might easily imagine that a time warp exists here—the town looks much the same today as it did when it was established near the turn of the twentieth century. A mining town named after a survivor of an infamous Indian attack, Oatman has braved rough economic times, but its gorgeous Mohave County scenery and Old West ambience continue to draw tourists. Oatman is a big rally point for Historic Route 66 cruisers, including motorcycle clubs, so don't be surprised if you pull into town and glimpse a line of Corvettes or Harleys.

Clark Gable and Carole Lombard, two of the town's most famous visitors, arrived in 1939. After a ceremony in Kingman, they spent their wedding night (though some claim it was night number two) in Room 15 of the ***Oatman Hotel*** (928-768-4408), a two-story adobe building on Main Street. The hotel, built in 1902, is the largest adobe structure in Mohave County. Although you can't rent a room here, you can check out the decorated rooms upstairs. Downstairs you'll find an ice-cream parlor, and a full bar with dining room wallpapered in dollar bills. The tradition dates back to the old days when miners would post dollars with their names written on them on payday so they could continue to drink even when they were broke.

Visitors to Oatman can see staged gunfights on Main Street every day, get a cold one at the town's two bars and browse the shops that fill the historic buildings. Of course, Oatman's most famous attraction is the herd of wild burros that wander into town each day. Descended from the pack animals of the early miners that were turned loose, these wily creatures have learned there's an easier way to make a living than trying to forage in a desert land. They simply mosey into town and stand around, often in the middle of the road, and people feed them. Please don't offer them junk food. Just about every business in town sells bags of alfalfa cubes for a buck. This helps keeps the animals healthy. And while the baby burros may be adorable, don't give them anything as they can easily choke. You'll notice all the youngsters wearing a Don't Feed sticker on their head. Those are placed there by the residents who are very protective of their herd. If you want to know the name of any of the animals, just ask a local.

Just past Oatman the distinctive humped promontory of **Boundary Cone** rises over the road. From here, you'll have a couple of options. If you continue on Historic Route 66 it's about 22 miles to Topock. This is the last Arizona town on Historic Route 66, on the banks of the Colorado River across the border from California. Or you can take a detour on Boundary Cone Road heading almost due west to **Bullhead City** (928-754-4121; bullheadareachamber.com). This is another Colorado River town except this one sits across the border from Nevada. Bullhead City began life more than fifty years ago as a camp for workers building the Davis Dam on the southern end of Lake Mohave. A rock formation here that resembled a bull's head led to the city's name, but it's now submerged in the lake. The dam was completed in 1953. It regulates water delivery to Mexico and generates electrical power that goes to substations in Arizona, California, and Nevada.

Andy Devine Country

If you're a fan of old-time western movies, no doubt you're familiar with Kingman's most famous native son, *Andy Devine.* Born in 1905 in Flagstaff, he grew up in Kingman. He began his film career in the mid-1920s as a Hollywood bit player. His shambling, bearlike gait and raspy voice caused him to be cast as the comic relief in numerous westerns, including the John Ford classic *The Man Who Shot Liberty Valance.* Devine also took roles in many vintage TV shows such as *Gunsmoke, Bonanza, The Twilight Zone, Flipper,* and *Love, American Style.* He continued working in colorful character roles until shortly before his death in 1977.

Bullhead City languished for years as a sparsely populated bedroom community. It began to grow in the mid-1960s when entrepreneur Don Laughlin began casino and resort development just across the Colorado River in Laughlin, Nevada, creating a need for visitor services on the Arizona side. Bullhead City was finally incorporated in 1984. Today, more than two million people a year visit Laughlin, and many of them launch their vacation from Bullhead City, where there's an airport that can accommodate planes as big as the Boeing 737. When visiting Bullhead City, stop at the **Colorado River Museum** (1239 AZ 95; 928-754-3399; coloradoriverhistoricalsociety.org). Located in Bullhead Community Park, the museum has exhibits on local Native American tribes, evidence of European exploration dating back to 1540, steamboat travel on the Colorado River, and the wagon and camel trains that passed through this area. Hours vary seasonally. Admission.

Lake Mohave can be reached by driving north on AZ 95. Lake Mohave is part of the **Lake Mead National Recreation Area** (702-293-8990; nps .gov/lake). Admission. Both narrow and shallow compared to Lake Mead, it is pinned between Arizona's Black Mountains and the Eldorado and Newberry Mountains of Nevada. The lake has fishing for largemouth and striped bass, catfish, sunfish, and bluegill. Fishing licenses, tackle, and bait are available at Katherine Landing at **Lake Mohave Marina** (928-754-3245; katherinelanding .com). The marina also rents boats from personal watercraft to patio boats that can accommodate up to 10 passengers. There's a campground, 16 motel rooms with mid-century décor and a café serving breakfast and lunch. $$.

If lounging in a casino sounds like more fun than lounging on a lake, there are several casinos only minutes away in Laughlin, Nevada, most of them lining the western bank of the Colorado.

A favorite place to stay in Bullhead City is the **Lodge on the River** (1717 AZ 95; 928-758-8080 or 888-200-7855; bullheadlodgeontheriver.com). The riverfront suites offer views and it's within walking distance of restaurants. $.

Another option on the waterfront is the **Colorado River Oasis** (1641 AZ 95; 928-763-4385; coloradoriveroasis.com). The resort also doubles as an RV park and includes such amenities as a boat dock, sand beach, swimming pool, fitness center, and a clubhouse. The resort offers a wide range of vacation rental rooms, some with kitchenettes. $$.

After a day on the river, join the locals at the **River Dog Grill** (2046 AZ 95; 928-704-3644). Wings and cold brew are the favorite things to order, but this jukebox joint also serves up a menu of salads, sandwiches, and seafood. The bar is the place to be, but the outdoor patio is a nice alternative. $.

Lake Havasu Area

South of Bullhead City and south of the Historic Route 66 junction with AZ 95 is **Lake Havasu City** (928-453-3444 or 800-242-8278; golakehavasu.com). Founded in 1963, it's one of Arizona's youngest municipalities. The lake itself isn't much older, having been created in 1938 when Parker Dam was built on the California border of the Colorado River. **Lake Havasu** attracts a huge number of visitors, especially in the winter with the influx of snowbirds, and spring when college students flock there for some sunny water-based (and possibly alcohol-fueled) spring break fun. It used to clear out in the summer, when Lake Havasu City often records the hottest temperature in Arizona—and sometimes in the nation. Today, though, southern Californians and Arizonans alike appear to ignore their thermometers and have turned the area into a popular summer getaway for water sports of all types.

Lake Havasu is a 45-mile-long playground perfect for waterskiing, jet skiing, powerboating, swimming, and fishing. **Lake Havasu State Park** (928-855-2784; azstateparks.com) is a popular place for surf and sand during the summer with its four boat ramps, swimming beach, picnic areas, nature trail, and numerous campsites, many of them right on the water.

Of course, Lake Havasu City offers more than just fun in the sun. As most of the free world knows, the city is home to the **London Bridge,** all 10,276 granite blocks of which were brought over from England in 1968 by city founder Robert McCulloch of McCulloch Chainsaw fame. When the city of London put the bridge up for sale because it began sinking due to the flow of modern traffic, McCulloch bought the bridge in a terrific publicity stunt for a mere $2,460,000. What you may not realize is that the city has gone to great lengths to complete the illusion of an English community. At the base of the bridge is the Tudor-style **English Village.** The shops, the streets, and even the phone booths resemble those in London. Stores in the village sell curios and gift items—some British, some not—such as glassware and candles. This is also where you'll find the Visitor Information Center (422 English Village; 928-855-5655). If you're here during the cooler months (Oct through Apr), sign up at the visitor center for a guided walking tour of London Bridge. They leave Tues, Thurs, and Sat at 11 a.m. and will give you plenty of history and a few ghostly tales. Admission.

Be sure to grab a bite or a drink at **Burgers by the Bridge** (928-854-6874; burgersbythebridge.com) nestled at the base of the bridge. The open-air restaurant serves as Lake Havasu's unofficial patio, with a perfect view and full bar. Everything in the kitchen is made fresh. The juicy burgers are good as the name would imply. The lightly battered fish and chips may be the best in town. $.

The English motif continues in enterprises like the **London Bridge Resort** (1477 Queen's Bay Rd.; 928-855-0888; londonbridgeresort.com), the facade of which mimics a stone castle. The resort has boat docks, several pools, a nine-hole executive golf course, tennis courts, a workout room, and other amenities. Like many other properties around the country, the London Bridge Resort is a time-share resort. Some suites have views of London Bridge. $$.

The Heat Hotel (1420 McCulloch Blvd. N; 928-854-2833; heathotel.com) is a hip, boutique property that sits on the water right in the heart of town. Rooms and suites are bright and cheerful with contemporary furnishings and private balconies. $$.

For a look at a different point of view, stop by the **Lake Havasu Museum of History** (320 London Bridge Rd.; 928-854-4938; havasumuseum .com). This popular museum features displays on the history of the region in a 3,000-square-foot building. Admission.

To explore more of the lake, take a *Bluewater Jet Boat Tour* (70 London Bridge Rd.; 928-855-7171; coloradoriverjetboattours.com). They offer three options including the popular narrated ride through the Havasu National Wildlife Refuge and scenic twisting Topock Gorge. Admission. If you'd prefer to pilot a boat yourself, try the *Rubba Duck Safari* (402 English Village; 928-208-0293). Take a single or double-manned rigid inflatable craft through Bridgewater Channel and into the open water on an interactive guided tour. Admission.

Landlubbers will enjoy a leisurely stroll along the Shoreline Trail, a 2-mile paved walkway that starts at London Bridge and traces the edge of the lake. As you walk past white sand beaches and swaying palm trees, watching the sun sparkling on the water and seagulls flying overhead, you'll begin to understand that Arizona does in fact have an impressive West Coast.

arizonatrivia

Lake Havasu City's London Bridge is the largest "antique" ever sold.

When you stop to eat, you can indulge at *Javelina Cantina* (1420 McCulloch Blvd.; 928-855-8226; javelinacantina.com). The family-friendly casual Mexican eatery features a patio overlooking London Bridge. $$. Or try *College Street Brewhouse & Pub* (1940 College Dr.; 928-854-2739; collegestreetbrew houseandpub.com) where they serve handcrafted beers and a menu of fresh-made food from flat bread pizzas to teriyaki shrimp skewers. $.

Quartz and Camels

Heading south from Lake Havasu City on AZ 95 you'll pass ***Cattail Cove State Park*** (928-855-1223; azstateparks.com) with a beautiful blend of desert hiking trails and white sand beaches. There are campsites, a picnic area and even a dog-friendly beach at this park that hugs the southern edge of Lake Havasu. Admission.

Birders can catch an eyeful at the ***Bill Williams River National Wildlife Refuge*** (928-667-4144; fws.gov/refuge/bill_williams_river). Look for such migratory waterfowl as vermillion flycatchers, yellow warblers, and summer tanagers. This is an odd collision of habitats, where the Sonoran Desert meets the Mojave Desert with a riparian corridor slashing through the middle. A few nature trails, and a short rugged scenic drive (high clearance 4WD recommended) provide access to the landscape. Many visitors prefer to see it via kayak. There's also a handicap-accessible fishing dock. The 6,100-acre refuge is located off AZ 95 between mileposts 160 and 162. Free.

AZ 95 continues to snake its way south through rugged desert hills, with flashes of the river peeking through. Two more state parks are perched on the banks of the Colorado River. First up is the smaller of the two, ***River Island State Park*** (928-667-3386; azstateparks.com) offering an intimate campground (only 37 sites), beach, boat ramp and a short but scenic hiking trail. Admission. Just over a mile further south ***Buckskin Mountain State Park*** (928-667-3231; azstateparks.com) commands an impressive view of the Parker Strip—an 18-mile stretch between Parker Dam and Headgate Dam that's especially popular with recreationists. The visitor center here serves both parks and there is a larger campground, more trails that lead through desert hills to old mine sites, a boat ramp, and a slender strip of beach. Admission.

Keep traveling south a few more miles on AZ 95 to reach the community of ***Parker*** (928-669-2174; parkeraz.org). This is the site of one of Arizona's greatest off the beaten path adventures. The ***Nellie E. Saloon*** (thedesertbar .com) sits 5 miles down a bouncy dirt road in the mountains surrounding Parker. At first glance, such an obscure hard-to-reach location might seem to be a detriment to business but it turns out, that's a big part of its charm. Better known as ***Desert Bar,*** the unexpected watering hole occupies the site of an old mining camp. Nearly everything is made from recycled material and it operates on solar power. It's only open from noon to sunset on Sat and Sun from Oct through Apr. Bands perform live music, food is cooked on big grills and cold beer flows freely. It's a winter party in the middle of the desert. 'Nuff said.

You'll find several restaurants and motels in the town of Parker that's strung along the highway. A few miles south of Parker is **Poston,** a name that doesn't mean much to most Arizonans but that played a major role in one of the saddest chapters in American history. Beginning in the summer of 1942, and continuing until the end of World War II, nearly 18,000 Japanese-Americans were interned at three Poston camps on the **Colorado River Indian Tribes Reservation** (928-669-9211; crit-nsn.gov). Though the detainees were able to create the semblance of a real community by building a pavilion and staging theatrical and musical entertainments, they were clearly prisoners within their own country.

In 1992, a monument to the camp's detainees was erected in Poston, which still contains the camp's original auditorium. The monument's single concrete column symbolizes "Unity of Spirit." It is 30 feet high and 7 feet wide with a hexagonal-shaped base representing a Japanese lantern with plaques that tell the story of the internment. The staff at the **Colorado River Indian Tribes Museum** (133 W. Riverside Dr.; 928-669-8970; crit-nsn.gov/critmuseum) in Parker can answer some questions about the Poston camp. The museum also has displays of artifacts from vanished tribes like the Anasazi and Hohokam, as well as rugs, baskets, and other

arizonatrivia

Palm Canyon, southeast of Quartzsite, is the only place in Arizona where native California palm trees grow in their natural habitat.

Quartzsite Camels

Besides being a rich mining district, **Quartzsite** also has an interesting connection to the United States Camel Corps. The army had employed Hadji Ali, a Syrian camel driver, to train the troops in the fine points of managing these "ships of the desert." Known as Hi Jolly to his friends, this Middle-Easterner who'd been transplanted to the American Southwest was regarded as a rather colorful character and something of a local hero. Despite Ali's best efforts, the experiment, carried out from the mid-1850s to 1864, was less than a rousing success. One explanation is that the camels couldn't get along with the army's pack mules. In any case, the hapless animals were finally sold at auction and a few escaped and were spotted wandering the Arizona desert years later.

Ali died in 1902, and thirty-three years later, Governor Benjamin Moeur dedicated the **Hi Jolly Monument**, a stone pyramid topped with a metal silhouette of a camel. The monument is easily reached off the west-end bypass of I-10.

crafts made by contemporary tribes like the Mohave, Navajo, and Chemehuevi. They're open Mon through Fri 8 a.m. to 5 p.m. Free.

No town fluctuates so dramatically with the seasons as **Quartzsite** (which you can reach by driving south on AZ 95 from Parker to I-10 and heading east on I-10 for a few miles). For much of the year this community of about 2,000, just across the border from Blythe, California, is little more than a quiet sun-baked desert outpost. But winter brings hordes of snowbirds. While the numbers have declined in recent years, still a million or more visitors show up to occupy the 70 RV parks and the thousands of acres of BLM land where dispersed camping is allowed. It's during this time that a series of gem and mineral shows take place, including some of the largest in the country, attracting rockhounds from all over. Vendor stalls spring up and food booths open as an epic swap meet spreads across much of the burg. For more information on Quartzsite gem shows, contact the Quartzsite Chamber of Commerce (928-927-5200; quartzsitetourism.com).

Continue east on 1-10 and then angle northeast on US 60 and you'll reach the turnoff for Alamo Lake in the small town of Wenden. Take this winding road 37 miles where it ends at an unexpected body of water. Far off the beaten path, **Alamo Lake State Park** (928-669-2088; azstateparks.com) is the most remote of Arizona's state parks. The lake fills the valley at the base of the Rawhide and Artillery Mountains and is regarded as one of the best bass fishing lakes in Arizona. Come prepared because you're a long way from anywhere. But if you're looking for a quiet getaway and some dark skies, this may be a good fit. Along with a campground and a few cabins, there's a market in the park that carries some supplies. Admission. Located just beyond the park boundary about 3 miles down a dirt road, **Wayside Oasis** (928-925-3456; waysideoasisrvpark.com) is a combination saloon/cafe/store/RV park where you can do your laundry and throw a game of horseshoes. Places in the outback have to provide for many needs. They serve a full breakfast and burgers and sandwiches the rest of the day, when they're open, which is during the cooler months. Call ahead for hours. $.

You'll soon leave the desert behind if you continue east. Turn on AZ 71 from US 60 until it ends at AZ 89, and then bear northeast on 89 toward Yarnell. Near the top of the hill before reaching the small town is a most significant stop. The **Granite Mountain Hotshots Memorial State Park** (azstateparks.com) honors the elite wildland firefighters that died battling the Yarnell Hill Fire on June 30, 2013. There's a roadside pullout with about a dozen parking spaces. A moderately steep trail winds its way up the slopes of the Weaver Mountains. Along the path 19 plaques have been placed to honor each man. They include a photo and a little of their story. It's a bit less than 3 miles to an observation deck overlooking the fatality site and the community beyond that the men were battling to save. Another trail follows the final route the hotshots took that day to the touching memorial where they fell. It's a heartbreaking spot but at the same time, there is a sense of peace and healing to be found here. For those that can't make the entire 7-mile round trip hike, a commemorative display with statue and photos can be found in the parking area. The park can only be accessed from the southbound lanes of 89, so you will have proceed toward Yarnell and backtrack. Free.

Sitting at the top of the hill, ringed by mountains, **Yarnell** survived that tragic fire. More than 100 buildings burned but most have since been rebuilt. People who move to a community like Yarnell do not want to give it up and when you see the views and wide-open spaces, you'll understand why. A few shops and eateries line the main drag through town. Watch for the turnoff to the **Shrine of St. Joseph of the Mountains**, a half-mile west of AZ 89. Created in 1939 by Felix Lucero, the hillside shrine depicts the Way of the Cross, the Garden of Gethsemane and the Last Supper. All life-sized pieces are sculpted out of reinforced concrete and set among the oak trees and boulders. Visitors can walk a trail through the Stations of the Cross. Open during daylight hours. Free.

Heading toward Prescott, you'll notice a turnoff to one of those locations where you just know there's a story to go along with the name. Although things are quiet now, there were many Indian wars fought here during Arizona's frontier days. **Skull Valley,** just west of Prescott, is named for the grisly aftermath of an 1864 battle between Apaches and Maricopas. The dead warriors were not buried, and white settlers were greeted by the sight of human skulls bleaching in the sun. For years Skull Valley was a stage stop as well as the location of Fort McPherson, established here to protect settlers and overland freighters from Indian attacks. The fort was removed after only a few years of use. A number of historic buildings, however, remain. These include the Santa Fe Depot, which was built in 1898; a one-room schoolhouse built in 1917; a 1916 general store; and a 1925 gas station. You can see the outside of the old buildings on your own. To learn more, visit the museum in the historic depot maintained by the **Skull Valley Historical Society** (3150 Old Skull Valley Rd.; skullvalley.org) on Sun afternoons Memorial Day to Labor Day from 2 to 4 p.m. Admission.

A Piece of the Old West

Nestled in a forested bowl at an elevation of 5,300 feet, Prescott is affectionately known as "everybody's hometown." But don't call it Pres-cott. Locals prefer the pronunciation *Press-kit.* ("Just like *biscuit,"* they'll tell you). The town was named after historian William H. Prescott and began its life in 1864 as a mining and ranching community.

In some respects, **Prescott** (928-445-2000 or 800-266-7534; prescott.org) looks like a cross between Flagstaff—because of its high altitude and pine trees—and Bisbee—because of its many Victorian, wood-frame homes. Residents compare it with the sorts of communities you come across in the Midwest. Of course, if you're from the Midwest, maybe that's not so exciting. We Arizonans think it's pretty cool. Perhaps that scenic setting and old-fashioned charm is why Prescott was also designated as "Arizona's Christmas City."

For visitors the town offers bed-and-breakfast inns, hotels, and motels. Prescott also has accommodations that are listed in the Historic Hotels of America registry. The **Hassayampa Inn** (122 E. Gurley St.; 928-778-9434 or 800-322-1927; hassayampainn.com) was built in the late 1920s as a getaway hotel for wealthy residents of Phoenix. The architecture is Pueblo art deco, done in red brick, and includes Arizona's first porte cochere. The inn has been redecorated on a regular basis without taking away the traditional character of its rooms. $.

Near the Courthouse Square and Whiskey Row is **Hotel Vendome** (230 S. Cortez St.; 928-776-0900; vendomehotel.com) which is listed on the National Register of Historic Places. It's a grandmother's cottage sort of place with quilts on the beds and a bed-and-breakfast ambience. Legend has it there's a ghost (and a ghostly cat!) in the house, which may be why the brochure says it's a unique lodging experience, not just a place to sleep. $$.

You won't starve in Prescott: Restaurants range from big-name chains to mom-and-pop establishments. **Murphy's** (201 N. Cortez St.; 928-445-4044; murphysprescott.com) is a former general store that is now transformed into an elegant eatery. Murphy's offers fresh fish daily, as well as ribs, lobster tail, and other examples of American and Continental cuisine. The restaurant's lounge affords a view of **Thumb Butte,** where Virgil Earp—before becoming a US marshal for Pima County—once ran a sawmill. $$. **Iron Springs Café** (1501 Iron Springs Rd.; 928-443-8848; ironspringscafe.com) occupies an old railroad depot. They serve up an intriguing mix of Southwest and Cajun dishes, along with made-from-scratch comfort food. $$.

arizonatrivia

Prescott was named Arizona's first territorial capital in 1864, a title it relinquished to Tucson in 1867 before regaining it in 1877. The capital was moved—permanently—to Phoenix in 1889.

If you want to find out more about the area's history, the best place to go is the **Sharlot Hall Museum** (415 W. Gurley St.; 928-445-3122; sharlot.org). Hall was an early twentieth-century historian, originally from Kansas, who grew up in and around Prescott. Later in life she purchased the former governor's mansion (Prescott was twice the territorial capital) and began a museum of items relating to Arizona history. On the grounds are the Museum Center, housing the archives and research library; the Sharlot Hall Building, a rock and pine log house; the Fremont House of more sophisticated construction; a Victorian-style Bashford House; Fort Misery (which is the oldest log building associated with Arizona); the Transportation Building, exhibiting the vehicle collection; and the Governor's Mansion, built in 1864. In addition there's a ranch house, a schoolhouse, a windmill, and several gardens, including the Pioneer Herb Garden. The museum is open Mon through Sat from 10 a.m. to 5 p.m. (May through Sept), 10 a.m. to 4 p.m. (Oct through Apr), and Sun from noon to 4 p.m. year round. Admission.

Another museum that attracts its share of visitors is the ***Phippen Western Art Museum*** (4701 AZ 89 N.; 928-778-1385; phippenartmuseum.org). Named after George Phippen, one of the founders of the *Cowboy Artists of America,* the museum has permanent and traveling exhibitions. Much of the work presented in the museum involves realistic depictions of cowboy life—roundups, campfires, bronc busting—but there are also impressionistic portraits of ranch hands, Native Americans, and other frontier dwellers that give startling insight into the life, work, and soul of the people of the Southwest. The museum also frequently hosts lecturers and special events related to cowboy art. The museum is open Tues through Sat from 10 a.m. to 4 p.m. and Sun from 1 to 4 p.m. Admission.

Historic ***Whiskey Row*** is a stretch of Montezuma Street between Gurley and Goodwin. In the "bad old days" of the West, this avenue of saloons and red light establishments was the scene of much debauchery and gunplay, not to mention a horrendous fire in 1900. One of the best places to visit on the Row is the ***Palace Restaurant and Saloon*** (120 S. Montezuma St.; 928-541-1996; whiskeyrowpalace.com). The original Palace burned down in the 1900 fire, but the hand-carved mahogany bar was carried (by hand) out into the street and later incorporated into the rebuilt structure. Opened in 1877, the Palace is the oldest bar in Arizona and has served customers like Wyatt and Virgil Earp, Doc Holliday, and Steve McQueen, who filmed several scenes of the 1972 movie *Junior Bonner* here.

Downtown walking tours are offered during summer weekends courtesy of the Chamber of Commerce. Led by knowledgeable guides the tours circle Courthouse Plaza and visit nearby attractions and dish up plenty of dirt on some of the town's early residents. Tours take place May to Oct on Fri, Sat and Sun at 10 a.m. unless there is a special event on the Plaza. They depart from the Visitor Information Center at 117 W. Goodwin St.

Chino Valley's Claim to Fame

Although Prescott claims the privilege of being the first Arizona territorial capital, that honor rightly belongs to the little community of **Chino Valley** (928-636-2493; chino valley.org), a bedroom community 15 miles to the north on AZ 89. In 1863 there was a mining camp in Chino Valley under the command of Lt. Amiel Whipple, and he established the capital at his fort. The most logical choice, Tucson—a much larger town with more amenities—was ruled out because of its large number of southern sympathizers. The territorial capital was moved to Prescott the following year.

Nearby, the ***Lynx Lake Recreation Area*** (928-443-8000; fs.usda.gov/prescott) offers plenty of outdoor recreational opportunities. In addition to bass and crappie, rainbow trout are periodically stocked in the 55-acre lake. Boating is restricted to electric motor-powered watercraft, but is also open to oar, paddle, or sail-powered boats. If you don't have your own, you can rent a boat at the ***Lynx Store and Marina*** (928-778-0720; lynxlakestore.com) or grab a bite in their cafe. Other area activities include hiking, camping, mountain biking, horseback riding, and bird-watching.

FOR MORE INFORMATION ABOUT WESTERN ARIZONA

Arizona Office of Tourism
visitarizona.com

Bullhead City
bullheadareachamber.com

Chloride Chamber of Commerce
chloridechamber.com

Grand Canyon West
grandcanyonwest.com

Havasupai Tourist Enterprise
theofficialhavasupaitribe.com

Hoover Dam
usbr.gov/lc/hooverdam

Kingman Tourism Bureau
gokingman.com

Lake Havasu Tourism Bureau
golakehavasu.com

Lake Mead National Park
nps.gov/lake

Oatman Chamber of Commerce
oatmangoldroad.org

Parker Area Chamber of Commerce
parkeraz.org

Prescott Chamber of Commerce
prescott.org

Prescott National Forest
fs.usda.gov/prescott

In recent years the city of Prescott, along with a hardy group of volunteers have added an incredible system of trails for hikers and mountain bikers. These include **Prescott Circle Trail,** a network of non-motorized trails that form a 54-mile loop around the town. Other popular trails weave among the Granite Dells, dramatic outcroppings of exposed rocks, encircle **Watson Lake** and **Willow Lake,** and follow an old railroad bed as part of the Rails-to-Trails system. You can find more information at prescott-az.gov.

Places to Stay in Western Arizona

KINGMAN

Days Inn by Wyndham Kingman West
3023 E. Andy Devine Ave.
(928) 753-7500
wyndhamhotels.com
A reasonably priced choice on the main drag. Includes a free continental breakfast and a heated outdoor pool. $.

LAKE HAVASU CITY

The Nautical Beachfront Resort
1000 McCulloch Blvd.
(928) 855-2141 or
(800) 892-2141
nauticalbeachfrontresort
.com
One hundred thirty-nine beachfront suites, each with a lake view and balcony or patio. $$.

MEADVIEW

Grand Canyon Western Ranch
3750 E. Diamond Bar Rd.
(928) 788-0283 or
(800) 798-0569
grandcanyonwesternranch
.com
This historic, working cattle ranch takes guests on an adventure to the Old West. Enjoy the ranch's rustic cabins or glamping tents. Horseback riding, wagon rides, and a helicopter tour of Grand Canyon West are available for an additional fee. $$.

PARKER

Blue Water Resort and Casino
11300 Resort Dr.
(928) 669-7777 or
(888) 243-3360
bluewaterfun.com
Rooms and suites, two restaurants, casino, live entertainment, pool and water park, marina, and sandy beach. $.

Havasu Springs Resort
2581 AZ 95
(928) 667-3361
havasusprings.com
Four separate hotels at this resort cater to a wide range of needs. The Marina Hotel is closest to the inner harbor, Lakeview Motel offers panoramic views, Vista Suites is geared for families, and the Poolside Motel offers a central location. $.

PRESCOTT

Prescott Pines Inn
901 White Spar Rd.
(928) 445-7270
prescottpinesinn.com
This Victorian bed-and-breakfast offers a romantic getaway in the ponderosa pine forest. Breakfast is a delight; it's even served on rose-patterned china. $$.

SELIGMAN

Canyon Lodge
22340 W. Route 66
(928) 422-3255
route66canyonlodge.com
Enjoy clean rooms, each
with a different theme, in
this classic motor court.
The comfortable beds are a
nice bonus. $.

Places to Eat in Western Arizona

KINGMAN

Floyd & Co. Wood-Fired Pizza
418 E. Beale St.
(928) 753-3626
floydandcompany.com
Artisanal wood-fired pizzas
are topped with hand-
pulled mozzarella and
perched on a soft, luscious
crust that retains a bit of a
crunch. $$.

Rickety Cricket Brewing
312 E. Beale St.
(928) 263-8444
ricketycricketbrewing.com
Besides the full slate of in-
house beers, they serve a

full menu of everything from
thin crust pizzas to piled
high burgers. $$.

LAKE HAVASU CITY

Chico's Tacos
1641 McCulloch Blvd.
(928) 680-7010
chicostacoslakehavasu
.com
This casual fast-food
Mexican joint serves up
such standard dishes as
tacos, enchiladas, flautas,
burritos, and fajitas. Six
specialty salsas at the salsa
bar spice things up. $.

Juicy's River Cafe
42 Smoketree Ave. S.
(928) 855-8429
juicysgreatfood.com
This cozy cafe is a great
place for breakfast. The
lunch and dinner menu
feature homemade cooking
at reasonable prices. $$.

Mudshark Brewing Company
210 Swanson Ave.
(928) 453-2981
mudsharkbeer.com
Handcrafted beers,
gourmet pizza, steak,
seafood, and burgers. $$.

PRESCOTT

Gurley Street Grill
230 W. Gurley St.
(928) 445-3388
gurleystgrill.com
This casual eatery serves
up a nice selection of ribs,
steak, pizza, burgers, and
pasta. Specials include
roasted chicken potpie, fish
and chips, and home-style
pot roast. $$.

Prescott Brewing Company
130 W. Gurley St.
(928) 771-2795
prescottbrewingcompany
.com
Handcrafted premium
beer and pub-style dining
overlooking Courthouse
Plaza. $$.

SELIGMAN

Roadkill Café
22830 W. Route 66
(928) 422-3554
Despite names like Swirl
of Squirrel and Fender
Tenders, you can expect a
tasty selection of burgers,
steaks, ribs and hearty
chili. $$.

Eastern Arizona

Indian Country

The ***Navajo Nation*** covers a staggering 27,000 square miles of northeastern Arizona, southeastern Utah, and northwestern New Mexico—making it larger than ten of the fifty United States. With a population of more than 330,000, it's easy to figure out that there are many miles of wide-open territory without a human being in sight. You can see vast expanses of unbroken near-wilderness area, then, suddenly, modern homes or a collection of hogans—traditional, one-room, dome-shaped Navajo dwellings—pop into view. The solitude of the land is a keen reminder of what this country was like hundreds of years ago.

Therein lies one of the primary attractions of ***Navajoland*** (928-810-8501; discovernavajo.com), along with one of the biggest problems for travelers. Few people means plenty of areas with no automotive services, so if your radiator overheats, you break an axle on a rutted road, or you just get very hungry, you can be out of luck.

Here's some advice for anyone planning a trip to the reservation:

EASTERN ARIZONA

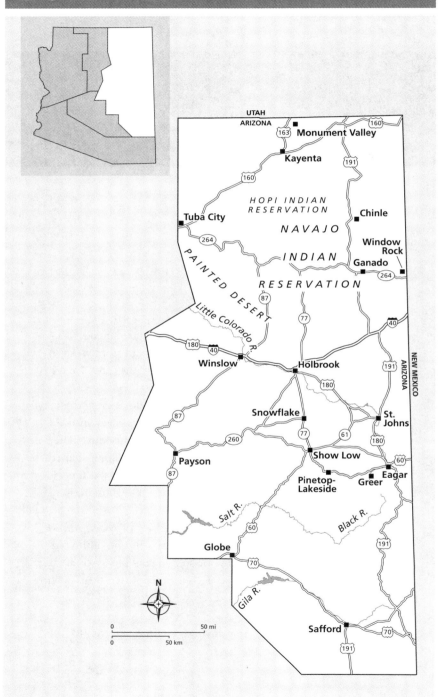

UTAH
ARIZONA

Monument Valley
163
160

Kayenta
191

160

HOPI INDIAN
RESERVATION

Chinle

NAVAJO

Tuba City
264

Window
Rock

INDIAN
Ganado
264

PAINTED DESERT

RESERVATION
87

Little Colorado R.

77

40

180
40

NEW MEXICO
ARIZONA

Winslow

Holbrook
191

180

Snowflake
St.
Johns

77
61
180

260
Show Low
60

Payson
87

Pinetop-
Lakeside
Eagar
Greer

Salt R.

Black R.

60

Globe
191

70

Gila R.

N

0   50 mi
0   50 km

Safford
70

191

Buy a good, detailed map of the area, showing dirt roads, and plan your route well in advance. Make sure your vehicle is in tip-top physical shape. Calculate distance and gas mileage. There may not be a service station for many, many miles, so make sure you have more than enough fuel to reach your destination and get back. Whenever you come to a gas station, top off your tank. Bring provisions in a cooler: water, trail mix, and fruit that travels well (like oranges).

And keep this very important fact in mind: When you enter the reservation, you're actually entering another nation's territory. Show respect for its laws, customs, and culture. A good practice is to stop at the visitor center first and get the rundown on what you can and can't do on the reservation. You may not be allowed to attend certain ceremonies, and at others you may be required to dress conservatively (no shorts and Hawaiian shirts). Alcohol is usually outlawed on reservation land.

In general, cameras, camcorders, tape recorders, and sketch pads are forbidden in the villages. Visitors who want some record of the colorful, expressive ceremonies or powwows will have to rely on memory to preserve that experience. Occasionally Native American tribes will stage dance or drum competitions (often off the reservations) where cameras and recorders are allowed.

While you're driving, you'll notice that in many well-traveled areas of the reservation roadside vendors sell everything from katsina dolls (which are made to teach children about Hopi katsina spirits) to rugs, baskets, pottery, and jewelry.

Native American craftspeople can spend months or even longer working on a single piece. A lot of time and painstaking work have gone into creating the olla (*oy-yah,* a pot), bracelet, or finely woven rug you're handling. The artist has a good idea of how much it's worth. There are definite established prices, and trying to haggle over money is usually considered an insult.

AUTHOR'S FAVORITES IN EASTERN ARIZONA

Canyon de Chelly

Gila Box Riparian National
Conservation Area

La Posada Hotel

Monument Valley

Navajo National Monument

Petrified Forest National Park

Sunrise Park Resort

Tonto Natural Bridge State Park

TOP ANNUAL EVENTS IN EASTERN ARIZONA

APRIL

Historic Home and Building Tour, Antique and Quilt Show
Globe/Miami
(928) 425-4495 or (800) 804-5623
globemiamichamber.com
Enjoy the territorial architecture of the mining communities and learn some of the stories from the past. Transportation to the historic homes is provided by tour guides.

MAY

Native American Art Auctions
Ganado
(928) 755-3475
nps.gov/hutr
This biannual auction at the historic Hubbell Trading Post includes authentic Native American art ranging from Navajo rugs to Hopi katsina dolls. The preview for the auction is from 9 to 11 a.m., with the auction starting at noon. The second annual auction is held in Sept.

JUNE

Strawberry Festival
Pine/Strawberry
(928) 978-0487
psbcaz.com
This arts and crafts fair also includes food booths, children's activities, and live entertainment at the Pine-Strawberry Community Center.

AUGUST

Eagar Days
Eagar
(928) 333-4128
eagaraz.gov
This local event includes a variety show, horseshoe tournament, junior rodeo, arts and crafts fair, kids' zone, and logging competition.

Suvoyuki Day
(928) 289-4106
azstateparks.com
This annual event features the Hopi Indians through traditional dances, a corn roast, artist demonstrations, cultural exhibits, and storytelling at Homolovi Ruins State Park.

SEPTEMBER

Fall Artisans Festival
Pinetop-Lakeside
(928) 367-4290
pinetoplakesidechamber.com
More than 150 artists display their wares at this arts and crafts fair, along with live entertainment, in this heritage event.

Navajo County Fair & Rodeo
(928) 524-4757
navajocountyfair.com
For more than 80 years, folks have been gathering for this county fair. Highlights include a rodeo, junior pageants, a livestock show, a carnival and midway, and a demolition derby at the Navajo County Fairgrounds in Holbrook.

Though Native American art is often cross-cultural (for example, every tribe has its share of oil painters and sculptors), as a rule of thumb the Navajos are best known for weaving and jewelry; Hopis are revered for their katsina dolls; Zunis are respected for their fetishes and jewelry; and Tohono O'odham (pronounced *Tahano Autum*) and Pima Indians are known for basketry.

Navajo Nation Fair
Window Rock
(928) 810-8501
discovernavajo.com
More than 70 years old, this fair features arts and crafts, contests, exhibits, concerts, horse racing, powwow, rodeo, and traditional song and dance.

OCTOBER

Apache Jii Day
Globe/Miami
(928) 425-4495 or (800) 804-5623
globemiamichamber.com
All-Indian celebration, crafts, paintings, baskets, quilts, dolls and clothing, and entertainment by various tribes.

Old West Fest
Holbrook
(928) 524-6558
holbrookazchamber.com
Enjoy gunfight reenactments, an arts and crafts fair, a quilt show, a talent contest, pie baking contest, children's activities, and live entertainment at the Navajo County Historic Courthouse.

NOVEMBER

Christmas Parade
Winslow
(928) 289-2434
winslowarizona.org
More than sixty years old, this event features the longest-running hometown Christmas parade in Northern Arizona.

DECEMBER

Festival of Lights
Globe/Miami
(928) 425-4495 or (800) 804-5623
Besh-Ba-Gowah Archaeological Park, luminarias, Christmas program and bonfire.

Parade of Lights
Holbrook
(928) 524-6558
holbrookazchamber.com
Arizona's oldest Electric Light Parade works its way down Historic Route 66. Day activities include a holiday arts and crafts fair, visits with Santa Claus, and live entertainment at the Navajo County Historic Courthouse.

In the last few decades, Native American artwork—everything from Pima ollas to Zuni bracelets—has become highly collectible. Blankets and rugs from the 1880s or earlier can sell for hundreds of thousands of dollars. Experts predict that prices for the works of contemporary Native American artists, who often spend as long as a year laboring on a single rug or other piece, will continue to rise.

Some trading posts are worth a visit if for no other reason than to marvel at their wealth of wonderful arts and crafts as well as their sense of history. One of the best places to look or buy is the **Hubbell Trading Post** (928-755-3475; nps.gov/hutr), about a mile west of the tiny town of **Ganado** off AZ 264 west of Window Rock. Founded in 1878 by John Lorenzo Hubbell, this establishment has been frequented by celebrities, visiting dignitaries, and US presidents. If you can't find the katsina doll, basket, or blanket you want here, it probably doesn't exist. Next door to the trading post at the visitor center, for a small fee, you can take a guided tour of the Hubbell home and see exhibits on Hubbell and the history of trading posts on the western frontier. Quite often Native American artisans use the area around the visitor center as a work space, and for a tip of a few dollars they'll pose for pictures. Hours vary seasonally. Free.

Native American Art

Living in Arizona we understand and appreciate so much of what the Indian cultures of our country are all about. For one thing, their love of the land is saving the open spaces of the West. Their reverence for the earth is also reflected in their pottery, made from the rich clay of the Arizona mesas. Utilitarian in origin, native pottery is an art form that dates back 2,000 years. Each tribe has its own way of decorating and coloring their grain and water pots—Hopi Tewa pottery is distinguished by the intricacy of their designs; Zuni use an owl motif, and the Acomas prefer figures of both animals and birds.

The Navajos are known for their weaving, which is a 300-year-old craft passed from mothers to daughters, possibly with a grandmother also providing both instruction and tribal lore as part of the learning process. There are more than thirty styles of Navajo rugs, each named for the various regions of their vast reservation (nearly five million acres in total size). Geometric shapes and representations of their deities are the distinguishing features.

Katsina dolls are a Hopi tradition given as gifts and teaching tools to their children. Carved from the root of a cottonwood tree, they represent dancers and spiritual beings who carry the prayers of the living to the deities who control events of everyday life.

Women are particularly fond of buying Native American jewelry when they visit Arizona. The Navajos and the Zunis are the tribes associated with necklaces, bracelets, rings, belts, and cluster work. Among the Navajo motifs are squash-blossom necklaces and crescent-shape pendants. Zunis are known for their combination of silver and stones. Zunis also produce fetishes, which are either polished stones that appear in the shape of a bear or carvings of wildlife (for example, a snake) that are thought to contain a spirit.

Every year the trading post hosts the popular ***Native American Art Auctions*** in May and September.

The best place to start an exploration of the Navajo Reservation is the pueblo-style complex that houses the ***Cameron Trading Post, Motel, and Restaurant*** (928-679-2231 or 800-338-7385; camerontradingpost.com), which was established in 1916. The hotel features spacious rooms decorated in a rustic southwestern style. The restaurant has specialties like Navajo stew and fry bread, as well as traditional burgers and sandwiches. More spectacular than the food, however, is the view from the dining room of the Little Colorado River. The trading post offers a vast assortment of katsinas, rugs, baskets, sand paintings, and pottery. Additionally, an attached gallery has high-end items, including ceremonial headdresses. Prices in the trading post and gallery are reasonable, and you can be assured of the authenticity.

Motorists unfamiliar with this vast land should understand that though many towns appear on the typical road map, services like food, water, and gasoline can be dozens of miles apart. Heading northeast to ***Kayenta*** and Monument Valley or southeast towards Window Rock, the town of ***Tuba City,*** near the intersection of US 160 and AZ 264, is a good place to stop, fill up, and stock up on supplies.

The capital of the Navajo Nation is ***Window Rock,*** located on AZ 264 just a few miles west of the New Mexico border. There are several interesting attractions near Window Rock. About 3 miles west on AZ 264 you'll see the ***St. Michaels Historical Museum*** (928-871-4171). This stone building was a home for Franciscan friars during the 1890s. The friars came to Arizona to spread the gospel and establish schools for Native Americans. They were instrumental in helping to create a written language for the Navajos, and there are displays in the museum of some of the original Franciscan translations. There are also photographs and exhibits depicting the friars' daily lives. The museum is open Mon to Fri from 9 a.m. to 5 p.m.

Back at Window Rock, the ***Navajo National Museum*** (928-871-7941) and the ***Navajo Arts & Crafts Enterprise*** (928-871-4090; gonavajo.com) are located downtown next to the ***Quality Inn Navajo Nation Capital*** (48 W. AZ 264; 928-871-4108). $. The museum houses intricate exhibits featuring life-size mannequins involved in tribal ceremonies and everyday activities. The arts and crafts enterprise is a Navajo organization that dates back to 1941. The purpose of this guild is to assure the quality, innovativeness, and authenticity of the

arizonatrivia

Near **Tuba City,** the desert is crisscrossed by Dilophosaurus tracks, evidence that the plant-eating dinosaur the size of a horse roamed this countryside.

crafts of its artisans. The guild also purchases arts and crafts from the Hopi, Zuni, and Santo Domingo tribes, so the selections here are very good. If you like Native American jewelry, make sure you see the Zuni pieces—especially the bracelets, which are for men as well as women.

Take Indian Route 12 north to **Tségháboodzání** (the Navajo name for "the rock with the hole in it"). This red sandstone landmark that gave the town its name is several stories tall, with a 130-foot hole in the center. There are picnic areas nearby, as well as the hogan-shaped **Navajo Nation Council Chambers** where the tribe's eighty-eight council members meet four times per year. Nearby, you can visit the **Window Rock Tribal Park and Veterans' Memorial** (928-871-6647; navajonationparks.org). The park features a monument to the Navajo Code Talkers—a group of Navajo soldiers who created a code during WWII that was never broken. Other symbolic structures within the park include a circular path pacing to the four cardinal directions, angled steel pillars engraved with the names of Navajo war veterans, and a healing sanctuary featuring a sandstone fountain.

One of the most spectacular sites on the reservation is **Canyon de Chelly National Monument** (928-674-5500; nps.gov/cach). Canyon de Chelly (Shay) is the scene of the final defeat of Navajo warriors who were holding out against troops commanded by General James Henry Carleton, who had waged a relentless scorched earth campaign spearheaded by Colonel Kit Carson. Carson swept through the canyons destroying hogans, orchards and livestock. In January 1864, after the final battle, the entire Navajo Nation began their Long Walk to Fort Sumner in New Mexico. Many died along the 300-mile march and it would be four painful years in captivity until they were allowed to return to their homeland. It's hard to imagine such cruelty and violence when gazing at the pastoral beauty of the canyon today. You can reach Canyon de Chelly by traveling west on AZ 264, then north on AZ 191 to **Chinle**, perched at the mouth of the canyon and offering food, gas and lodging. This route is about 80 miles. Follow the highway signs to the visitor center. The center has a museum that traces the history of Native Americans in the canyon. It also has an art gallery, demonstrations of Indian arts and crafts, and an information desk. Navajo guides can also be hired here.

Canyon de Chelly National Monument includes two large canyons, Canyon de Chelly to the south and Canyon del Muerto to the north. At the visitor center you can get a map that will show you the route of the rim drives that follow each canyon stopping at broad overlooks. You can take these roads unescorted and there is no admission fee to enter the national monument. If you want to experience Canyon de Chelly more fully, you must hire a Navajo guide to enter the canyon. There are jeep tours, hiking tours and horseback rides available for which there will be a fee. Cameras are permitted on these trips, and usually the guides will pose for a picture provided you don't want to sell it to a photo stock agency or some such thing. Some guides will be willing to take you to homes where you can see jewelers and rug weavers at work and watch scenes of contemporary Navajo life. In some of these locations, you may be asked to leave your camera or sketch pad in the Jeep.

The moderately steep 3-mile round-trip trail to **White House Ruin** is the only place where visitors can enter Canyon de Chelly without a Navajo guide. With sixty rooms in the lower section and another twenty tucked away in the cliff, this Ancestral Puebloan structure housed as many as one hundred people at a time during the years between AD 1060 and AD 1275. The trailhead begins at the White House Overlook on the South Rim Drive.

If you're interested in learning more of the Ancestral Puebloans (formerly known as the Anasazi), make the journey west of Canyon de Chelly. Off US 160, 20 miles south of Kayenta, lies the lonely **Navajo National Monument** (928-672-2700; nps.gov/nava). The 360 acres protected by the Navajo National Monument contain three of the most intact Ancestral Puebloan cliff dwellings in Arizona. Stop at the visitor center 9 miles north of US 160 on AZ 564. Like most visitor centers on the reservation, there is an exhibit hall, an arts and crafts shop, and presentations on Navajo history. Best of all, the center is next to a moderately strenuous 5-mile round-trip hiking trail that takes you for a closer look at **Betatakin.** The large cliff dwelling known as Betatakin can only be reached via a ranger-guided hike. It is situated about 700 feet below the rim of

Exploring Canyon de Chelly

When you arrive at the entrance to **Canyon de Chelly,** the canyon walls are only about 30 feet high, but they eventually soar to 1,000 feet above the sandy floor. The South Rim Drive ends at perhaps the most dramatic vista in the national monument, **Spider Rock Overlook.** Spider Rock is an 800-foot-tall chunk of sandstone about which there are many legends. In one Navajo version of a Bogey Man story, Navajo children are told by their parents that if they don't behave, Spider Woman—a demigod who also supposedly taught the Navajos how to weave—will take them away and leave them on top of the rock to die. From the rim you'll see gardens and orchards, and livestock grazing. Many of the Diné—as the Navajo call themselves—still live and farm on the canyon floor. Also, if you're physically able, a hike into the gorge to see the White House Ruin is an experience you won't forget. There are three overlooks on the North Rim Drive overlooking **Canyon del Muerto** ("the canyon of the dead," so named because of burial sites uncovered here by archaeologists in the 1880s). At each spot you'll gaze at the remains of the cliff dwellings of the Ancestral Puebloans dating back centuries.

the canyon, has about 135 rooms that were built sometime between AD 1250 and AD 1300. You'll need binoculars or a spotting scope to see much detail, but even from a distance they are impressive.

For those with limited time, the monument includes three gentler hiking trails that visitors can explore on their own, including the paved Sandal Trail that leads to an overlook with cross-canyon view of Betatakin.

If you're feeling adventurous and want a truly off-the-beaten-path experience on the Navajo reservation, sign up for a hike to ***Keet Seel*** (928-672-2700), a 160-room pueblo. After trekking the 8.5 miles to the remote cliff dwelling, you can climb up ladders with a ranger to walk the streets of this ancient civilization. People began settling in Keet Seel in AD 950, nearly 300 years before construction began in Betatakin. In AD 1250, a new group of settlers arrived and a steady influx kept the village growing until it contained more than 150 rooms—making it the largest of its kind in the state. The diversity of Keet Seel residents is reflected in the building styles used to construct the four distinctly different kivas, three common streets, and a retaining wall stretching 180 feet along the eastern half of the village.

Both Betatakin and Keet Seel sites can only be visited on ranger-guided tours. Each is a strenuous outing. Do not attempt if you have hip, knee, heart, respiratory problems or recent surgery. Betatakin tours are conducted daily from Memorial Day weekend through Labor Day weekend, while Keet Seel is closed Tues and Wed. Free tickets for the guided Betatakin hike are handed out at 8:15 a.m. and 10 a.m. daily on a first-come, first-serve basis with a limit of twenty-five hikers for each tour. Free permits are available

Exploring Canyon Mysteries

The sandstone walls of the extensive ***Tsegi Canyon*** system cradle the remains of an ancient civilization that inhabited lands that are now part of the vast Navajo Nation. The Ancestral Puebloans inhabited the vivid landscape found in southeastern Arizona for nearly a thousand years before finally mysteriously abandoning their far-flung dwellings.

Deep within the sandstone canyons, three cliff dwellings are protected by Navajo National Monument—Inscription House, Betatakin, and Keet Seel. Visitors can take a 5-mile round-trip hike led by Navajo guides to the base of a looming cave measuring 450 feet high and 370 feet wide. Nestled inside are the weathered remains of Betatakin. A 17-mile round-trip hike into a tributary canyon of the system leads to Keet Seel, one of the largest and best preserved cliff dwellings in the state. However, the location of Inscription House is kept secret in hopes of preserving the crumbling vestige of the small dwelling.

Monuments of Time

Pulitzer-prize winner N. Scott Momaday described **Monument Valley:** "You see the monoliths that stand away in space, and you imagine that you have come upon eternity. They do not appear to exist in time. You think: I see that time comes to an end on this side of the rock, and on the other side there is nothing forever."

This desert highland, situated at 5,564 feet, began to form twenty-five million years ago as a vast inland sea. When the waters receded, all that remained were expansive beds of red sandstone, which the wind used to sculpt the massive monuments— grain by grain, year by year.

Hogans nestle along the road and farther out into the valley, where the Navajo people live and play as they have since they first came to this region in the late fifteenth century. Since that time, the Navajo were only parted from its stark beauty after their forced removal to New Mexico between 1864 and 1868. Ninety years later, the Navajo Tribal Council designated the 29,816-acre **Monument Valley Navajo Tribal Park** to preserve the lifestyle of the Navajos residing within its boundaries.

for the Keet Seel tour with a limit of twenty people a day. Orientation is mandatory to receive a permit and takes place at 3 p.m. the day before the hike. Reservations can be made up to two months in advance for Keet Seel. Hikers have the option to try to complete the 17-mile round trip hike to Keet Seel in a day, or to stay overnight in a primitive campground near the dwelling. The Navajo Nation is on daylight saving time and is one hour ahead of other Arizona locations during the summer months. Guided hikes to Betakin are occasionally available in the winter months, depending on weather conditions, scheduling, and staffing. Check with the visitor center for more information.

While on the hikes, beware of rockfall hazards, watch for flash floods and stay on trails to avoid quicksand. Livestock pollute the stream so all water must be carried in. Take a minimum of two liters of water per person for the Betatakin hike and four quarts for the Keet Seel hike. The trails run primarily through Navajoland, and all hikers must stay on designated paths.

Don't leave the Navajo reservation until you've seen **Monument Valley** (928-871-6647; navajonationparks.org), where numerous westerns have been filmed. You can reach Monument Valley Navajo Tribal Park by driving north on US 163. Though it straddles the Utah–Arizona border, most of the park is actually within Arizona. The nearly 30,000-acre valley spills across the landscape like a watercolor set of purples, reds, and golds. Jutting up at irregular intervals are tremendous mountains of sand-sculpted rock. The valley is unquestionably one of Arizona's most widely photographed sites, with its soaring sandstone monoliths and cliff formations that bear curious names like the Three Sisters, Totem Pole and Rain God Mesa. *Goulding's Trading Post, Lodge and Museum* (435-727-3231; gouldings.com) is located just north of the Arizona border. The museum features the role Monument Valley played in director John Ford's memorable movies, including *Stagecoach, The Searchers,* and *She Wore a Yellow Ribbon,* all starring actor John Wayne. *Goulding's Lodge* offers great views of Monument Valley, the *Stagecoach Dining Room,* and an indoor pool. $$$.

The only lodging within the tribal park is the Navajo-owned *View Hotel* (435-727-5555; monumentvalleyview.com). Perched on a low mesa overlooking the iconic Mittens and Merrick Butte, each room in the View features a private balcony. Also on the property is a trading post, a restaurant with floor-to-ceiling windows, cabins and a campground. $$$. The View is adjacent to the *Tribal Park Visitor Center* (435-727-5870; navajonationparks.org) that includes a small museum and trail information. There are three hiking trails that visitors can take on their own without a guide. There's also a 17-mile loop drive through the valley, but the road is poorly maintained and bumpy. You'll have a much better time if you hire a guide in the parking lot kiosk at the visitor center to take you by Jeep or horseback on a tour of the full valley. Admission.

One place that nearly everyone visits on the Navajo Reservation is *Four Corners National Monument* (928-871-6647; navajonationparks.org), the only place in the nation where four states (Arizona, Utah, Colorado, and New Mexico) converge. There's a marker at this point, and few Arizona vacations are complete without a photo of the travelers straddling this landmark. Tribal vendors selling arts and crafts and traditional foods are also on hand. Four Corners is easily reached by taking US 160 northeast. Admission.

There isn't an endless array of motels and eateries on the reservation, but of the few, most are well known and time-tested. In *Kayenta the Wetherill Inn* (928-697-3231; wetherill-inn.com), located on US 163, has fifty-four rooms, no restaurant, but a small gift shop and an indoor pool. $$. In *Chinle* the *Thunderbird Lodge* (928-674-5842 or 800-679-2473; thunderbird.com) has a cafeteria that's open until 8 p.m. and a gift shop. $$. Half-day, all-day and sunset tours of Canyon de Chelly can be booked in the gift shop.

For restaurants try *Amigo Cafe* (928-697-8448), off US 163 just north of US 160; it serves Mexican, American, and Navajo cuisine, some of the best on the reservation. $$.

Tucked entirely within the Navajo Nation is the comparatively tiny 1.5-million-acre *Hopi Reservation*, home to about 8,000 people. This rocky terrain has been inhabited by the Hopi and their ancestors for hundreds of years. In fact the village of *Oraibi* on the third mesa (plateau) is the oldest continuously inhabited town in the United States, having been settled around AD 1100.

A good place to start is ***Moenkopi Legacy Inn & Suites*** (928-283-4500; experiencehopi.com) in Tuba City. The Upper Village of Moenkopi is one of twelve Hopi villages situated on First, Second, and Third Mesa. The hotel architecture reflects the style and colors of Hopi villages and includes tribal symbols throughout the grounds. That same welcoming feel carries over to the 100 guestrooms and suites. $$. You can also sign up for a variety of Hopi-led tours at the front desk that will provide insight into Hopi art, culture and unique landscapes.

Visitors are welcome to drive across the Hopi Reservation on their own but it's important to follow proper etiquette. Photography, videotaping and sketching are prohibited. Do not explore non-designated areas. Do not pick up loose feathers, rocks, pottery shards or other items. If you are fortunate enough to encounter a ceremony or dance, observe quietly from the background. AZ 264 connects all three Hopi mesas. You'll see a few galleries along the way, part of the ***Hopi Arts Trail*** (hopiartstrail.com). It's always a good idea to stop to see the woven-baskets, hand-carved katsina dolls, pottery, painting, silver inlay jewelry and more. While there, don't be afraid to ask questions. The ***Hopi Cultural Center*** (928-734-2401; hopiculturalcenter.com) is accessible from the second mesa off AZ 264. Here you'll find a motel, restaurant and gift shop. The rooms are clean and casual and the restaurant dishes up everything from American favorites to traditional Hopi dishes. $.

The motel's front desk staff is an excellent source for information about any tribal dances and ceremonies that the public may view. Though friendly, the Hopi closely guard their privacy and religious rituals. Some areas of the Hopi Reservation are open to tourists, whereas others are not. And although the Hopi do invite visitors to observe many of their colorful ceremonies, the use of cameras, video or audio recorders, and sketch pads is strictly forbidden. Hopi dances traditionally begin in December, with ceremonies stopping in July, but call ahead if you'd like to plan your visit to coincide with these events. *One other note:* Like Arizona, the Hopi Reservation does not observe Daylight Savings Time. Yet the Navajo Nation does, so that can be a bit confusing when traveling in the area.

Wild West Country

Just south of the Navajo Nation, near the junction of AZ 77 and I-40, is the town of ***Holbrook*** (928-524-6558; holbrookazchamber.com). More than one hundred years ago, Holbrook was known as "the town too tough for women and children." Cowboys shot it out in saloons like the Bucket of Blood, and some of the killings associated with the Pleasant Valley War took place here. To get a look at what the town used to be like, drop by the 1898 *Navajo County Courthouse* (100 E. Arizona St.; 928-524-6558) where you'll find a terrific museum. (The Holbrook Chamber of Commerce is also located in the courthouse building.) You can tour the sheriff's office and the jail and see exhibits depicting everything from the area's geologic history to an old-time barbershop. It's open daily from 8 a.m. to 5 p.m. For a special treat, stop by the courthouse on weeknights during June and July and enjoy Native American dance performances from 6:30 to 8:30 p.m.

Once a year (usually in Jan or Feb) the town offers visitors a chance to obtain a very unusual souvenir: a letter delivered by the *Pony Express.* In commemoration of the area's history and as a kickoff to other festivities, a team of riders known as the *Hashknife Pony Express Riders* (hashknifepony express.com) sets off from the Holbrook Post Office on a three-day trek to Scottsdale, traveling over 200 miles from the Mogollon Rim through the Mazat-zal Mountains. They carry thousands of letters with them, and each is canceled with a special mark that designates it as a Pony Express delivery.

For restaurants in Holbrook, *Romo's Cafe* (121 W. Hopi Dr.; 928-524-2153) has been serving up Mexican favorites since the 1960s. $$. Across the street, *Joe & Aggie's Café* (120 Hopi Dr.; 928-524-6540) has been at it even longer, dishing up traditional American and Mexican dishes since 1943 and is now being managed by the third generation of family members. $.

Holbrook does not have any bed-and-breakfast inns but it does have more than 1,000 motel rooms, ranging from simple mom-and-pop–style lodging to more elaborate chain accommodations. *The Best Western Arizonian* (no, we don't normally spell it that way) *Inn* (2508 E. Navajo Blvd.; 928-524-2611; bestwestern.com) offers 72 comfortable rooms and has a pool. $. A favorite place to stay for families is the Historic Route 66 icon *Wigwam Motel* (811 W. Hopi Dr.; 928-524-3048; sleepinawigwam). This classic slice of Americana has been delighting Route 66 travelers for decades. $. Reservations are highly recommended.

The *Petrified Forest National Park* (928-524-6228; nps.gov/pefo) is a short drive north from town on I-40. The Painted Desert portion of the park lies north of the freeway and provides vistas of green desert vegetation with mountains of red and purplish hues. The startling hues of these rugged bad-lands are most vivid when the sun is low in the sky.

Across the road, the *Petrified Forest* is a marvel of the unique properties of nature. Littered across the landscape are giant chunks of what were once logs, part of a conifer forest that thrived millions of years ago. Long before humans walked the earth, the forest was covered by water, and sediments settled on the trees. Gradually, as the trees decayed, all that was left was hardened stone in the shape of the original tree. Look close to see the array of colors lurking in the stone. Admission.

Before heading off to see the sights, stop at the visitor center and grab a descriptive brochure. You'll probably want to see *Agate Bridge,* where a petrified log fell over a canyon. One story has it that more than one hundred years ago, on a ten-dollar bet, a cowboy rode his horse over that bridge—not a feat I'd care to duplicate! Another place to stop is *Newspaper Rock,* where ancient Indian tribes chiseled in all the news that was fit to chip. The park is book-ended by a couple of excellent museums near the south and north entrance where you can learn more about the forces that petrified the fallen trees, the ancient creatures that roamed the landscape and the people who lived here much, much later. There are several short hiking trails branching off the scenic drive that slices through the park, large pueblo sites and even some Off the Beaten Path routes for adventurous types who want to hike cross country.

By the way, it's illegal to remove any pieces of wood from the park, and, really, the stuff is so nice in the gift shops you'd be foolish to risk the fine. Stop by *Jim Gray's Petrified Wood Co.* (928-524-1842; petrifiedwoodco.com) gift shop on US 180 at AZ 77, and you'll see many crafts made from petrified wood, as well as polished chunks of the material.

The Winslow area has long been inhabited. Hopi archaeological remains in the nearby *Homolovi State Park* (928-289-4106; azstateparks.com) date back many hundreds of years. The park, located off I-40 via AZ 87, sprawls over 4,000 acres at 4,900 feet and has campsites and hiking trails, some of which will take visitors to petroglyphs and an old Mormon cemetery above the Little Colorado River. Two of the sites are open to the public. Several other sites are still being excavated. Exhibits of Hopi artwork and artifacts recovered from the pueblos are on display in the visitor center. Admission.

arizonatrivia

Arizona has its own "Triassic Park," actually the *Petrified Forest National Park*, where the remains of Triassic reptiles have been unearthed and ancient trees turned to stone 225 million years ago.

Winslow (928-289-2434; winslow arizona.org) itself, founded in 1881, has quite a history. Named for Gen. Edward F. Winslow, president of the St. Louis & San Francisco Railroad, the community was raised on the three Rs: ranching, railroading, and Route 66. The *Old Trails Historical Museum* (212 N. Kinsley Ave.; 928-289-5861; oldtrails museum.org) has displays of all three stages of the area's history, as well as artifacts from the region's Native American history. The museum is open Tues through Sat from 10 a.m. to 3 p.m.

No visit to Winslow is complete without a stroll over to the park to see the two-story mural at **Standin' on the Corner Park** (standinonthecorner.com). The Glenn Frey/Jackson Browne song "Take It Easy"—recorded first by the Eagles on their debut album and later by Browne—recounts an incident that occurred in Flagstaff. It was just one of those youthful moments that Browne experienced, with a girl slowing down and catching the eye of the young balladeer. But Browne exercised a bit of poetic license (she was also driving, not a flatbed Ford, but a red Datsun). Somehow the line from that song, "Well, I'm standin' on a corner in Winslow, Arizona" resonated and turned this spot into one of the ultimate photo ops for Route 66 travelers. Murals on the wall recreate the scene, along with a bronze statue of a young guitar-toting troubadour leaning against the lamppost. And each and every day people stop to be part of it. The town estimates that more than 100,000 people visit the corner every year. After Glen Frey passed away in 2016, another bronze statue bearing his likeness was added to the plaza. In September, the town holds the **Standin' on the Corner Park Festival,** which features food, fun, classic cars and Eagles tribute bands. Any guesses on the most requested song?

arizonatrivia

In its heyday, Winslow's historic **La Posada Hotel** housed such celebrity guests as Clark Gable and Carole Lombard, Douglas Fairbanks and Mary Pickford, Charles and Anne Morrow Lindbergh, Gary Cooper, John Wayne, Howard Hughes, Will Rogers, Harry Truman, and Franklin Roosevelt, as well as Japanese royalty.

One of the most exciting projects in Winslow in years was the renovation and reopening of the historic **La Posada Hotel** (303 E. Second St.; 928-289-4366; laposada.org), a Fred Harvey hotel located by the Santa Fe Railroad tracks. The hotel, a National Historic Landmark, is a 60,000-square-foot Spanish Mission–style palace designed by famed architect Mary Jane Colter and built in 1929 at a cost of more than $1 million dollars; it was frequented by many celebrities. During World War II, as many as 3,000 troops were fed in the dining hall each day. It closed in 1957 as the result of declining rail travel. In 1997 Allan Affeldt and his wife, Tina Mion, purchased the building and along with partner Dan Lutzick, did an amazing job of restoring it to its former glory. Today it is filled with an intriguing mix of Mission-style antiques, Mexican furniture and artwork, and contemporary sculpture and art. The hotel has a restaurant—the Turquoise Room, one of the finest eating establishments in the state—gardens, an art gallery, trading post, and museum. $$

Winslow has many chain restaurants as well as mom-and-pop places, such as the ***Brown Mug Cafe*** (308 E. Second St.; 928-289-9973). $$. Open for more than fifty years, the ***Casa Blanca Cafe*** (1201 E. Second St.; 928-289-4191) is a local favorite serving Mexican and American fare. $.

Apache and Mormon Country

The ***Apache-Sitgreaves National Forests*** (928-333-6280; fs.usda.gov/asnf) is an impressive stand of vegetation (about two million acres) that stretches along the Mogollon Rim and into the White Mountains. The landscape ranges from about 3,500 feet in elevation to more than 11,000 feet above sea level. Flora and fauna from many diverse environments can be seen here. Three dozen campgrounds, several hundred thousand acres of wilderness or primitive area blocked to vehicles, and nearly 900 miles of trails are here for those who love hiking and camping.

Many small towns, including Heber, Show Low, Pinetop-Lakeside, and Alpine, lie within the forest boundaries, and quite a few others are within an hour's drive or less. Widely used by vacationers during ski season, this area is also a cool summer retreat. High country lakes, clear-running rivers, hiking and biking trails, campgrounds, cabins and inky dark skies make this a desirable destination for the recreation-minded.

Settled in 1878, ***Snowflake*** was one of the first Mormon communities founded in Arizona. Believe it or not, it wasn't named after an ice crystal—rather, it was built by Erastus Snow and William J. Flake. Like many Mormon settlers in Arizona, Flake met with hostility regarding his religious beliefs and, in 1884, he was arrested for polygamy and spent some months in the gruesome Yuma Territorial Prison.

The town follows Brigham Young's City of Zion design—wide boulevards and neatly squared-off city blocks. Today in the downtown area, many of the original homes—ranging in style from Greek revival to Victorian to bungalow—look exactly as they did more than one hundred years ago. Snowflake and the neighboring town of ***Taylor*** manage to feel both vibrant and quaint at the same time. These are the kinds of communities that make you want to slow down, stroll the shady sidewalks and explore. And they encourage you to do just that. Take a tour of the pioneer homes. There are 45 listed on the Historic Registry. You can take a self-guided tour of the exterior of the historic homes year-round. You can also arrange for an interior tour of several of the homes that includes museums, cabins and a one-room schoolhouse. Pick up a walking tour map at the Chamber of Commerce office (113 N. Main St.; 928-536-4331; snowflaketaylorchamber.org) in Snowflake. Details on tours for both towns are listed on the website.

Mogollon Rim Overlook

If you visit the forest, be sure to take the *Mogollon Rim Interpretive Trail*, which is accessible from AZ 260 in Lakeside. This easy, 1-mile hike through pine forest along the edge of the Rim affords magnificent canyon views. The Mogollon Rim is a 200-mile long escarpment characterized by towering cliffs that extend from Sedona to New Mexico. As it separates the high plateau country from the low deserts, it provides exquisite and far-reaching views.

For a relaxing base to explore the area, check into the **Heritage Inn Bed & Breakfast** (161 Main St.; 928-536-3322 or 866-486-5947; heritage-inn.net) in Snowflake. Choose from 10 charming rooms decorated with country provincial flair in this 1890 Victorian. Guests are treated to a full gourmet breakfast. $$. Reservations are highly recommended.

Situated along US 180, **St. Johns** (928-337-4517; sjaz.us), the Apache County seat, prides itself on having a major **Equestrian Center** (928-337-4517) located next to the airport. The center has facilities for cross-country competition, dressage, and other events; however, no riding rentals for visitors are offered here. Call to find out if any horse shows are scheduled during your visit to the White Mountains. The **Apache County Museum** (180 W. Cleveland Ave.; 928-337-4737) is also located here. Artifacts of the area's history and prehistory—including a 24,000-year-old set of woolly mammoth tusks—are on display. The museum is open Apr through Nov, Tues, Thurs and Sat from 10 a.m. to 2 p.m. Free.

For a cool summer treat, enjoy water sports at one of the largest lakes in northeastern Arizona at **Lyman Lake State Park** (928-337-4441; azstateparks .com). Located 11 miles south of St. Johns on US 191, this state park is a great place for boating, fishing, waterskiing, camping, and hiking. The park also rents cabins overlooking the water. Admission.

You can certainly be forgiven if you think the communities in the White Mountain region blend together. It's easy to forget which town is on what side of which lake. In simple terms, **Show Low** (928-537-2326; showlowchamber .com) was named after a card game in the 1870s that supposedly established the town's ownership. It is west on US 60 and just south of **Fool Hollow Lake Recreation Area** (928-537-3680; azstateparks.com). The 800-acre recreation area is located in the Apache-Sitgreaves National Forest and offers year-round fishing and boating on the 150-acre lake. Other outdoor activities include camping, hiking, and wildlife watching. Admission.

The conjoined towns of *Pinetop-Lakeside* (928-367-4290; pinetoplake sidechamber.com) are south of Show Low along AZ 260. Nestled in heavy forest and surrounded by a network of trails, they make a good base camp to explore more of the White Mountains. Sunrise Park Resort lies to the southeast along AZ 273.

The entire *White Mountain Apache Reservation* (928-338-4346; white mountainapache.org) area is loaded with recreational opportunities: lakes, streams, nature trails, golf courses, and even *Hon-Dah* (Apache for "welcome") *Resort Casino* (800-929-8744; hon-dah.com) on AZ 260 just south of Pinetop-Lakeside. Many of these enterprises are owned by the White Mountain Apache Tribe, which has done a phenomenal job developing visitor services while maintaining the natural look of the terrain.

One of their finest accomplishments is the *Sunrise Park Resort* (928-735-7669 or 855-735-7669; sunriseskiparkaz.com), Arizona's largest ski resort on AZ 273, 4 miles south of 260. Three mountains—Sunrise Peak (10,700 feet), Apache Peak (11,100 feet), and Cyclone Circle (10,700 feet)—comprise the skiable terrain, which is laced with sixty-five trails and served by modern, high-speed quad, triple, and double chairlifts.

Day lodges on each of the peaks provide food and full rental facilities for skis and snowboards. Additionally the one-hundred-room *Sunrise Park Lodge* (928-735-7669 or 800-772-7669; sunriseskiparkaz.com) provides accommodations, whirlpool spas, and saunas just 3 miles from the base of the moun-

arizonatrivia

The world's largest contiguous ponderosa pine forest stretches across Arizona and is on vivid display in the White Mountains.

tain. The season starts in early Dec and, weather permitting, runs through late Mar or longer. Because the resort has extensive snowmaking equipment, it isn't totally dependent on Mother Nature. During summer months, Sunrise becomes a different kind of playground with zip line, mountain biking, climbing walls, archery, horseback riding and more. The lodge includes a restaurant noted for its Western Apache cuisine, a gift shop, an indoor pool and hot tub, and a game room. $.

About 30 miles south of Hon-Dah Resort Casino on AZ 73 is *Fort Apache Historic Park* (928-338-1230). This historic piece of frontier and military history operated from 1870 to 1922. Its primary mission was to keep the peace between white settlers and northern tribes of Apaches. General George Crook used the fort as a base of operations during his expeditions against Geronimo and Cochise. Today the fort doubles as a museum, with many of its buildings intact, including officers' quarters, horse barns, and a cemetery. Among the exhibits on display at the *Fort Apache Museum,* which is located in the *White Mountain Apache Cultural Center* (928-338-4625) are some on the history of the White Mountain Apache Tribe in Arizona. Hours vary seasonally. Admission. While at the Cultural Center ask about visitation to the *Kinishba Ruins,* a National Historic Landmark five miles away. The large pueblo contains nine masonry buildings constructed between AD 1250 and 1350 by the pre-Columbian Mogollon Culture. Those wishing to visit Kinishba must check in at the Cultural Center first.

There's little evidence of it now, but more than one hundred years ago *Springerville* (928-333-2321; springervilleeagarchamber.com) was one of the toughest towns in the Arizona territory. Springerville and sister city Eagar are tucked away in the high mountain basin known as the Round Valley, Because the dense foliage of what is now the Apache-Sitgreaves National Forests provided so many excellent hiding places and made tracking difficult, a countless number of stolen horses and cattle ended up here. Even the tattered remnants of the Clanton clan, after an infamous shoot-out in Tombstone, decided to avail themselves of this area's greater tolerance of lawless activity. It's also a place John Wayne fell in love with. His former 26-Bar Ranch lies just west of Eagar.

Springerville's history as a pioneer outpost is honored by being one of twelve sites in the nation to have a *Madonna of the Trail Statue.* These statues, made of algonite stone that incorporates Missouri granite to achieve a glowing hue, were placed on points along the National Old Trails Road by the Daughters of the American Revolution in the late 1920s. The statue depicts a sturdy, stoic pioneer woman in homespun clothes, cradling one child in her left arm and holding a rifle in her right, while another child clings to her skirts. To find the statue, drive down Main Street to the post office; the Madonna is directly across the street.

arizonatrivia

Ike Clanton ran away from the Gunfight at the O.K. Corral but never gave up his lawless ways when he arrived in Springerville. In 1887, detectives attempted to arrest Ike and his brother Phineas for cattle rustling. Phin surrendered but Ike attempted to draw his rifle and was shot dead.

About 2 miles north of town is *Casa Malpais* ("house of the badlands") *Archaeological Park* (928-333-5375; casamalpais.org). This Ancestral Puebloan village and National Historic Landmark site was first reported by an archaeologist in 1883. Stone walls, pottery, and other features of the site indicate that it was occupied for nearly one hundred years before being abandoned in the fourteenth century. Tours begin from a museum on Main Street in

Springerville where you'll watch an informative video. The visit to the pueblo involves a ¾ mile hike over some rocky sections. Guided tours are offered Mar through Nov, Tues through Sat at 9 and 1 p.m., weather permitting. Admission. The museum at 418 E. Main St. is open year round and is free.

The tiny towns of **Greer** and **Alpine** offer quiet getaways off the beaten path. Nestled amid green mountains and lush meadows, Alpine is often called the "Alps of Arizona." It sits south of Springerville along the **Coronado Trail,** a designated National Scenic Byway. Luna Lake, where bald eagles nest, lies just outside of town. Be sure to stop for a meal, and a slice of homemade pie, at **Bear Wallow Café** (928-339-4310) on Main Street in Alpine. Everything is made from scratch and you'll likely run into everyone in town over the course of a day. $. The hamlet of Greer is tucked down a road just east of Sunrise, flanked by small lakes and the Little Colorado River flowing right through the heart of town. Bring your fishing gear. Both towns have some visitor services, including quaint lodges and cabins, but most shops and restaurants in the area are in Springerville. For a quick meal, try **Booga Reds** (521 E. Main St.; 928-333-2640), which offers homemade Mexican and American. $.

Motels, guest ranches, and cabins are spread throughout the White Mountains area, including **Greer Peaks Lodge** (1 Main St.; 928-735-9977; greer peakslodge.com) in Greer. Spacious rooms and suites (fireplaces in each suite), complimentary breakfast, and equipment rentals are available for every season so whether you're fishing or sledding, they've got you covered. $$. Another great place to kick up your feet is at the **Tal Wi Wi Lodge** (928-339-4319; talwiwi.com) in Alpine. The Tal Wi Wi Lodge, incidentally, features some suites that have fireplaces and hot tubs. There is also an on-site restaurant and saloon. $.

Payson and Tonto

If you take AZ 260 west from Show Low, you'll travel a scenic route through the Apache-Sitgreaves National Forests, across the Mogollon Rim and down into the **Tonto National Forest** (602-225-5200; fs.usda.gov/tonto). There are many small towns along the way in which you can stop for gas and travel supplies. The area also features scads of national forest campgrounds and developed hiking trails. You'll soon reach **Payson** (928-472-5110; paysonrimcountry.com), only about 90 miles from the major metropolitan area of Phoenix, yet close to immense stands of ponderosa pine and numerous lakes and streams. As you might expect, this small community of about 15,000 is a recreational stop for people on their way to the White Mountains, as well as a vacation spot for world-weary warriors from the Phoenix area.

Nature trails, campgrounds, and various frequent festivals keep this area active. In August, Payson is the location of ***The World's Oldest Continuous Rodeo.*** In September, the ***Old Time Fiddlers' Contest*** brings the region's finest pickers and fiddlers to the pine country. Although Payson lacks a true downtown, they have something even cooler—a park. ***Green Valley Park*** at the end of Main St. features a grassy play area, picnic tables and three small lakes as the centerpiece. Paved paths circle the water that's punctuated by an occasional fountain. The lakes are part of an urban fishing program. Also in the park is the ***Rim Country Museum*** and ***Zane Grey Cabin*** (700 S. Green Valley Pkwy.; 928-474-3483; rimcountrymuseum.org). The small museum and friendly staff of volunteers will provide lots of history of the region. Admission price also includes a tour of the Zane Grey Cabin, a replica built after the famed Western writer's original cabin was destroyed in a forest fire. Hours vary seasonally.

Just north of here up AZ 87 is the ***Tonto Natural Bridge State Park*** (928-476-4202; azstateparks.com), a limestone formation that's believed to be the largest travertine arch bridge in the world (183 feet high, 400 feet long). Overlooks of the bridge can be reached from the parking area. Short but steep trails lead down to the creek below and into the massive water-gnawed tunnel. Another trail leads to an elvish waterfall cascading down a wall of hanging ferns and flowers. Trails may be closed in winter if conditions turn icy. Admission. A bit farther north are the tiny mountain towns of ***Pine*** and ***Strawberry*** (928-474-4515; rimcountrychamber.com). The ***Strawberry Schoolhouse*** (pinestrawhs.org), built in 1884 is often called the oldest standing schoolhouse in the state but is actually a bit younger than the Arivaca Schoolhouse, which opened its doors in 1879. But the Strawberry Schoolhouse is a beauty. It held its last classes in 1907, and today it's a historic state monument that's open for tours on the weekends from mid-May to Mid-Oct.

Globe (928-425-4495 or 800-804-5623; globemiamichamber.com), a town of about 7,500, is a mining community with strong links to Arizona's past. You can reach Globe by driving south on AZ 87 to AZ 188, which passes the ***Tonto National Monument*** (928-467-2241; nps.gov/tont). This often-overlooked national monument preserves prehistoric cliff dwellings lived in by the Salado Indians more than 700 years ago. The Lower Cliff Dwelling can be viewed on the observation deck at the visitor center or by a half-mile hike along the Lower Cliff Dwelling Trail. The Upper Cliff Dwelling can only be reached by a guided hike along the 3-mile round-trip Upper Cliff Dwelling trail, which is only open from Nov through Apr. Reservations are required. While you are here you might want to check with the park rangers on special activities including full-moon hikes, living-history demonstrations, and off-site hikes. Admission.

Continue south on this scenic route and you'll soon enter Globe. From the Phoenix area, it's an easy jaunt east on US 60. In the downtown area, more than two dozen historic buildings date from just before the turn of the twentieth century until the late 1920s. They range in style from territorial adobe to Queen Anne Victorian. You can drop by the **Gila County Historical Museum** (1330 North Broad St.; 928-425-7385; gilahistoricalmuseum.org)—the former Globe-Miami Mine Rescue Station, built in 1920—on US 60 next to the chamber of commerce, to look at exhibits of how the community grew and changed. The museum is open Tues through Sat from 11 a.m. to 3 p.m. Also worth a look is the town's **Cobre** ("copper") **Valley Center for the Arts** (928-425-0884; cobre valleyarts.org), in the building that used to be the Gila County Courthouse on 101 N. Broad St. It has been lovingly restored as a venue for the local theater. They also offer workshops and classes, and it also houses visual arts studios. You can take a self-guided tour and browse in the gift shop, which sells every-thing from hand-painted furniture to stationery. Hours vary with the season. Follow Broad Street through Globe for about 1.5 miles, and you'll see a clearly marked road leading to **Besh-Ba-Gowah** ("place of metal") **Archaeological Park** (928-425-0320). This Salado pueblo settlement was built around AD 1225 on top of what was once a Hohokam pit house. The site has been restored to allow visitors a self-guided tour. You can climb around in the ancient settle-ment using ladders to follow the same paths original occupants took to get to the roof or down to the first floor. An on-site museum houses artifacts retrieved from the excavation, including an extensive collection of Salado pottery. Admis-sion. It's open from 9 a.m. to 4:30 p.m., closed Mon and Tues during summer.

After you've worked up an appetite crawling in and out of the pueblo, try a home-style meal at **Judy's Cook House** (5412 S. Russell Rd.; 928-425-5366) in Globe. $. Refreshed, you can prowl Globe's numerous antiques or gift shops, such as the jam-packed **Pickle Barrel Trading Post** (404 S Broad St.; 928-425-9282; picklebarreltradingpost.com).

As for accommodations, several bed-and-breakfast inns in Globe provide rest for the weary. **Noftsger Hill Inn** (425 North St.; 928-425-2260; noftsger hillinn.com) has guests sleeping in the actual classrooms and janitor's closet of the old Noftsger Hill School. Owners Rosalie and Dom Ayala purchased the property in 2001 and have six rooms currently available—all furnished in "comfortable antiques." A delicious homemade breakfast wakes you up in the morning. $.

One reason to visit the **Safford** (928-428-2511 or 888-837-1841; visitgra hamcounty.com) area is to drive up the 35-mile **Swift Trail** to the summit of **Mount Graham** (928-428-4150; fs.usda.gov/coronado), a 10,713-foot peak in the Pinaleño Mountains known as "sky islands," isolated mountains surrounded by low desert creating islands of distinct and separate habitats. This mountain has had an interesting history over the years. More than one hundred years ago when there was a fort nearby, injured soldiers were taken up Mount Graham to recuperate in the pine-scented air. For a number of decades there have been cabins, Christmas tree farms, and campgrounds on the mountain. As an aside, on your way up Swift Trail you'll pass *Safford Federal Prison Camp* on your left, where Watergate conspirator John Ehrlichman was imprisoned for a while.

The Swift Trail is a narrow road with lots of sharp curves and steep drop-offs with no guardrail. The upper section is unpaved. It's not for the faint of heart. That being said, there are many beautiful areas on the mountain where you can pull off and have a picnic. There are also several scenic overlooks where you can see gorgeous, sweeping vistas of the valley all the way down to Safford. If hiking is on your agenda, there are nine major trails on Mount Graham. One of the best is the moderately difficult 14-mile *Round the Top Mountain Trail,* which meanders through shady pine forest and also offers some good views of the countryside. Check with the Coronado National Forest Safford Ranger District (711 Fourteenth Ave., Ste. D; 928-428-4150; fs.usda.gov/coronado) for detailed hiking maps. Whenever you visit Mount Graham, bring a jacket, because it's chilly even in the summer.

For adventures closer to the ground, pay a visit to *Roper Lake State Park* (928-428-6760; azstateparks.com). The 30-acre lake is ringed by campgrounds and cabins and is especially popular with families for the shady "island," a thumb of land with shade trees, picnic tables and a small beach jutting into the water. There's also a natural stone hot tub, taking advantage of one of the many hot springs in the area. Sister unit to the park, *Dankworth Pond* is 3 miles away and features a short educational hiking trail and beautiful mountain panoramas. Admission.

If you're itching for backcountry, head to the 23,000-acre *Gila Box Riparian National Conservation Area* (928-348-4400; blm.gov), where bird-watchers can keep an eye out for the more than 200 species of birds that inhabit the region. This riparian area features four waterways (the Gila and San Francisco Rivers and Bonita and Eagle Creeks), cliff dwellings, sandy beaches, hiking trails, and shady woodlands. Favored activities in the area include kayaking, canoeing, fishing, wildlife watching, swimming, and camping. The Gila Box Riparian National Conservation Area is located 20 miles northeast of Safford. For an adventurous backcountry drive, take the 21-mile-long *Black Hills Back Country Byway,* which travels between Safford and Clifton. Along the way, you'll travel through desert grasslands and the Gila Box Riparian National Conservation Area. Access to the backcountry road is from US 191. The southern end of the road is at milepost 139 and the northern end is at milepost 160.

Arizona Shoot-out

On a summer evening in 1877, a scuffle broke out in George Atkins' Saloon near the Camp Grant Army Post in southeastern Arizona. The row was between a burly blacksmith named Windy Cahill and a skinny teenager working as a teamster, whom Cahill had shoved around on prior occasions. After insults were traded, Cahill quickly threw the youngster to the ground. During the scuffle the teen managed to pull his pistol, shoot the blacksmith point blank and flee. Cahill died the next day. The skinny teamster returned to New Mexico where he would soon became embroiled in the bloody Lincoln County War. More shootings followed and he soon earned a reputation as a gunman. Yet it was in Arizona that Billy the Kid killed his first man. Just four years after putting a bullet into Cahill's belly, the Kid would be gunned down by Sheriff Pat Garrett, dead at the age of 21.

The rugged, dirt road is only for high clearance and four-wheel-drive vehicles. For driving directions or more information on the Gila Box Riparian National Conservation Area or the Black Hills Back Country Byway, contact the Bureau of Land Management's Safford Field Office (711 Fourteenth Ave.; 928-348-4400; blm.gov/arizona).

Places to Stay in Eastern Arizona

GREER

Greer Lodge Resort and Cabins
80 N. Main St.
(928) 225-7620
greerlodgeaz.com
This mountain resort offers lodge rooms and cabin rentals, a full-service spa, two restaurants, a gift shop, and three private lakes. $$$.

HOLBROOK

Globetrotter Lodge
902 W. Hopi Dr.
(928) 297-0158
hotelsholbrookaz.com
This historic Route 66 motel has been beautifully restored by an Austrian couple and filled with personal, homey touches. Sitting right across the road from the Wigwam Motel, guests enjoy a classic mother road view. $.

KAYENTA

Kayenta Monument Valley Inn
Jct. US 160 and US 163
(928) 697-3221 or
(866) 306-5458
kayentamonumentvalley
.com
This property is conveniently located in the closest town to Monument Valley. Amenities include an outdoor swimming pool, coin-operated laundry, and fitness center. Remember: Navajoland is alcohol-free! $$.

PAYSON

Days Inn & Suites by Wyndham
301-A South Beeline Hwy.
(928) 478-7445
wyndhamhotels.com
Comfortable rooms at this popular chain hotel include refrigerators, microwaves, and fireplaces (some). Other amenities include an indoor pool and hot tub, and a deluxe continental breakfast. $.

Mountain Meadows Cabins
1075 E. Ranch Rd.
(928) 478-4415
mountainmeadowscabins.com
The six cozy cabins are tucked away in the forest under the Mogollon Rim. Cabins come complete with kitchens, fireplaces, and porches. There is a two-night minimum stay on weekends. $$.

PINETOP-LAKESIDE

Antlers Inn
1023 E. White Mountain Blvd.
(928) 367-4146
antlersinnaz.com
The friendly staff and clean spacious rooms help put you in vacation mode right away. Pets are welcomed, a continental breakfast is served in the office and there's a 9-hole miniature golf course and picnic tables in the courtyard. $.

FOR MORE INFORMATION ABOUT EASTERN ARIZONA

Apache-Sitgreaves National Forests
fs.usda.gov/asnf

Arizona Office of Tourism
visitarizona.com

Coronado National Forest
fs.usda.gov/coronado

Globe-Miami Chamber of Commerce
globemiamichamber.com

Graham County Chamber of Commerce
visitgrahamcounty.com

Holbrook Chamber of Commerce
holbrookazchamber.com

Navajo Nation Tourism Office
discovernavajo.com

Payson Department of Tourism
paysonrimcountry.com

Petrified Forest National Park
nps.gov/pefo

Pinetop-Lakeside Chamber of Commerce
pinetoplakesidechamber.com

Rim Country Regional Chamber of Commerce
rimcountrychamber.com

Show Low Chamber of Commerce
showlowchamber.com

Springerville Chamber of Commerce
springervilleeagarchamber.com

Tonto National Forest
fs.usda.gov/tonto

White Mountain Apache Reservation
whitemountainapache.org

Winslow Chamber of Commerce
winslowarizona.org

Whispering Pines Resort

237 White Mountain Blvd.
(800) 840-3867
whisperingpinesaz.com
This older resort offers
something for everyone
with 38 cabins from
studios to three bedrooms
spread across 13 acres
of woodlands. Some even
have spa tubs. $$.

SAFFORD

Cottage Bed and Breakfast

1104 S. Central Ave.
(928) 428-5118
cottagebedandbreakfast
.com
Originally built in 1890, this
B&B offers a cozy cottage
and a two bedroom guest
house. They also operate
the adjacent bakery
and each morning a full
breakfast is served. $.

SHOW LOW

KC Motel

60 W. Deuce of Clubs
(928) 537-4433
kcmotelshowlow.com
It's an old-fashioned road
trip experience at this older
motel with spotlessly clean
rooms and good prices. $.

TUBA CITY

Quality Inn

10 N. Main St.
(928) 283-4545
choicehotels.com
This pet-friendly hotel is
centrally located on the
Navajo Reservation and
is less than two hours

away from Grand Canyon
National Park, Monument
Valley, and the Navajo
National Monument. $$.

Places to Eat in Eastern Arizona

PAYSON

El Rancho Mexican Restaurant

200 S. Beeline Hwy.
(928) 474-3111
elranchorestaurant.net
Tacos, enchiladas, burritos,
and other Mexican favorites
are served up at this family-
friendly restaurant. $$.

Macky's Grill

201 W. Main St.
(928) 474-7411
mackysgrill.com
This casual Payson
restaurant serves American
food for lunch and dinner
and offers a full children's
menu. $.

PINE

Old County Inn

3502 N. AZ 87
(928) 476-6560
oldcountyinn.com
Delicious pizzas, inventive
small plates and pine-
shaded patio make this
restaurant popular with
locals and visitors alike. $$.

PINETOP-LAKESIDE

Chalet Restaurant and Bar

348 W. White Mountain
Blvd.
(928) 367-1514
chaletrestaurantaz.com
Seafood, ribs, and a sushi
bar. Open Tues through
Sat for dinner only. $$.

Charlie Clark's Steakhouse

1701 White Mountain Blvd.
(928) 367-4900
charlieclarks.com
This local favorite has been
serving up everything from
salad to steak since 1938.
Patio dining is offered
during summer months.
$$.

SAFFORD

El Coronado

409 Main St.
(928) 428-7755
Mexican specialties and
American favorites are the
mainstays at this casual
eatery. $.

Manor House Restaurant and Rockin' Horse Saloon

415 East Hwy. US 70
(928) 428-7148
visitsaffordmanorhouse
.com
This bustling restaurant
serves up a full menu of
seafood, steaks, pasta and
Mexican entrees. $$

WINSLOW

Turquoise Room

303 E. 2nd St. (Route 66)
(928) 289-2888
theturquoiseroom.net
Located in the historic
La Posada Hotel, this fine-
dining establishment serves
a stylish southwestern-
inspired menu of dishes
such as pork carnitas,
Churro lamb cassoulet,
and elk medallions. Open
for breakfast, lunch, and
dinner. $$.

Central Arizona

The Valley of the Sun and Phoenix

The **Valley of the Sun** cuts a diagonal swath from Wickenburg in the northwest to Florence in the southeast with Arizona's primary gateway, **Sky Harbor International Airport,** located almost exactly in the center and encircled by the major interstates and highways that provide access to every region of the state. Covering approximately 2,000 square miles of the **Sonoran Desert,** the Phoenix metro-plex is made up of twenty-two separate cities and towns, the best-known of which are Phoenix (the core city), Scottsdale (filled with resorts and art galleries), and Tempe (home of Arizona State University). Other prominent communities include Mesa and Apache Junction in the east valley, Florence and Casa Grande to the south, and Glendale (known for its antiques shops and as the home for the NFL Arizona Cardinals and the NHL Arizona Coyotes) and Wickenburg (filled with Old West charm) in the west valley.

For information about the Valley of the Sun, your best starting point is the **Greater Phoenix Convention and**

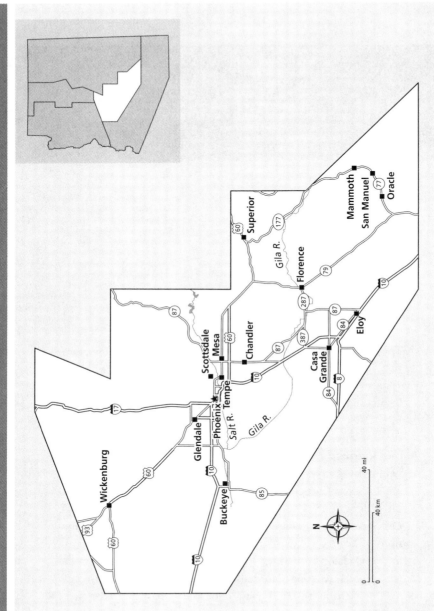

Visitors Bureau (125 N. Second St., Ste. 120; 602-254-6500 or 877-225-5749; visitphoenix.com) in Phoenix. When you get to town, the CVB has a downtown walk-in information center open Mon through Fri from 8 a.m. to 5 p.m.

Phoenix is the fifth largest city in the nation, with more than 1.6 million residents within city limits and about 4.7 million total in the greater Phoenix area. Towns spread out along I-10 and I-17 like strands of a giant spiderweb, covering the Valley of the Sun with attractions that are sure to ensnare travelers. The Valley is made up of a myriad of pseudo-, micro-, and full-scale communities. To the west of Phoenix are the suburban communities of Sun City West, Surprise, El Mirage, Youngtown, Sun City, Peoria, Glendale, Buckeye, Wickenburg, Litchfield Park, Goodyear, and Avondale. To the east are Paradise Valley, Scottsdale, Tempe, Mesa, and Apache Junction. Farther south are Guadalupe, Ahwatukee, Chandler, Gilbert, Sun Lakes, Higley, Queen Creek, and Casa Grande. And that's just a partial list!

Phoenix emerged from the ashes of Hohokam settlements, prospector claims, and military camps around 1850. It was long an agricultural center, diverting water from the Salt River to irrigate many acres of farmland. In true colorful western fashion, the man most credited with envisioning the irrigation potential of the Valley was Jack Swilling, a drug-addicted Confederate deserter.

Those who imagine the desert as flat, brown and lifeless will be startled by the lushness of Phoenix. This is the heart of the Sonoran Desert, the most biologically diverse of all North American deserts. It is a surprisingly green

AUTHOR'S FAVORITES IN CENTRAL ARIZONA

Apache Trail	Lost Dutchman State Park
Arcosanti	McDowell Sonoran Preserve
BC Jeep Tours	OdySea in the Desert
Boyce Thompson Arboretum State Park	Old Town Scottsdale
	Picacho Peak State Park
Cerreta Candy Company	Pinal County Historical Museum
Desert Botanical Garden	Taliesin West
Heard Museum	White Tank Manta Regional Park
Historic Heritage Square	

JANUARY

Arizona National Horse Show
Scottsdale
(602) 258-8568
anls.org
One of Arizona's largest horse shows, this annual event includes a quarter horse show, 4-H/FFA horse show, and a saddlebred show at WestWorld in North Scottsdale.

Litchfield Park Native American Fine Arts Festival
Litchfield Park
(623) 935-9040
litchfieldparkgathering.com
Enjoy the work of more than 100 Native American artisans at this popular annual event.

Waste Management Phoenix Open
Scottsdale
wmphoenixopen.com
"The Greatest Show on Grass" tees off one of the PGA Tour's top events in late Jan/early Feb, featuring some of the finest golfers in the world.

FEBRUARY

Arizona's Renaissance Festival
Gold Canyon
(520) 463-2600
arizona.renfestinfo.com
This traveling festival (Feb and Mar) is situated at a permanent site east of Apache Junction, built to resemble a sixteenth-century European village. Visitors can shop in the village market with over 200 authentic shops including an apothecary, blacksmith, toy-maker, potter, and glassblower. The festivities are highlighted by daily jousting matches and meals at various food stands loaded with turkey legs, cold beer, and roasted nuts.

Gold Rush Days
Wickenburg
(928) 684-5479
wickenburgchamber.com
A senior rodeo (age fifty and older) includes gold panning, carnival, western dances, arts and crafts, barbecue, gem show, and mucking and drilling.

Native American World Championship Hoop Dance Contest
Phoenix
(602) 252-8840
heard.org
The Heard Museum hosts top Native American dancers from the United States and Canada in a national hoop dancing competition. Lawn seating only, so bring folding chairs or blankets.

Scottsdale All-Arabian Horse Show
Scottsdale
(480) 515-1500
scottsdaleshow.com
Two thousand of the world's most beautiful Arabians, Half-Arabians, and National Show Horses compete in this annual equestrian display.

MARCH

Arizona Scottish Highland Games
Mesa
arizonascots.com
This exciting festival, sponsored by the Caledonian Society of Arizona and honoring Scottish heritage, features piping and drumming, a dance competition, and clan/society registration.

Heard Museum Guild Annual Indian Fair and Market
Phoenix
(602) 252-8840
heard.org
This annual fair features more than 300 of the nation's top Native American artists.

Scottsdale Arts Festival

Scottsdale
(480) 499-8587
scottsdaleartsfestival.org
The festival is rated among the top in the country and includes 200 selected artists. The event includes live music from local performers as well as fresh food and wines from the area.

Tempe Spring Festival of the Arts

Tempe
(480) 355-6060
tempefestivalofthearts.com
This event attracts more than 200,000 people to Downtown Tempe over the course of the 3-day weekend.

APRIL

Scottsdale Culinary Festival

Scottsdale
(480) 945-7193
scottsdalefest.org
Sample the best in food and drinks from around the area, along with chef demos, cooking challenges, and live music at this grand picnic in the heart of downtown Scottsdale.

MAY

Summer Concerts in the Park

Scottsdale
(480) 312-2312
therailroadpark.com
This free concert series features local bands from the Phoenix Valley. The concerts are held at the McCormick Ranch Park. The train runs at night and refreshments are available for purchase.

JULY

Summer Spectacular ArtWalk

Scottsdale
scottsdalegalleries.com
A meandering trail through the streets of downtown Scottsdale leads to some of the best galleries in the city. Patrons can cool off during the hot summer nights as they pop in and out of shops hosting the work of local artists.

SEPTEMBER

Bye Bye Buzzards

Superior
(602) 827-3000
btarboretum.org
Celebrate a flock of turkey buzzards at Boyce Thompson Arboretum State Park, before they depart for their winter home in Mexico.

Fiesta Septiembre

Wickenburg
(928) 684-5479
wickenburgchamber.com
The festival at the Desert Caballeros Western Museum features arts and crafts, folklorico dancers, mariachi bands, mercado, and a salsa contest.

NOVEMBER

Feeling of Fall Festival

Superior
(602) 827-3000
btarboretum.org
The Boyce Thompson Arboretum celebrates the sights and smells of fall, with their Chinese pistachio trees ablaze with color. Enjoy Arizona apple cider, live music, and special events for kids.

Fountain Festival of Arts and Crafts

Fountain Hills
(480) 837-1654
fountainhillschamber.com
Over 200,000 visitors attend this festival featuring 500 visiting artists.

TOP ANNUAL EVENTS IN CENTRAL ARIZONA (CONT.)

Fantasy of Lights
Tempe
(480) 355-6060
downtowntempe.com
Downtown Tempe celebrates the holidays with the city tree lighting, parade, boat parade, and live entertainment.

DECEMBER

Cowboy Christmas Poetry Gathering
Wickenburg
(928) 684-5479
wickenburgchamber.com
A night of poetry, ballads, stories, and songs, evoke the hard but rewarding life on the range.

landscape punctuated by mountains in and around town. While the summers can be scorching hot (also a great time to snag deals at swanky resorts) the climate is superb for eight months of the year. That bounty of sun and mild temperatures is sure to coax visitors outside for the championship golf courses, sprawling county parks, desert preserves, and even a collection of cactus-guarded lakes.

While the golf courses still provide a carpet of green, traditional lawns are rarely seen as residents continue to embrace their desert home by utilizing xeriscaping techniques. Using drought resistant plants in landscape design conserves water and blends with the natural surroundings. There's a wide range of plants that thrive in arid conditions. This is a place where flowers bloom every day of the year. That may not seem like a huge deal but it really is lovely.

Sports fans may want to begin their exploration of the Valley in downtown Phoenix. **Talking Stick Resort Arena** (201 E. Jefferson St.; 602-379-7800; talkingstickresortarena.com) is the home of the National Basketball Association's Phoenix Suns, as well as the Women's National Basketball Association's Phoenix Mercury, and the American Football League's Arizona Rattlers. Talking Stick Resort Arena is also one of the best places in the Valley to see musical performers, ice shows, rodeos, and whatever. On the first level of the arena, the **Team Shop** (602-514-8321) sells posters, key chains, wearables, and other items related to the Suns and other Phoenix-area teams. Down the street, **Chase Field** (401 E. Jefferson St.; 602-462-6500; mlb.com/dbacks/ballpark) opened in 1998 as the home field for the Arizona Diamondbacks. Even when the Arizona Diamondbacks aren't playing, this massive, $350-million, retractable-roofed stadium is worth seeing—perhaps over lunch at **T.G.I. Friday's Front Row** (602-462-3506; frontrowphoenix.com), a casual

The Cactus League

Spring comes early to the desert and nowhere is that more evident than with the iconic crack of the bats signaling the return of the *Cactus League* (cactusleague .com). Major League Baseball's spring training runs through Feb and Mar, when everyone's a potential Hall of Famer. The Cactus League was started to avoid some of the racial tensions in post-war Florida. In 1946, Bill Veck, owner of the Cleveland Indians decided to train his team in Tucson. He convinced the New York Giants to relocate to Phoenix and the Cactus League was born. Veck signed Larry Doby, the second African-American to play Major League Baseball, and the first in the American League. Today the Cactus League is comprised of 15 teams playing more than 200 games in cozy stadiums across the Valley. Enjoy plenty of sunny weather, affordable tickets, and seats that are practically on the field with the players. For baseball fans, it's a reminder why they fell in love with the game in the first place.

eatery built right into the stands that's open daily. Here, too, you can shop for sports memorabilia at *Team Shop* (602-462-6701). As an aside, Chase Field is the first ballpark ever to be built with its own swimming pool off right field. Only in Phoenix!

Naturally the area is rife with sports bars for fans to celebrate (or mourn) before, during and after each game. More eclectic offerings can be found at the *Phoenix Convention Center & Venues* (100 N. Third St.; 800-282-4842; phoenix conventioncenter.com) another anchor of downtown. The facilities include 900,000 square feet of exhibit space for a variety of shows, complemented by 2,300-seat Symphony Hall and the Historic Orpheum Theatre.

Your best bet to sample the range of Phoenix nightlife is to explore *Roosevelt Row* (602-829-5259; rooseveltrow.org), downtown Phoenix's walkable arts district, home to galleries and studios, restaurants, bars and boutique shops. An active nightlife scene keeps RoRo jumping anytime but show up on the first Friday of the month from 6 p.m. to 10 p.m. and you'll enjoy a bustling art walk with plenty of extra activities. The hip and trendy eateries include *Cibo* (603 N. 5th Ave.; 602-441-2697; cibophoenix.com), an urban pizzeria in a charming 1913 bungalow. $$. *Carly's Bistro* (128 E. Roosevelt St.; 602-262-2759; carlysbistro.com) is known for the soups and salads featuring a bit of a Mediterranean flair. $$. With a selection of handcrafted beers and elevated pub fare, *Mother Bunch Brewing* (825 N. 7th St.; 602-368-3580; motherbunchbrew .com) makes welcome sanctuary. Enjoy small plate specials during the "Traffic Hours," weekdays 3-6 p.m. $$.

Phoenix also features the classy downtown complex called *The Arizona Center* (602-271-4000; arizonacenter.com). Located between Third and Fifth

Streets north of Van Buren Street, it's a complete dining, shopping, and enter-tainment complex. There's the ***AMC Arizona Center 24 Theatres,*** a twenty-four-plex movie theater (602-307-5371; amctheatres.com) that shows first-run features in their full digital sound splendor and offers reduced ticket prices for the early shows. You'll find local favorites: ***Mi Amigos Mexican Grill*** (602-256-7355; miamigos.com) and ***Canyon Cafe*** (602-252-3545; canyoncafe.com). For something quicker and cheaper, stop by one of the smaller eateries where you can get everything from gourmet coffee at ***Starbucks*** (602-258-8472; star-bucks.com) to ice cream concoctions at ***Cold Stone Creamery*** (602-252-5572; coldstonecreamery.com).

For concert lovers, ***Ak-Chin Pavilion*** (2121 N. 83rd Ave.; 602-254-7200; ak-chinpavilion.com) offers about three dozen events per year, including most of the top pop/rock and country acts that tour Arizona. The Pavilion, which seats about 20,000 under the stars, has provisions for video screens and adja-cent areas for booths that sell everything from bottled water to concert tees to margaritas. During major events such as Jimmy Buffett's annual visit, the Pavil-ion turns into Party Town, with a forest of colorfully decorated Parrotheads—which is what Buffett fans call themselves—bopping to the tunes.

The Valley is a great place to hear up-and-coming musical acts, and as you might expect, there are a lot of hip clubs. Your best bet for finding the hot new spots in town is to look for one of the local freebie publications distributed from street stands and in local restaurants and shops.

They may have built this city on sports and rock-and-roll, but art and architecture also offer significant appeal. Several key buildings were designed, built, or influenced by master architect Frank Lloyd Wright; some of them are private residences, but four are public buildings that can be toured. The most impressive is ***Taliesin*** (Welsh for "shining brow") ***West*** (12621 Frank Lloyd Wright Blvd.; 480-860-2700; franklloydwright.org). Built against the foothills of the McDowell Mountains just outside of Scottsdale, this winter retreat was begun in 1937 by Wright, who made many changes to it over time (the original structure used canvas flaps instead of glass windows). Today, it's the head-quarters of the ***Frank Lloyd Wright Foundation,*** which operates a school of architecture and maintains an archive of the master's designs. Taliesin West has a gift shop and offers tours that range from a one-hour overview to an in-depth, behind-the-scenes study. Special events at the site include desert walks and nighttime city-light gazing.

Wright also had an influence on one of Phoenix's best-known resorts, the ***Arizona Biltmore Resort and Spa*** (2400 E. Missouri Ave.; 602-955-6600; arizonabiltmore.com), which at one time was run by the Wrigley chewing gum family. Though most believe that the resort was designed by Wright, it was actually at the hand of his former apprentice, Albert Chase McArthur. The story goes that McArthur invited the famous architect to oversee construction of the hotel, which he did quietly for a few months before completely removing himself from the project. Nevertheless, Wright's touch can be seen in the block structure of the resort as well as in its distinctive spire. You have to be a guest to get a guided tour, but you're welcome to look around the lobby and other public areas.

If you're still looking for the "Wright stuff," drop by **Grady Gammage Memorial Auditorium** (480-965-3434; asugammage.com) on Apache Boulevard and Mill Avenue in Tempe. This structure, on the grounds of Arizona State University, was actually begun after Wright's death and was completed in 1964. The circular building has been extensively praised for its physical beauty as well as its acoustics. Tours are conducted during the academic year from September through May, and the center regularly hosts touring Broadway groups that perform such hits as *Cats, Wicked,* and *Rent* to sold-out crowds.

Architecturally, **Downtown Phoenix** has a lot to admire. The copper-domed 1901 historic **State Capitol** building (1700 W. Washington St.; 602-926-3620; azlibrary.gov) is now a historical museum. (The actual government offices now occupy the modern, nine-story tower that rises behind the historic dome.) You can wander about at your own pace, or take one of the guided tours to peer into exhibits on the state's political past. The State Capitol building is open Mon through Fri from 9 a.m. to 4 p.m., Sat 10 a.m. to 2 p.m. from Sept through May. Guided tours are free but reservations are required. Also worth a look in the downtown area are Heritage Square, St. Mary's Basilica, and the Old County/City Hall complex.

The **Historic Heritage Square** complex (602-262-5070; heritagesquare phx.org) at Seventh and Monroe Streets is a group of historic houses from the original Phoenix town site. Now the buildings house museums, boutiques, a bistro, and a gift shop/tearoom surrounding a cool, green courtyard. The **Rosson House Museum** is a fully restored 1895 Queen Anne Victorian that offers a stylish peek at the past. The house is only accessible through guided tours. It's open Wed through Sat 10 a.m. to 5 p.m., and Sun noon to 5 p.m. Last tours are given at 4 p.m. Admission. Along with the history, you have a couple of amazing dining options at Heritage Square where you'll find two of the best restaurants in the city/state/nation. Housed in a cozy turn-of-the-century bungalow, **Nobuo at Teeter House** (602-254-0600; nobuofukuda.com) serves vibrant award-winning modern Japanese cuisine. $$. For foodies, a visit to **Pizzeria Bianco** (602-258-8300; pizzeriabianco.com) is a pilgrimage. Chris Bianco's simple yet elegant pies were the driving force behind the artisanal pizza movement. $$. Chefs at both eateries are James Beard award winners.

The **Arizona Science Center** (600 E. Washington St.; 602-716-2000; azscience.org) is the kind of place where Carl Sagan would have felt right at home. Now located in a $47-million building just east of the Phoenix Convention Center, the facility is a hands-on (and in some cases, whole-body-on) learning complex that encompasses Arizona's largest planetarium, a wide-screen theater, and 350 interactive exhibits that beg to be touched and explored. The center is open from 10 a.m. to 5 p.m. daily. Admission. There are separate fees for the planetarium and the IMAX shows.

St. Mary's Basilica (231 N. Third St.; 602-354-2100) is a soaring edifice that seems out of place, yet is oddly natural amid all the modern downtown structures. Founded in 1881, it is the oldest Catholic church in the city and a popular place for weddings and other major events. If there aren't any services taking place when you visit, you can walk around inside and marvel at the various forms of architecture that were used in constructing this Phoenix land-mark (call for hours). It also, interestingly enough, has its own gift shop selling religious articles and mementos.

The **Herberger Theater Center** (222 E. Monroe St.; 602-254-7399; her-bergertheater.org) is an understated earth-tone structure that provides space for several performing arts groups—including the very popular (and deservedly so) Arizona Theatre Company, which uses professional actors from stage and screen to perform original and time-tested works in Phoenix and Tucson. The company's season usually runs Oct through May.

If you're hungry after a downtown tour, **1130 The Restaurant** (455 N. Third St.; 602-368-3046; 1130therestaurant.com) is located in the Arizona Center. There's a nice bistro vibe to the place, good for lunch or happy hour. $$.

The Old County Courthouse

No tour of the downtown area is complete without a look at the historic **Maricopa County Courthouse** at 125 W. Washington St. The county structure, thought to be the largest terra-cotta–surfaced structure in the state, is a grand old courthouse built in the late 1920s. On the second floor is the courtroom where the famous Miranda trial took place. The 1963 case, involving Ernesto Miranda, who was arrested for a rape that occurred near Bethany Home Road and Seventeenth Street in Phoenix, threw a harsh spotlight on police interrogation tactics and resulted in the Miranda Rights ruling ("You have the right to remain silent. If you give up the right to remain silent . . . ") The structures in the county/city complex are public buildings; as such they are open to visitors, but no tours are offered.

America's Heroes: Phoenix's Firefighting Museum

Among the many unusual places to visit in Phoenix is the largest firefighter museum in the world. *The Hall of Flame* (6101 E. Van Buren St.; 602-275-3473; halloflame .org) has 130 antique and classic fire engines as well as firefighting artifacts of all types. The fire engines date as far back as 1725 and are as new as 1969. One of the carriages was used to fight the 1871 Chicago Fire. Photos, artwork, badge and arm patch displays, and even a fire safety exhibit for kids round out the items of interest here. Admission. It's open Mon through Sat from 9 a.m. to 5 p.m., and Sun from noon to 4 p.m.

Another choice in the neighborhood is *Seamus McCaffrey's Irish Pub & Restaurant* (18 W. Monroe St.; 602-253-6081; seamusmccaffreys.com). $$.

While you're downtown, be sure to get a look at the Spanish Colonial–style *Orpheum Theatre* (203 W. Adams St.; 602-262-6225 for tickets). Built in 1929, the theater was used for films and vaudeville performances. Mae West and W. C. Fields both graced this stage. Following an exhaustive, meticulous $14-million restoration project, the Orpheum reopened in early 1997. Broadway road shows play here.

Before leaving central Phoenix, the *Heard Museum* (2301 N. Central Ave.; 602-252-8840; heard.org) is an Arizona "must-see" near Monte Vista Road. Long known for its vast collection of Native American art, this museum features the craftsmanship and design abilities of the Native people of the Southwest. Barry Goldwater's collection of hand-carved katsina dolls is there; so is the doll collection of the Fred Harvey Corporation. Also fascinating to see and study are baskets, jewelry, pottery, and

arizonatrivia

Arizona is known as the Copper State. It produces more than 65 percent of the nation's domestic supply.

textiles. The artist-in-residence program gives you a chance to meet and hear artists discuss their work; plus, you can see replicas of traditional Indian dwellings including a Navajo hogan, an Apache wickiup, and a Hopi corn-grinding room. The museum is open Mon through Sat from 9:30 a.m. to 5 p.m., and Sun from 11 a.m. to 5 p.m. Admission.

There's a twofer waiting to be discovered at Phoenix's *Papago Park,* and they're side-by-side on Galvin Parkway east of downtown. *The Phoenix Zoo* (455 N. Galvin Pkwy.; 602-286-3800; phoenixzoo.org) is the largest privately funded zoo in the country; it's spacious, neat, and amusing, which is why it's also regarded as one of America's finest. Designed as a series of habitats, it includes an African veldt, a South American rain forest, and a traditional Arizona farm. Docents and teen volunteers make the exhibits come alive, and a Disney-style tram covers the entire complex. Two worthwhile special events during the year are "Howl-o-Ween," when children visit wearing Halloween costumes, and during the holidays, "Zoo Lights," a must-do. It's a month-long celebration (late Nov to early Jan) when the trees and the cacti are lit every evening until 10 p.m., and mimes, magicians, and carolers appear in the central courtyard or on the pathways. The zoo is open 364 days of the year (closed only Dec 25); hours vary seasonally. Admission.

Next along the road is *Desert Botanical Garden* (1201 N. Galvin Pkwy.; 480-941-1225; dbg.org), home to one of the world's largest and most diverse collections of desert plants as well as fine examples of Native American housing styles. It's a great place to learn more about cacti and their nasty habits before you set off on a desert hike; it's also an eye-opener to the beauty and delicacy of desert wildflowers, bushes, and small trees. Events here during the year include spring and fall plant sales, Music in the Garden, and Jazz in the Garden, and like its neighbor the zoo, the garden holds a winter holiday celebration of lights called *Las Noches de las Luminarias* each year. The Botanical Garden is open every day except July 4, Thanksgiving, and Dec 25; hours are from 7 a.m. to 8 p.m. May through Sept, and from 8 a.m. to 8 p.m. Oct through Apr. Admission.

North on Central Avenue from downtown is the *Phoenix Art Museum* (1625 N. Central Ave.; 602-257-1880; phxart.org), which houses a wide-ranging collection of artworks, including American, European, Spanish Colonial, Latin American, and Asian paintings and sculptures. Of particular interest to visitors may be the museum's collection of western American works featuring the works of southwestern artists. Children will enjoy the Thorne Miniature Rooms, which show how people lived during historic periods in the United States and Europe. Admission. Guided tours are offered at various times throughout the week. The museum is closed Mon.

One of the Valley's most unusual attractions is the *Mystery Castle* (800 E. Mineral Rd.; mymysterycastle.com) near South Mountain Park in Phoenix. This eighteen-room stone structure, which incorporates such unusual building materials as salvaged rail tracks, telephone poles, and wire rims from a Stutz Bearcat, was put together completely by hand. The mystery comes from the fact that the builder never told his family about the work. He had always promised his daughter that he would build her a castle, and after being diagnosed with tuberculosis he left their home in Seattle and came to Phoenix to undertake the project. She only found out about the castle when his will was read, and she lived there until her death in 2010. The castle has thirteen fireplaces, lots of antiques, and the general sense of being smack dab in the midst of somebody's dream. You can tour this unique home Thurs through Sun from 11 a.m. to 3:30 p.m., Oct through May only. Admission.

The ***Pueblo Grande Museum and Archaeological Park*** (4619 E. Washington St.; 602-495-0901; pueblogrande.org) is an actual Hohokam village that was abandoned around AD 1450. The museum's exhibit rooms have permanent displays of artifacts and also serve as a venue for workshops such as pottery making and archaeology. A hiking trail leads through the site and past a platform mound, a ball court, and replicated houses. Since 1976 the museum has held an annual Indian market (usually in Dec), where more than 200 artists sell their works. The market also features traditional music and dancing, food, and beverages. The museum is open Mon through Sat from 9 a.m. to 4:45 p.m., and Sun from 1 to 4:45 p.m. The museum is closed Sun and Mon, May through Sept. Admission.

A surprising attraction is the ***Musical Instrument Museum*** (4725 E. Mayo Blvd.; 480-478-6000; mim.org). More than 6,000 instruments from around the world are on display. Move through the open space at your own pace while being magically serenaded with a lush exotic soundtrack. Each exhibit senses your presence and plays audio in the wireless headphones provided by the museum. Enjoy snacks or lunch from the global cuisine in the café. There's also a theater hosting 200+ concerts each year. Open daily from 9 a.m. to 5 p.m. Admission.

Scottsdale and its Neighbors

Scottsdale, as a community, began in 1888 when army chaplain Winfield Scott purchased land to grow citrus and other crops. Over the years the town has emerged as a world-renowned resort destination, offering great shopping, public parks, nationally recognized museums, frontier-type attractions, and galleries galore.

In fact Scottsdale is loaded with galleries. In at least three separate areas—Main Street Arts and Antique District, Marshall Way, and Fifth Avenue Shopping Area (in which there are more than 200 specialty shops)—you can stroll for hours and get a close-up look at everything from traditional Native American

arizonatrivia

The Phoenix/Scottsdale area is home to more Mobil Five-Star and AAA Five-Diamond resorts than any other destination in the United States.

Cosanti and Cause Bells

In addition to the architectural work of Frank Lloyd Wright that is so much a part of the Phoenix-Scottsdale landscape, you'll also want to try to see the more fantastical and futuristic work of Italian architect **Paolo Soleri. Cosanti** (6433 E. Doubletree Ranch Rd.; 480-948-6145; cosanti.com) in Scottsdale is an example of his concept of blending desert landscaping with earth-formed concrete structures. Everywhere you walk among the courtyards, terraces, and gardens, there are bronze and ceramic wind bells tinkling. Designed by Soleri and his artisans, these Cause Bells, as they are known, represent national and global issues. You can watch them being made; you also can buy them to provide funding for the various organizations that work on solving world problems. Cosanti is open Mon through Sat from 9 a.m. to 5 p.m. and Sun from 11 a.m. to 5 p.m. The foundry is open to the public in the morning—it's best to call first. Donations accepted.

arts and crafts to nineteenth-century fine art. You can easily walk or take Scottsdale's local transportation—a free trolley—to these various areas, but you may want to take your car, because you'll no doubt buy something!

Faust Gallery (7100 E. Main St.; 480-200-4290; faustgallery.com) represents emerging and established Native American artists, with katsinas, pottery, paintings, and other works. **American Fine Art Editions, Inc.** (3908 N. Scottsdale Rd.; 480-990-1200; americanfineartgallery.com) represents the contemporary art scene very well with an eclectic collection of original work by internationally acclaimed twentieth-century artists (Neiman, Wyeth, Picasso). **On The Edge Gallery** (7050 E. Fifth Ave.; 480-265-8991; ontheedgegallery .com) is owned by more than 40 Arizona artists and covers just about any genre you can imagine. Come out on any Thurs evening to experience the nation's longest-running ArtWalk.

Explore the romance of a past era at **Western Spirit: Scottsdale's Museum of the West** (3830 N. Marshall Way; 480-686-9539; scottsdalemuseum west.org). Located in Old Town Scottsdale, the museum features ongoing and rotating exhibits of artwork, rare artifacts, and cultural treasures. A Smithsonian Affiliate, docent-led tours are also offered at various times. The museum is open Tues through Sat 9:30 a.m. to 5 p.m., Sun 11 a.m. to 5 p.m., with extended Thurs hours in winter. Admission.

While Scottsdale may be known for its resorts, galleries, restaurants and ultra-trendy nightclubs, it also has a backyard that must be seen to be believed. Years ago a handful of residents banded together and managed to save large tracts of pristine desert from development. Established in 1995, the **McDowell Sonoran Preserve** (480-998-7971; mcdowellsonoran.org) encompasses more than 30,000 acres, making it the largest urban preserve in the country. More than 200 miles of hiking and biking trails fan out across the expanse spread across North Scottsdale, departing from multiple trailheads. And if you're hesitant to venture into the desert on your own, free guided hikes are offered from mid-Sept through mid-Apr. Dates and locations are posted on the website, where maps are also available.

If it's too warm for an outdoor adventure but you still want to feel close to nature, head for *OdySea in the Desert* (9500 E. Via de Ventura; odyseainthe desert.com) an entertainment district packed with world-class attractions. Some highlights include the *OdySea Aquarium* (480-291-8000; odyseaaquarium .com) combining theme park-style entertainment with the largest aquarium in the Southwest. Take an underwater escalator through the Sharks of the Deep habitat if you dare. *The Butterfly Wonderland* (480-800-3000; butterflywonder land.com) is inside the largest rainforest conservatory in the United States, where more than 3,000 butterflies wobble and flutter among the foliage and flowers. Other exhibits include a butterfly emergence garden, reptile exhibit, honeybee extravaganza, tropical waters teeming with sharks, stingrays and more, and a 3D Theater. Other attractions include animatronic dinosaurs, a laser maze and more. Shops and eateries round out the roster. There are admission fees to each exhibit. Check the website for hours.

About 12 miles east of Scottsdale is the community of *Fountain Hills* (480-837-1654; fountainhillschamber.com). Fountain Hills is the community of a dazzling array of contemporary African art. The picturesque town has a number of local sights that are worth a look. The *World Famous Fountain* sits in a large manmade lake and sprays water for 15 minutes every hour from 9 a.m. to 9 p.m., except during days of high winds. When it was built it was the world's tallest fountain, launching plumes of water to 560 feet. Those dizzying heights are saved for special occasions these days, with most normal eruptions cresting about 330 feet.

If you want to try for your own record, hit the jackpot at *Fort McDowell Casino* (800-THE-FORT; fortmcdowellcasino.com), where visitors challenge Lady Luck twenty-four hours a day, seven days a week. Located on the Fort McDowell Yavapai Nation, this is also home to outfitters *Fort McDowell Adventures* (480-789-5300; fortmcdowelladventures.com) offering trail rides, cattle drives, Salt River kayaking tours and off-road exploration in rugged Tom-cars. *Saguaro Lake,* an artificial reservoir on the Salt River, offers a number of boating, waterskiing, and swimming opportunities, as well as the **Desert Belle** steamboat paddle wheeler (480-984-2425; desertbelle.com) that does regular tours and dinner cruises. The *Saguaro Lake Marina* (480-986-5546; saguarolakemarina.com) has boat rentals, a general store, and the *Lakeshore*

A Carefree Life

About twenty minutes north of Fountain Hills are the twin communities of **Cave Creek** and **Carefree.** Cave Creek was a mining community one hundred years ago, and over time it has become a diverse town filled with cool shops, eateries and saloons. It's where the Old West meets Jimmy Buffet's Parrotheads. Nearby Carefree is a bedroom community that began development in the 1950s. Carefree is also the location of one of the largest sundials in the United States, standing 35 feet tall, extending 72 feet and is 90 feet in diameter. This impressive timepiece, which sweeps out of the earth like a giant scimitar, can be found off Cave Creek Road and Sunshine Way.

Restaurant (480-984-5311). You can reach Saguaro Lake by taking AZ 87 north until you reach Bush Hwy. Head south on Bush Hwy., and it will take you to the lake.

While you're in Fountain Hills, drop by for a bite at *Que Bueno* (13207 N. LaMontana Dr.; 480-837-2418). This Mexican restaurant has won plaudits for its homemade salsa and features savory desserts like chocolate chimichangas.

The West Valley

On the western side of the Valley—accessible by heading west out of downtown Phoenix on I-10—are cities such as Avondale, Goodyear, Tolleson, and *Litchfield Park* (623-932-2260; southwestvalleychamber.org). *Litchfield Park* sprang to life as a company town in 1916 after Goodyear Tire and Rubber executive Paul Litchfield purchased the land to use as a cotton farm back in the days when cotton cords were utilized in automotive tires. It took the name Litchfield Park a decade later. Today the town is best known as the location of *The Wigwam Golf Resort and Spa* (300 E. Wigwam Blvd.; 866-976-6894; wigwamarizona.com). This four-star resort is composed of charming adobe casitas that were initially built for Goodyear officials. The Wigwam is especially favored by golfers because it features three eighteen-hole golf courses.

arizonatrivia

There are more than 185 golf courses in Greater Phoenix—making it one of the top five golf destinations in the world!

Two of these, the Gold Course and the Blue Course, were designed by well-known golf-course architect Robert Trent Jones Sr. The Gold Course, which has earned several accolades and awards, is a whopping 7,345 yards long.

Not surprisingly for an area that was raised by the rubber giant, nearby **Avondale** is home to **ISM Raceway** (623-463-5400 or 866-408-RACE; ismrace way.com), currently hosting two NASCAR race weekends annually.

The city of **Glendale** (623-930-4500; visitglendale.com) has some delightful off-the-beaten-path surprises to offer. The city is an interesting blend of old and new, quaint shops and adorable homes to go along with cheering crowds at championship sporting events. **Historic Downtown Glendale** is where you'll find a great antiques shopping area, and the **Catlin Court Historic District,** where the Craftsman bungalow-style homes have been turned into shops and restaurants; there's a walking tour leaflet you can use to see the entire neigh-borhood. A fairly easy walk from Old Town is **Cerreta Candy Company** (5345 W. Glendale Ave.; 623-930-9000; cerreta.com), a family-operated choco-late factory where you can watch candy being made, buy gift assortments, and enjoy a sample or two. Thirty-minute factory tours are offered Mon through Fri at 10 a.m. and 1 p.m. The **Deer Valley Petroglyph Preserve** (3711 W. Deer Valley Rd.; 623-582-8007) is a museum and easily accessed archeological site. A quarter-mile interpretive trail leads to a jumble of boulders where ancient people etched thousands of symbols. The preserve is open Wed through Sat 9 a.m. to 3 p.m. Admission.

In recent years, Glendale has established major league sports venues—acquiring both the NHL Arizona Coyotes and the NFL Arizona Cardinals. You can watch the Arizona Coyotes play at the **Gila River Arena** (623-772-3800; gilariverarena.com). It's also a great place to catch high-profile concerts. The Arizona Cardinals (azcardinals.com) play ball next door at the **State Farm Sta-dium,** (623-433-7101; statefarmstadium.com). The stadium, designed by archi-tect Peter Eisenman, is built in the shape of a barrel cactus and seats 63,000. It opened for the 2006 season and hosted its first Super Bowl, Super Bowl XLII, just two years later.

State Farm Stadium Fun Facts

- The stadium's 63,400 seats would stretch 18 miles if they were set in a straight line.

- There is enough concrete in the stadium to lay 900 miles of sidewalk, enough to reach from Phoenix to San Francisco.

- The stadium's grass field is the first of its kind in North America. The 18.9-million-pound tray is rolled outside and kept there for optimal grass growth until game day.

Anchoring the far western edge of the Valley is **White Tank Mountain Regional Park** (602-506-2930; maricopacountyparks.net). At nearly 30,000 acres it is the largest regional park in Maricopa County. It's spread across the desert lowlands and sharp-rising peaks of the White Tank Mountains, accessed by 40 miles of trails. The most popular is the Waterfall Canyon Trail that leads to a pool in a narrow box canyon. And yes, after a hard rain, there really is a waterfall. Following rainy winters, the desert at the base of the mountains erupts in colorful display of wildflowers. Admission.

If you're looking for a larger expanse of water than just a canyon pool, you don't have far to travel. **Lake Pleasant Regional Park** (602-506-2930; maricopacountyparks.net) sits at the northern edge of Peoria, a 10,000-acre reservoir popular with boaters, anglers, kayakers, campers, and even scuba divers. At the Lake Pleasant Discovery Center, visitors learn about the history of the area and desert wildlife. Two marinas feature restaurants, fuel, and boat rentals. Admission.

Wickenburg and Points North of Phoenix

At the junction of US 93 and US 60, **Wickenburg** (928-684-5479; wickenburg chamber.com) is a frontier town that's been a popular getaway destination for decades. Once known as "The Dude Ranch Capital of the World," Wickenburg was where city slickers came to get in touch with their inner cowpoke. But times change and only a few guest ranches remain. Wickenburg continues to thrive however. As a small western town surrounded by natural beauty, it still offers a special kind of escape.

Prospector/farmer Henry Wickenburg, a native of Prussia, founded the town in 1863 after discovering the largest gold-producing strike in the history of the state. He called his find the **Vulture Mine.** If you're interested in viewing the remains of Wickenburg's mining camp, it's about a dozen miles from town. Drive about 2.5 miles west of Wickenburg on US 60, turn left onto Vulture Mine Road, and continue for 12 miles. The remains of **Vulture City** (877-425-9229; vultureminetours.com) include weathered restored buildings surrounded by artifacts and mining equipment. A half-mile gravel path leads through the heart of the old camp. Open from 9 a.m. to 3 p.m. daily. Guided tours are offered most weekends at 10 a.m. Admission.

Mining is no longer a major portion of Wickenburg's economy. The lovely scenery—which ranges from creosote bush and cacti to oak and pine trees— draws visitors. Ranching and agriculture have helped to keep the city's coffers well stocked.

The Code of the West

If you're fascinated by the "Code of the West" (as is nearly anybody who grew up watching *The Rifleman* and *Wanted: Dead or Alive*), head for the Circle K store in Wickenburg near Tegner and Wickenburg Way. Behind the store is a 200-year-old mesquite tree, known as the "jail tree," which was used from 1863 to 1890 as a place to chain miscreants before the town had an actual cell.

If you drive in from the west off US 60, you can continue on the roadway that becomes Wickenburg Way, center of many of the area's hotels and restaurants. US 89/93 also leads into the town; once in the town limits, it's called Tegner Street. Either way, it's easy to get around, and most of Wickenburg's attractions are in the downtown center grid. Take some time to explore the century old buildings that line the streets. Grab a brochure from the visitor center housed in the restored train depot at 216 N. Frontier St. and take a self-guided tour. You'll also encounter some interesting characters from the past, several bronze sculptures represent much of Wickenburg's history.

Don't miss the **Desert Caballeros Western Museum** (21 N. Frontier St.; 928-684-2272; westernmuseum.org). The museum displays modern artwork from members of the **Cowboy Artists of America** in addition to pieces by American masters like Frederic Remington. There are also period rooms depicting Wickenburg's early years. The small park adjacent to the museum features a life-size statue by Joe Beeler of a cowboy kneeling beside his horse. The museum and museum store are open year-round, Mon through Sat from 10 a.m. to 5 p.m. and Sun from noon to 4 p.m. In the summer, from May through Aug, the museum is closed on Mon. Admission.

arizonatrivia

Hassayampa is actually a Yavapai word that means "following the water as far as it goes." Oddly, the preserve is one of the few locations where the river does not run underground.

Wickenburg is better known for its current hospitality than for its earlier law enforcement policies. Its guest ranches range from a cozy, historic hacienda to an elaborate resort that has its own golf course. **Kay El Bar Ranch** (928-684-7593; kayelbar.com) is a traditional adobe guest ranch with a pool and horseback riding; it is open mid-Nov to May 1. Rates include lodging, meals, and riding. $$$. **Flying E Ranch** (928-684-2690; flyingeranch.com) is an actual working cattle ranch that also has a tennis court, horse stables, pool, spa, and sauna; its season is Oct to Apr. $$$. **Rancho de los Caballeros** (928-684-5484 or 800-684-5030; ranchodeloscaballeros.com) caters not only to horse lovers but also to tennis buffs and especially golfers. The Los Caballeros course was rated as one of the top 100 in the nation by *Golf Digest*. It is open from mid-Oct to mid-May. $$$.

In keeping with Wickenburg's frontier history, area restaurants include steakhouses and several establishments serving Mexican fare, but you also can find other options as well. *The Horseshoe Cafe* (207 E. Wickenburg Way; 928-684-7377) has American cuisine and is known for its big downhome breakfasts. $. Another cool hangout is *Avi's Screamers Drive-In* (1151 W. Wickenburg Way; 928-684-9056), a 1950s-style diner featuring a variety of dishes, including chicken, fish, hamburgers (even a Hawaiian Burger), hotdogs, and more. $.

A must-see attraction is the *Hassayampa River Preserve* (928-684-2772; maricopacountyparks.net), about 4 miles southeast of town on US 60 at mile marker 114. The 770-acre preserve is a refuge area for birds like the zone-tailed hawk and the yellow-tailed cuckoo. It's not unusual to see the white posteriors of mule deer as they frolic through the brush. You may also see tracks made by raccoons, bobcats, and javelinas. The preserve's office is in a restored 1860s ranch house. After more than a quarter of a century as a Nature Conservancy preserve, the oasis is now managed by Maricopa County Parks and Recreation Department. It will serve as a gateway to the planned Vulture Mountains Recreation Area. Hours vary seasonally. Admission.

Ghost towns are scattered throughout this rugged area, including Stanton, where prospectors are said to have picked up gold nuggets the size of potatoes, and Congress, home of a legendary tunnel that led from the general store to the town's hotel. If you'd like to explore some the ghost towns, or the scenic beauty of the rugged landscape, try *BC Jeep Tours* (928-684-7901; bcjeeptours .com). The family-owned Wickenburg business will get you to places you won't find on your own and provide great information along the way.

Hidden *Castle Hot Springs* (877-600-1137; castlehotsprings.com), east of Wickenburg and west of Lake Pleasant, was at one time an exclusive spa where soothing natural hot spring water provided therapeutic relief for an impressive guest list that included President John F. Kennedy. After closing, the place was virtually abandoned for nearly 40 years. Following a complete ground-up reconstruction, luxury has once again returned to the desert. The digitally disconnected environment allows you to reconnect to the spectacular and healthful surroundings. $$$.

If you travel north from the Valley of the Sun, the *Pioneer Living History Museum* (3901 W. Pioneer Rd.; 623-465-1052; pioneeraz.org) on I-17, 1 mile north of Carefree Hwy., is a group of more than two dozen buildings, some authentic, and some reproductions that are used by reenactors to re-create the image of the frontier West. Visitors can see metalworking, dressmaking, carpentry, and other activities going on just as they were more than one hundred years ago. Hours vary seasonally. Admission.

Be sure to stop in ***Black Canyon City*** at one of Arizona's iconic restaurants for a meal or at least a slice of pie. ***Rock Springs Café*** (623-374-5794; rocksprings.cafe) started as a small general store in 1918 and continued to evolve into a hotel and café. While the full-service restaurant does a bustling business, it's the 24 types of pie that fly off the shelves, especially the popular Jack Daniels pecan. Rock Springs sells more than 100,000 pies a year and that number will likely grow with the planned addition of a free-standing bakery.

Arcosanti (928-632-7135; arcosanti.org) sits only a few minutes away, just off I-17 near Cordes Junction at exit 262. Although Arcosanti is visible from the interstate, uninformed motorists may not know what to make of the odd-looking structures perched on the cliffside and simply zip on by unaware of what they've missed. A sort of glorious urban experiment, Arcosanti, established in 1970, is the brainchild of Italian architect Paolo Soleri. Soleri's theories of "arcology" (a meld of architecture and ecology) prompted him to construct a self-sufficient community that would produce crops and create marketable products.

The buildings of Arcosanti look like nothing you've ever seen before: round and square shapes combining in asymmetrical forms amidst walls of basalt, splashed with color throughout. The effect is sort of "Frank Lloyd Wright *Through the Looking Glass*" (not surprising, given that Soleri was a Frank Lloyd Wright Fellow). In some ways the community will remind you of the styles and decor of the early seventies—a lava lamp would look right at home here—yet it all seems timeless, like a fairy-tale kingdom. Soleri died in 2013.

Visitors to Arcosanti, which is open year-round, can tour the ten-acre facility, browse in the gift shop (which sells everything from Soleri's famous ceramic or bronze abstract bells to posters and T-shirts), take part in crafts and building workshops, and attend concerts. Some concerts are preceded by dinner and followed by a light show projected on the canyon wall.

Arcosanti also has a bakery and a cafe. Admission to the gift shop and cafe is free, but a donation is requested for the one-hour tour (offered every hour from 10 a.m. to 4 p.m., except at noon). Architecture and specialty tours can be arranged with advance planning. Overnight accommodations are available in one-of-a-kind guest rooms.

The East Valley and Points South

On the opposite side of the Valley, *Tempe* (480-894-8158 or 800-283-6734; tempetourism.com) is known as the home of *Arizona State University* (480-965-2100; asu.edu). ASU is one of the largest public universities in the country and that youthful and passionate energy is apparent throughout the town. The previously mentioned Grady Gammage Memorial Auditorium is definitely worth your time.

For a different kind of artwork, wander into the ASU campus and head for the *Nelson Fine Arts Center.* The 49,700-square-foot center, designed by Antoine Predock, is itself a work of art. The lavender-hued structures that make up the center are boldly geometric yet reflect the shapes you find in the Sonoran Desert. Inside, along with performing arts spaces, are 12,000 works of art in the *ASU Art Museum* (480-965-2787; asuartmuseum.asu.edu), including an extensive collection of contemporary ceramics and Latin American folk and fine art. Hours vary seasonally. Free.

A prime attraction is *Tempe Town Lake* stretching for 2 miles just a short walk from downtown. A network of pathways circles the slender reservoir, popular with walkers, joggers, and bikers. The lake is stocked with trout, bass, catfish, and sunfish. If you're eager to get out on the water you can rent a variety of electric and human-powered craft at *Tempe Beach Park* on the south side of the lake next to the Mill Avenue Bridge. After your outing, you might enjoy a stroll along Mill Avenue, where you can flash back to your own college days. The lively street is crowded with that eclectic mix of restaurants, funky shops, and entertainment venues that seem to flourish close to a campus.

Just east of Tempe is *Mesa* (480-827-4700; visitmesa.com), another surprise in the Valley of the Sun. Arizona's third largest city, Mesa goes from urban to rural. Family farms have created numerous agritourism attractions. Mesa likes to proclaim "We had a Food Network before there was a Food Network." Check out Arizona's Fresh Foodie Tour on the Visit Mesa website to begin some yummy exploration. The vibrant downtown area, adorned with more than 200 public art sculptures, is the site of almost everything you might want to see or do. The expanded *Arizona Museum of Natural History* (53 N. Macdonald St.; 480-644-2230; arizonamuseumofnaturalhistory.org) has the largest exhibition of animated, full-scale, "roaring" dinosaurs west of the Mississippi, plus an exhibit of sea life from the Jurassic and Paleozoic periods. A 50-foot waterfall, caves, and re-creations of Hohokam Indian dwellings are also part of the museum's exhibits. The museum is open Tues through Fri from 10 a.m. to 5 p.m., Sat from 11 a.m. to 5 p.m., and Sun from 1 to 5 p.m. Admission.

Also near the museum is the ***Arizona Commemorative Air Force Museum*** (480-924-1940; azcaf.org), which is located adjacent to Falcon Field Airport near the crossroads of McKellips and Greenfield Roads. The museum displays several of the greats of World War II, restored and maintained not just for display in Arizona but in flying condition and ready for takeoff to events around the country each year. Among their aircraft is the American B-17 *Sentimental Journey,* which is considered the most authentically restored of all the B-17s flying today; plus there is an example of a C-47 Skytrain, and two restored B-25 bombers of the type Jimmy Doolittle flew. For a real thrill you can even go up in one of seven different warbirds. Go soaring over the Superstition Mountains in an open cockpit Stearman feeling the wind in your hair. How often will you get to do that? Typical flight days are Wed, Fri, and Sat. The museum is open daily from 10 a.m. to 4 p.m. Admission.

Don't leave town without trying the Latin comfort food at ***Republica Empanada*** (204 E. 1st Ave.; 480-969-1343; republicaempanada.com). You'll find almost two dozen varieties of empanadas, pillowy pastry pockets stuffed with both savory and sweet fillings. $.

The ***Lower Salt River Recreation Area,*** which can be reached easily from Mesa, is a popular summer spot for "tubing" and river rafting trips. Weather permitting, the Salt is crammed with people on inner tubes, drifting lazily while their portable stereos compete for audio dominance. Others take guided tours of the river. A few companies not far from Mesa that provide equipment and transportation are ***Salt River Tubing*** (480-984-3305; saltriver tubing.com) and ***Desert Voyagers Guided Raft Trips*** (480-998-7238; cliff creekoutfitters.com).

Just south of Mesa, the town of ***Gilbert*** (480-503-6913; discovergilbert .com) has emerged as another culinary hotspot. The strong agricultural roots of the community complement its Main Street charm. Visit ***Agritopia*** (agritopia .com) for a nostalgic return to simpler times. The live-eat-play neighborhood is centered around an 11-acre urban farm that supplies the numerous restaurants with produce, fruit, dates and olives. This is farm-to-table dining in its purest form. Diners at ***Joe's Farm Grill*** (3000 E. Ray Rd., Bldg 1; 480-563-4745; joesfarmgrill.com) tuck into burgers, sandwiches, and crisp salads at shade tree-draped picnic tables. $$.

The eastern edge of the Valley of the Sun comes to an abrupt end when it crashes against the rising wall of the Superstition Mountains. ***Apache Junction,*** located at the intersection of AZ 88 and US 60, is the gateway to this hauntingly beautiful landscape. Legend has it that sometime in the late 1880s German miner Jacob Walz (he would become known as the Dutchman) discovered a gold mine in the ***Superstition Mountains.*** The Superstitions, a 160,285-acre volcanic mountain range, are rocky and rugged throughout. When Walz died in 1891 without revealing the location of his mine, many treasure seekers flocked to the area to hunt for the Dutchman's riches. To this day no one has uncovered the location.

You can delve into the region's mining history any time of year by following the **Apache Trail,** a twisty, winding route into the **Tonto National Forest** (602-225-5200; fs.usda.gov/tonto). One of the first attractions you'll see as you turn northeast on AZ 88 is the **Superstition Mountain Museum** (480-983-4888; superstitionmountainmuseum.org). At the museum you can learn how prehistoric Indians lived in the area, and study exhibits that tell you about natural history—rocks, ores, animals, and reptiles. One exhibit contains photos, furniture, and equipment from a miners shack; another displays equipment and clothing from the mounted troops that are part of Arizona history; and, perhaps most fun, there are twenty-three maps that show possible locations of the Lost Dutchman Mine. The museum is open daily from 9 a.m. to 4 p.m. Admission. Just up the road is the **Goldfield Ghost Town** (480-983-0333; goldfieldghost town.com). The re-creation of an 1890s mining town features tours of a former mine, gunfights in the street, and a scenic railroad. Goldfield Ghost Town is open daily from 10 a.m. to 5 p.m. Free.

Across the road from Goldfield, **Lost Dutchman State Park** (480-982-4485; azstateparks.com) gives visitors a chance to explore the harsh landscape in relative safety. The campground includes a handful of camping cabins, and a network of trails slash across the slope to the base of the mountains. One trail, Siphon Draw, exits the park, enters the Superstition Mountain Park Wilderness Area, and scrambles up to a rocky basin. Carry plenty of water if you're attempting this hike. Wet winters can prompt an explosion of color at Lost Dutchman as a sea of golden poppies wash down the slopes in Feb and Mar. Admission.

The route continues to **Canyon Lake,** where you can ride the **Dolly Steamboat** (480-827-9144; dollysteamboat.com) through the inner waterways of the "Junior Grand Canyon" and learn more about plants and animals that live near the lake. To rent a boat of your own, check in at the **Canyon Lake Marina and Campground** (480-288-9233; canyonlakemarina.com).

Next stop, **Tortilla Flat,** Arizona (480-984-1776; tortillaflataz.com), population 6, where the combination restaurant, saloon, gift shop, grocery store, and US Post Office is a convenient place to stop for a burger, chili, or an ice-cream cone. This is a good place to turn around unless you're prepared for a driving adventure. The pavement ends soon after you leave Tortilla Flat and soon you're making a harrowing descent down Fish Creek Hill, a steep, curving one-lane route with pullouts. Traffic coming uphill has the right of way. After reaching the bottom of the grade, the road traces the edge of Apache Lake before ending at Roosevelt Dam. From here you can turn southeast on AZ 188 and make your way to the mining town of Globe.

Traveling east from Apache Junction on US 60 takes you to the mining town of **Superior** (520-689-0200; superiorarizonachamber.org). Nestled at the base of Apache Leap Mountain, the historic buildings create a picturesque downtown that has begun to flourish in recent years with the opening of new shops and eateries, restoration of old structures and an addition of colorful murals. History buffs will want to make the short trip to the ghost town of Pinal City, just west of Superior, accessible by hiking trail and jeep tour. The cemetery here is the final resting place for Celia Ann "Mattie" Blaylock, the common-law wife of Wyatt Earp, who died in 1888 of an alcohol and laudanum overdose.

Today visitors make the trek to Superior to tour the nearby **Boyce Thompson Arboretum State Park** (602-827-3000; btarboretum.org). The arboretum contains more than 3,900 species of plants, as well as many birds and animals. Its specialties are desert and arid-land plants, including cacti and wildflowers of many colorful varieties. Created in 1924, it's the oldest and largest botanical garden in Arizona. There are several hiking trails throughout the grounds. Ranging from easy half-mile strolls to moderate 3-mile hikes, these trails are especially popular in the fall and winter when the mild weather in this area encourages people to enjoy the great outdoors. In 1927, Colonel Boyce Thompson built a sprawling mansion known as **Picket Post House** atop a stony cliff overlooking the landscape. The arboretum is open daily from 8 a.m. to 5 p.m. (Oct through Apr), and 6 a.m. to 3 p.m. (May through Sept). Dogs are permitted if leashed, and picnic tables are available. Admission.

If your next destination is the Tucson area, take AZ 177 south and you'll soon skirt the edge of the gaping abyss of the **Ray Mine,** 6 miles long, 2 miles wide and hundreds of feet deep. The Ray represents one of the largest copper reserves in the United States. You'll pass through the small towns of Kearney and then Winkelman, at the confluence of the Gila River and San Pedro River. The **Winkelman Flats Public Park** sits on the banks of the Gila and offers camping, picnic areas, fishing, and tubing during high water periods.

Turn south onto AZ 77 and you'll pass the small town of **Oracle** (visitoracle.org), home of the famous (or, depending upon your perspective, infamous) **Biosphere 2** (520-621-4800; biosphere2.org) on AZ 77. The Biosphere 2 was originally designed by a team of researchers put together by Texas billionaire Edward Bass to create a totally self-contained environment in the form of a giant, pyramid-shaped greenhouse that could be used to study how ecosystems work and also provide a prototype for civilizations of the future (i.e., on other planets). Plagued by personnel problems and dogged by allegations of cultism, the project, which planned to seal a group of researchers inside the facility for two years, proved to be a large flop. The facility was taken over by the University of Arizona where it serves as a laboratory for controlled scientific studies. Today visitors can tour portions of the 7.2-million-cubic-foot greenhouse and see environments ranging from a tropical rain forest to a coral reef to mangrove wetlands. A variety of tours are offered at specific times. Check the website to find the one you want. Admission.

Nearby Oracle has a long history as a mining community. In fact, in 1902 Buffalo Bill Cody staked out a gold claim in this area and for a while lived in a cabin above one of his mines. He squandered a large portion of his fortune on what was essentially a hoax (there was virtually no gold, and the tungsten ore he found was not enough for him to recoup his investment).

Like many Arizona towns, Oracle has a dedicated group of artists of various disciplines and abilities. The artists range from potters to landscape painters to bronze sculptors. They host an annual weekend **Oracle Festival of Fine Art** (oraclestudiotour.com), usually in April. During the festival there are tours of the artists' studios, art discussions, and performing arts events. Oracle has a number of galleries and shops that display local artists' work year-round. Also in town is **Oracle State Park** (520-896-2425; azstateparks.com), a 4,000-acre wildlife refuge with more than 15 miles of hiking and biking trails cutting through the oak-grassland habitat, including a 4-mile segment of the Arizona Trail. The Mediterranean-style **Kannally Ranch House** is on the National Register of Historic Places. Visitors can explore the home on their own, but ranger-led tours are also offered Sat and Sun at 11 a.m. Park hours vary seasonally. Admission.

Another off-the-beaten-path route to Tucson is through **Florence** (520-868-9433; florenceazchamber.com). The visitor center is located in the old adobe courthouse, part of **McFarland State Historic Park** (24 W. Ruggles St.; 520-868-5216; azstateparks.com). Built in 1878 of adobe bricks, the courthouse is filled with exhibits of Florence's surprisingly rowdy past that involved bloody gunfights and prisoners being dragged from cells and lynched. There's also an exhibit on the large POW camp in town that held over 13,000 German and Italian prisoners during World War II. The adobe building later served as a hospital and was eventually purchased and donated to Arizona State Parks by Ernest McFarland, former Arizona governor. Free.

The old courthouse is just one of dozens of historic buildings that make up downtown Florence. Architectural styles range from elegant Victorians to Sonoran-style row houses to American bungalows. Grab a map for a self-guided walking tour at the visitor center. The **Florence Historic**

Home Tour is a popular event held every February. Another spot not to be missed is the *Pinal County Historical Museum* (520-868-4382; pinalcountyhistoricalmuseum.org). They house a fascinating collection that includes cactus furniture, cowboy memorabilia, and a display of nooses used for hangings at the state prison in town. The museum is open 11 a.m. to 4 p.m. Tues through Sat, and noon to 4 p.m. on Sun. They close from July 1 through Aug 31. Admission.

The *Pinal County Courthouse,* which replaced the old adobe structure, was built in 1891. It's located on North Pinal Street between Eleventh and Thirteenth Streets, a large, rather ornate redbrick building with a clock tower. Incidentally, this is the courthouse where Pearl Hart, the last known stagecoach robber in the United States, was tried in 1899 and sentenced to five years in the Territorial Prison at Yuma.

If you'd like to hang around Florence for a while, check into the *Rancho Sonora Inn* (9198 N. Hwy. 79; 520-868-8000 or 800-205-6817; ranchosonora .com), a 1930s adobe guest ranch. The comfortable rooms are decorated in classic western fashion, but with the modern comfort conveniences of dual-paned windows and air-conditioning. The inn also has a heated pool and a hot tub.

Rancho Sonora is not far from the *Tom Mix Monument,* a stone pillar topped by a metal silhouette of a riderless horse. This vaguely macabre statue commemorates the approximate spot where silent-movie western hero Tom Mix was killed in 1940 when he drove his speeding Cord Phaeton automobile off the road. The horse (Tony, Mix's favorite mount) has been stolen from the monument several times over the years, so don't be too surprised if it seems to have moseyed off!

From Florence you can take AZ 287 west and AZ 87 south to the *Casa Grande Ruins National Monument* (520-723-3172; nps.gov/cagr). Casa Grande was a Hohokam settlement

arizonatrivia

If any of the terrain around Florence looks to you like Martians could land and feel right at home, you're not alone in your opinion. The 1953 George Pal–produced film *War of the Worlds* was partially shot here.

built around AD 1350. Theories abound, including everything from family dwelling to astronomical observatory, regarding the purpose for the large adobe structure that still stands here in the midst of the desert. It's one of the best-preserved sites of its kind in the state. Stop by the visitor center to get a brochure and take the self-guided tour. If you have the time, stay for one of the informative talks given by a park ranger on the history of the Casa Grande ruins. The visitor center is open daily from 9 a.m. to 5 p.m. from Oct through Apr, and closes at 4 p.m. during the summer. Admission.

The major annual event for this area is the ***Casa Grande Cowboy Days & O'Odham Tash*** (casagrandecowboydays.com), combining a rodeo with a celebration of Native American culture and usually held in February. You'll hear traditional music of several varieties, including waila, a kind of rock-and-roll polka. Watch colorful ceremonial dancers compete for awards and browse through arts and crafts, including baskets, rugs, paintings, and jewelry. You can also sample O'Odham cuisine.

Continuing on AZ 87 south takes you past farming communities that sprout forth like an emerald beard across the stubbly face of the desert. AZ 87 merges into I-10 a few miles south of the tiny town of ***Picacho.*** Just east of the town is ***Picacho Peak State Park*** (520-466-3183; azstateparks.com), a craggy, saguaro-dotted mountain that in the spring is covered with wildflowers. This is the site of the Battle of Picacho Pass, the westernmost battle of the Civil War.

The military engagement took place on April 15, 1862. The California Column consisting of 2,000 Union volunteers was advancing on a Confederate force occupying Tucson. Wanting to maintain the element of surprise, Colonel Carleton of the California Column sent a cavalry detachment commanded by Lt. James Barrett to circle behind a group of Confederate pickets and prevent their escape as the main force swept down on them. Although ordered not to engage, Barrett, perhaps seeking battlefield glory, recklessly charged the sentries. In the ensuing action, Barrett and two Union privates were killed, three more were wounded, and three of the Confederates were captured. After 90 minutes of fierce combat, the leaderless Union cavalry broke off the attack, allowing the Confederates to mount up and carry warning of the advancing army to Tucson. Activities at Picacho Peak include picnicking, hiking, and camping. A short interpretive trail features more details of the Civil War battle and there's a stone memorial to brash Lt. Barrett, whose body was never recovered. Admission.

Places to Stay in Central Arizona

GLENDALE

Renaissance Phoenix Glendale Hotel & Spa
9495 W. Coyotes Blvd.
(623) 937-3700
renaissanceglendale.com
Located just a short stroll from Gila River Arena and State Farm Stadium, as well as plenty of dining and shopping options. $$$.

MESA

Starlite Motel
2710 E. Main St.
(480) 964-2201
For neon lovers, this is a pilgrimage. The no-frills motel is simple and clean, but is most famous for one of the all time great neon signs, the animated Diving Lady, plunging nearly 80 feet in a series of blinking dives. The 1960 icon was toppled in a 2010 storm but was painstakingly restored. $.

PHOENIX

Arizona Grand Resort & Spa
8000 S. Arizona Grand Pkwy.
(602) 438-9000 or
(877) 800-4888
arizonagrandresort.com
This luxury resort at South Mountain has championship golf, an athletic club and spa,
three restaurants and The Oasis—"Arizona's Ultimate Water Adventure." $$$.

Hyatt Regency Phoenix
122 N. 2nd St.
(602) 252-1234
hyatt.com
Right downtown across from the Civic Plaza, this hotel is renowned for the great views and fabulous cuisine at its revolving Compass Restaurant, which offers 360-degree views of the valley from the hotel rooftop. $$$.

SCOTTSDALE

Hotel Valley Ho
6850 E. Main St.
(480) 376-2600
hotelvalleyho.com
This chic and colorful hotel combines the best of two worlds, where mid-century architecture gets a contemporary makeover. A good restaurant, spa, and a swinging pool scene provides everything you need. $$$.

The Phoenician,
6000 E. Camelback Rd.
(480) 941-8200
thephoenician.com
Located at the base of Camelback Mountain, this renowned resort offers a golf course, a spa, a tennis garden, multiple pools, and eight restaurants and lounges. $$$.

The Scott Resort and Spa
4925 N. Scottsdale Rd.
(480) 945-7666 or
(800) 528-7867
thescottresort.com
This lovely resort is located in downtown Scottsdale near the art galleries and shops in the Old Town District. $$$.

TEMPE

Ramada by Wyndham Tempe Arizona Mills Mall
1701 W. Baseline Rd.
(480) 413-1188
wyndhamhotels.com
Right off I-10, this casual hotel is close to all the shopping and attractions, and not far from downtown Tempe. $.

Places to Eat in Central Arizona

GILBERT

The Farmhouse
228 N. Gilbert Rd.
(480) 926-0676
farmhouseofgilbert.com
This Gilbert favorite opened in 1989 in an actual farmhouse before relocating. Crowds flock here for the fresh homemade breakfasts, but they're open for lunch as well. $$.

FOR MORE INFORMATION ABOUT CENTRAL ARIZONA

Apache Junction Area Chamber of Commerce
ajchamber.com

Arizona Department of Tourism
visitarizona.com

Carefree/Cave Creek Chamber of Commerce
carefreecavecreek.org

Casa Grande Chamber of Commerce
casagrandechamber.org

Florence Chamber of Commerce
florenceazchamber.com

Fountain Hills Chamber of Commerce
fountainhillschamber.com

Gilbert Tourism
discovergilbert.com

Glendale Tourism
visitglendale.com

Mesa Tourism
visitmesa.com

Oracle Tourism
visitoracle.org

Peoria Tourism
visitpeoriaaz.com

Phoenix Tourism
visitphoenix.com

Scottsdale Tourism
experiencescottsdale.com

Southwest Valley Chamber of Commerce
southwestvalleychamber.org

Tempe Tourism
tempetourism.com

Tonto National Forest
fs.usda.gov/tonto

Wickenburg Chamber of Commerce
outwickenburgway.com

Joe's Real BBQ
301 N. Gilbert Rd.
(480) 503-3805
joesrealbbq.com
Lovers of slow-cooked 'cue will savor the smoky flavors of this down home feast. $$.

GLENDALE

Haus Murphy's
5739 W. Glendale Ave.
(623) 939-2480
hausmurphys.com
Enjoy authentic German food, the Bier Garten, and live music at this popular restaurant on the main street of Old Town Glendale. $$.

MESA

Baby Kay's Cajun Kitchen
2051 S. Dobson Rd.
(480) 800-4811
babykayscajunkitchen.com
Let the good times roll at this popular joint serving classic Cajun dishes like jambalaya, red beans and rice, and shrimp remoulade. $$.

Mango's Mexican Cafe
44 W. Main St.
(480) 464-5700
mangosmexicancafe.com
Mango's serves Mexican specialties in the heart of downtown shopping not far from Mesa Southwest Museum. $.

PHOENIX

Fry Bread House
4545 N. Seventh Ave.
(602) 351-2345
This small downtown restaurant has some of the best Indian fry bread in town. $.

Little Miss BBQ
4301 E. University Dr.
(602) 437-1177
littlemissbbq.com
Specializing in Central Texas-style barbecue that's dry rubbed and slow smoked. When the day's brisket is gone, it's gone. Save room for smoked pecan pie. $$.

Short Leash Hot Dogs +
Rollover Doughnuts
4221 N. Seventh Ave.
(602) 795-2193
shortleashhotdogs.com
Innovative gourmet wieners and veggie dogs come wrapped in pillowy naan bread. Then follow that with a decadent homemade doughnut for dessert. $.

SCOTTSDALE

Citizen Public House
7111 E. Fifth Ave.
(480) 398-4208
citizenpublichouse.com
Diners are treated to upscale comfort food and specialty cocktails at this gastropub in Old Town Scottsdale. $$$.

Craft 64
6922 E. Main St.
(480) 946-0542
craft64.com
Artfully designed wood-fired pizzas pair beautifully with 30 Arizona craft beers on tap. $$.

FnB Restaurant
7125 E. Fifth Ave.
(480) 284-4777
fnbrestaurant.com
This contemporary American restaurant was one of the pioneers in the seasonal farm-to-table cuisine and also highlights Arizona wines. $$.

TEMPE

Casey Moore's Oyster House
850 S. Ash Ave.
(480) 968-9935
caseymoores.com
Along with seafood dishes there are plenty of other options at this comfortable spot. Dine inside or on their roomy patio. $$.

The Chuckbox
202 E. University Dr.
(480) 968-4812
thechuckbox.com
One of Tempe's oldest restaurants makes some of the best burgers in the state, thick tender patties cooked over a mesquite grill. $.

Southern Arizona

The Southwestern Corner

Like so many towns, **Yuma** (928-783-0071 or 800-293-0071; visityuma.com), sprang up as a river crossing. Two granite outcroppings forced the volatile Colorado River into a narrower channel and from this passage, the city of Yuma grew, along with the booming architectural industry surrounding it.

If you haven't seen Yuma lately, then you haven't seen Yuma at all. The town that sits only minutes from the California state line and the Mexican border has undergone a renaissance in recent years. Despite the connection to the river, Yuma seemed to lose touch with its watery roots. The riverbanks had become hopelessly overgrown, a tangled jungle lined with trash dumps and hobo camps.

The **Yuma Crossing National Heritage Area** began implementing its master plan in the early 2000s. It was a massive undertaking that involved numerous agencies, opposing factions and a horde of volunteers. The results have been nothing short of remarkable. They hauled out the trash, eliminated invasive species, cleared the space, restored habitat, planted trees, and created a series of parks connected by walking and biking paths.

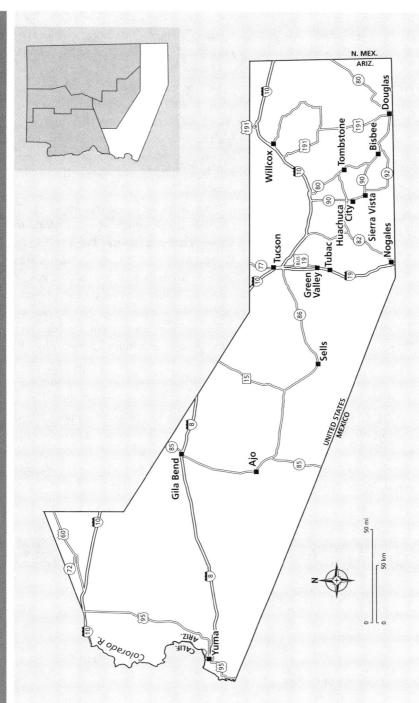

SOUTHERN ARIZONA

The riverfront is divided into three segments. The centerpiece of the West Wetlands is a sprawling kid-designed creative playground, along with a lake stocked with fish, a sandy beach, hummingbird garden and woodland trails. Gateway Park offers beaches and picnic ramadas, while East Wetlands has been returned to a natural state. Thousands of cottonwood and willow trees were planted and marshes were formed. This stretch of river now looks very much like it did a century ago. The Yuma Crossing National Heritage Area led the way in the revitalization of the historic downtown and also oversees the two state parks perched on the riverbank.

arizonatrivia

According to the *Guinness Book of World Records*, Yuma is the sunniest place on earth.

To help get your bearings, you'll find the visitor center at the ***Colorado River Historic State Park*** (201 N. Fourth Ave.; 928-783-0071; azstateparks .com). Stop in for maps, brochures or general information or to rent a bicycle, a great way to enjoy the miles of riverfront paths. While the visitor center is free, there is a small admission charge to explore the state park. Formerly known as Yuma Quartermaster Depot, the 10-acre property underwent a rebranding in 2017 and now tells the story of the past, present and future of the Colorado River.

In 1864, the US Army established the Quartermaster Depot on the high ground above the river. For nearly two decades, this compound served as a supply point for all military posts in the Southwest shipping ammunition, food and clothing on river steamers or overland by mule wagons. Many historic buildings have been preserved and are filled with artifacts and displays. While the Quartermaster Depot is still represented the scope has widened to include all chapters of the Colorado River story.

AUTHOR'S FAVORITES IN SOUTHERN ARIZONA

Arizona-Sonora Desert Museum	Mission San Xavier del Bac
Bisbee	Ramsey Canyon Preserve
Chiricahua Mountains	Sabino Canyon
Club Congress	Yuma Territorial Prison State Park
Kartchner Caverns State Park	

A variety of films on the river are shown throughout the day. Displays track where the river water goes, the impact of dams, the environmental challenges faced today and more. The park is open daily from 9 a.m. to 5 p.m. Oct through May. It's closed on Mon, June through Sept. Admission.

The ***Yuma Territorial Prison State Park*** (220 N. Prison Hill Rd.; 928-783-4771; azstateparks.com) at the east end of First Avenue is another popular attraction. No film about the Old West is complete without at least one reference to this infamous Iron Bar Hotel. Historians argue over whether the prison, built in 1876, was actually a "hellhole," as it's often depicted. Certainly inmates would have found it cramped, dark, and hot. Yet it had one of the first libraries in the state, electric fans, and many brief prison sentences. Visitors can enter through the sally port, tour the cellblocks, climb the guard tower and walk among the graves of the prison cemetery. The museum is filled with exhibits and artifacts such as prisoner-made weapons and art. Video presentations on the history of the prison are shown in a small theater. The park is open daily Oct through May (closed Tues and Wed during summer) from 9 a.m. to 5 p.m. Admission.

For another view of Yuma's rich history, visit ***Sanguinetti House Museum*** (240 S. Madison Ave.; 928-782-1841; arizonahistoricalsociety.org/yuma). Located downtown, the charming 19th century adobe was once home to E. F. Sanguinetti, Yuma's "merchant prince." The house contains period rooms and rotating exhibits and is surrounded by lavish gardens and an aviary. Guided museum tours combine history and storytelling. The museum also offers walking and trolley tours on select dates. They're open from 10 a.m. to 3 p.m. Tues through Sat. That changes to Mon through Fri during June through Sept.

If you eat a salad in the winter, you have Yuma to thank. Over 90 percent of all leafy vegetables consumed in this country between November and March are grown in Yuma. With more people wanting to know the origins of their food, Yuma Visitors Bureau created the ***Field to Feast Tours*** in 2011. The outings offer a peek behind the scenes of Yuma's multi-billion dollar agricultural industry, and allow visitors to harvest and sample a little fresh produce. Other food-based events have followed, like Date Nights (gourmet dinners in date groves) and Savor Yuma Culinary Tours. All agricultural tours take place during the winter and details are listed at visityuma.com.

One of Arizona's most intriguing off the beaten path attractions can be found in the harsh desert north of Yuma. ***Castle Dome Mines Museum*** (928-920-3062; castledomemuseum.org) can be reached by driving north on AZ 95 for about 30 miles to Castle Dome Road near mile marker 55, then northeast for 10 miles (watch for signs). The last few miles are unpaved but generally

JANUARY

Dillinger Days
Tucson
(520) 622-8848
hotelcongress.com
Celebrate the 1934 capture of gangster John Dillinger and his gang with a depression-era themed weekend of car shows, history re-enactments, and live music.

Wings over Willcox
Willcox
(520) 384-2272
wingsoverwillcox.com
Held on the third week of Jan, this Sandhill Crane Celebration includes guided tours, a "hawk stalk," seminars, workshops, field trips, and bird-watching.

FEBRUARY

Tucson Gem, Mineral and Fossil Showcase
Tucson
(520) 322-5773
tgms.org
This main event is billed as the "world's largest marketplace gem and mineral show." More than 250 vendors show their wares during the two-week-long festival.

Cochise Cowboy Poetry and Music Gathering
Sierra Vista
(520) 508-9359
cowboypoets.com
On the second weekend in Feb, you can listen to storytellers, reciters, singers and musicians, and nationally recognized artists at this popular event.

Tubac Festival of the Arts
Tubac
(520) 398-2704
tubacaz.com
This event features juried national and international artists, live entertainment, and artist demonstrations.

Vigilante Days
Tombstone
(520) 457-3434
tombstonevigilantes.com
Get into the spirit of the Old West with shoot-outs, hangings, concerts, a chili cook-off, and performances by saloon girls.

MARCH

O'odham Tash
Tumacácori National Historical Park
(520) 377-5060
nps.gov/tuma
Enjoy Native American traditions of the Tohono O'odham such as basket-weaving, painting, carving, singing, and traditional foods.

Tucson Festival of Books
Tucson
(520) 621-0302
tucsonfestivalofbooks.org
A celebration of literacy quickly grew into one of the largest book festivals in the country, drawing massive crowds to the University of Arizona Mall. Author presentations, panel discussions, a poetry venue, go along with chef demonstrations and a Science City Area.

APRIL

Pima County Fair
Tucson
(520) 762-9100
pimacountyfair.com
This exciting annual event runs daily for ten days, with rides, attractions, and livestock competitions.

Rose Festival
Tombstone
(520) 457-3326
tombstonerosetree.com
This is a chance to experience a softer side of Tombstone as the town celebrates the blooming of the world's largest rose tree. There's a parade, high tea, an art show, and a concert in the park.

MAY

Willcox Wine Country Spring Street Fair
Willcox
(520) 384-2272
willcoxwinecountry.org
This big town party takes place in Railroad Park, with arts and crafts booths, food vendors, live music and wine flowing freely.

Wyatt Earp Days
Tombstone
(520) 457-9317
tombstonechamber.com
Gunfights, a Wyatt look-alike contest, saloon girls, fashion show, parade, dancing, and live country-western music brings back the lifestyle of the Wild West over Memorial Day weekend.

JUNE

DeGrazia's Birthday
Tucson
(520) 299-9191 or (800) 545-2185
degrazia.org
Celebrate the life of famed artist Ted DeGrazia with a sweet event. Every June 14, the staff at the DeGrazia Gallery in the Sun serves cake and ice cream. Admission to the 10-acre grounds, a National Historic District, is free for the day.

JULY

Peach Mania Festival
Willcox
(520) 384-2084
appleannies.com
Love your peaches with all-you-can-eat breakfasts, wagon rides, pick-your-own peaches, peach products, and a country craft fair.

AUGUST

Southwest Wings Birding Festival
Sierra Vista
(520) 266-0149
swwings.org
Enjoy Arizona's oldest birding festival with field trips, displays, lectures, bat stalks, owl prowls, and arts and crafts.

SEPTEMBER

Labor Day Rodeo
Sonoita
(520) 455-5553
sonoitafairgrounds.com
A western rodeo complete with barrel racing, a wild-horse race, team roping events, and mutton busting at the Sonoita Fairgrounds.

Santa Cruz County Fair
Sonoita
(520) 455-5553
sonoitafairgrounds.com
This county fair includes an old-fashioned carnival, exhibits, and live entertainment.

OCTOBER

Bisbee 1000—The Great Stair Climb
Bisbee
(520) 266-0401
bisbee1000.org
This annual event is not only a fun and popular physical-fitness challenge for all ages and levels of fitness; it also helps to raise money for preservation of the local community.

TOP ANNUAL EVENTS IN SOUTHERN ARIZONA

Patagonia Fall Festival
Patagonia
(520) 797-3959
patagoniafallfestival.org
This southern Arizona community celebrates art and cooling weather with juried arts and crafts, country western, bluegrass, folk, mariachi, Latin jazz, rock 'n' roll, Saturday night dance, and western events.

Helldorado Days
Tombstone
(520) 457-9317
tombstonevigilantes.com
The oldest celebration in town is held every third weekend in Oct and includes shoot-outs, a fashion show, and street entertainment.

Rex Allen Days
Willcox
(520) 409-7123
rexallendays.org
Celebrate singing cowboy star Rex Allen the first weekend in Oct with a rodeo, parade, dances and cowboy poetry readings.

NOVEMBER
Bisbee Home Tour
Bisbee
(520) 432-3554
discoverbisbee.com
Relive eras gone by as you visit restored historic homes in varying architectural styles throughout the town.

Colorado River Crossing Balloon Festival
Yuma
(928) 343-1715
crcballoons.com
This festival includes sunrise balloon liftoffs, sunset balloon glow, fireworks, and live entertainment.

DECEMBER
Fourth Avenue Street Fair
Tucson
(520) 624-5004
fourthavenue.org
Over 300 international artisans, 40 plus food vendors, a community stage, entertainers, and a host of children's activities bring visitors to the heart of Tucson.

La Fiesta de Tumacácori
Tumacácori
(520) 377-5060
nps.gov/tuma
Entertainment and crafts, folklorico and Native American dancing, Mexican, Indian, and old-time Arizona music takes place the first full weekend in Dec.

Luminaria Nights
Tucson
(520) 326-9686
tucsonbotanical.org
Holiday lights and music by local groups and choirs at the Tucson Botanical Gardens.

passable in a sedan. Here at the base of the Castle Dome Mountains you'll find the restored remnants of a town once larger than Yuma.

Allen and Stephanie Armstrong have created a ghostly village using original buildings, others that were hauled in from nearby mines, and some that were constructed using salvaged materials. You'll be hard pressed to tell which is which. Visitors can roam through 50 buildings, including a hotel, doctor's office, church, blacksmith shop, jail and several saloons. Each are packed to the rafters with artifacts left behind or recovered from the surrounding mines. Plan to spend the day making discoveries at every turn.

In 2018, the Armstrongs opened a startling and vibrant attraction, the ***Hull Mine.*** They acquired the adjacent mine years earlier and began shoring it up to open for tours. The big surprise came when they discovered entire walls covered with fluorescent minerals. When the UV lights are turned on, the rocks blaze with a rainbow of colors. The other corridors are filled with an underground blacksmith shop, an outlaw hideout, and a variety of tools and equipment.

Castle Dome Mines Museum is generally open daily from mid-Oct through the end of Apr. Hours are spottier during the summer but as is the case with any destination located down a dirt road; it's always a good idea to call ahead. There's an admission fee for the museum and an additional cost for the guided Hull Mine tour.

While traveling AZ 95 keep an eye peeled for a small, roadside chapel at the edge of farm fields, 14 miles north of Yuma. A sign with the words "Pause Rest Worship" beckons to weary travelers. Loren Pratt, a farmer and Navy veteran, built the tiny church (8 x 12 feet) as a tribute to his late wife. When it was destroyed in a storm, neighbors stepped in to rebuild it. Take a quiet moment for yourself.

Yuma has evolved into a culinary hotspot with a wide-range of locally owned restaurants. ***The Chile Pepper*** (1030 W. 24th St.; 928-783-4213; bgfamilyltdpartnership.com) first opened its doors in 1954 so generations of Yumans have grown up on their family recipes. This casual Mexican eatery often lands on lists for best burritos in the country. Everything is made from scratch including the soft and tender tortillas. The exquisitely simple bean and cheese burrito is the most popular. $.

Another beloved family-owned eatery is ***Lutes Casino*** (221 Main St.; 928-782-2192; lutescasino.com), which is the oldest continuing pool hall and domino parlor in the state. Lutes offers sandwiches and other fast-food items in a somewhat wacky atmosphere. $.

For another dining spot that features a dash of history try the ***Yuma Landing Bar & Grill*** (195 S. Fourth Ave.; 928-782-7427; bestrestaurantinyuma.com). Along with serving up a hearty menu of homemade meals, this landmark restaurant is decorated with historical photographs and is located near the site of the monument marking the landing site of Robert G. Fowler, who touched down at this location on October 25, 1911, with his Wright model B biplane— the first airplane to land on Arizona soil. $$.

Perched on the edge of **Desert Hills Golf Course,** diners at **Patio Restaurant** (1245 W. Desert Hills Dr.; 928-344-1125; patioyuma.com) enjoy lovely views to accompany their meals. Chef Alex Trujillo, one of the driving forces in the Yuma culinary scene, opened the eatery in 2015. His passion for using fresh local ingredients is a lynchpin of the menu. $$.

Many national chains and family-owned motels are on standby to house road warriors visiting Yuma. Among the top choices are **Historic Coronado Motor Hotel** (233 S. Fourth Ave.; 928-783-4453 or 877-234-5567; best hotelinyuma.com). Built in 1938, this was one of the first motor courts in the state. The Coronado was one of the charter members of the Best Western chain but is independent again. In addition to being close to all of Yuma's historical sites, this Spanish-style hotel has two pools, a hot tub, and an exercise room. $$.

The **Best Western Yuma Mall Hotel and Suites** (1450 S. Castle Dome Ave.; 928-783-8341 or 800-780-7234; bestwestern.com) features luxurious suites complete with complimentary breakfast and evening cocktail hour. This pet-friendly hotel also has lighted tennis and basketball courts, a pool and hot tub, and a fitness center. $$.

Nearby the **Shilo Inns Yuma** (1550 S. Castle Dome Ave.; 928-782-9511 or 800-222-2244; shiloinns.com) offers a free buffet breakfast. Hotel amenities include an on-site restaurant and lounge, one of the largest pools in Yuma, and a fitness center complete with a sauna and steam room. $$.

Head east on I-8 and if you're not completely stuffed, pull over in **Dateland** for a delicious road treat. **Dateland Travel Center** (928-454-2772;

Sand Dune Stand-ins

Arizona's deserts are among the world's most verdant, so visitors looking for a Sahara-like landscape will find more vegetation than bargained for. However, a sandier setting exists 20 miles west of Yuma. Travel into California on I-8 to Gray's Well exit and follow the frontage road. You'll wind up surrounded by sand dunes that have served as stand-ins for Middle Eastern dunes in many TV shows and films, dating back to about 1921 when Valentino's *The Sheik* was filmed here. Three versions of *Beau Geste* were at least partially lensed in these dunes, as well as the Jimmy Stewart movie *The Flight of the Phoenix.* (At the very end of the film, a patched-together plane heads over these dunes and disappears from sight. In real life it crashed just out of camera range, killing the pilot.) The George Lucas film *Star Wars* was partially filmed here, as was the science fiction hit *Stargate.* There are no real markers or landmarks here to photograph—just miles of sand—so bring your imagination and maybe a few props like a light saber or your pet Ewok.

dateland.com) sits at exit 67, flanked by a grove of date trees forming an exotic oasis in this lonely landscape. Inside, you'll find a market and gift shop selling packaged dates grown a few yards from where you're standing (along with yummy free samples). The soda fountain spoons up homemade ice cream and luxuriously rich date shakes made from the regal Medjool date.

Continuing east, you won't find many signs of civilization until you approach **Gila Bend** (928-683-2255; gilabendaz.org). The town got its name from the sharp bend in the Gila River that used to occur at this point before the river was diverted for agricultural purposes.

Just west of town is a surprising display of ancient art, **Painted Rock Petroglyph Site.** The archeological gem sits about 11 miles north of I-8. Take exit 102 and follow the signs. Hundreds of petroglyphs are scratched into a cluster of basalt boulders overlaying a rock outcropping. From the parking area, an easy path loops around the mound showcasing the rock art with informational signage providing historic and cultural information. The exact meaning of these 1,000-year-old Hohokam etchings is unknown. Humans are represented, as well as animals, sun symbols, concentric circles, spirals and mazes. There's a dry campground adjacent and picnic tables on site so pack a lunch, bring a sketch pad and try to decode all the combinations of the unique language depicted at Painted Rock.

The **Agua Caliente Hotel and Hot Springs** ruins are also located just west of town. To reach them, exit from I-8 onto Sentinel Road. The former hotel and surrounding adobe buildings—constructed to take advantage of the area's status as a stage stop as well as the supposed therapeutic values of the water—are still partially standing. You can pose by a crumbling adobe wall and then send copies of the picture to your friends and family. Tell them you've picked out your retirement home. You won't be able to relax in the hot springs, however; they dried up years ago.

In downtown Gila Bend is the **Gila Bend Museum** (644 W. Pima St.; 928-683-2255). Dedicated to the preservation of archaeological and historical finds, it includes information gathered from the Hohokam Ceremonial Platform that's near town. The platform dates from AD 800; there are plans to re-excavate and open up some of the area. The museum is open Mon through Sat from 9 a.m. to 3 p.m.; donations accepted. The museum is also the visitor information center.

At first glance dining options in Gila Bend seem to be limited mostly to fast food. For more discerning travelers there are a couple of simple but tasty Mexican restaurants. But the surprise star is **Little Italy** (502 E. Pima St.; 928-683-2221, littleitaliapizza.com). While Gila Bend may feel like a long way from the Italian countryside, it won't when you tuck into any of the classic dishes

The Oatman Massacre

East of the Aqua Caliente ruins is the site of the Oatman Massacre. In 1851, Roys and Mary Ann Oatman and their seven children were part of a Mormon pilgrimage to the Arizona/California border area. They were camped on this spot when a group of Yavapai Indians approached and asked for food and tobacco. Roys complied but, fearful that he wouldn't have enough for his family, refused the Yavapais' request for seconds. The family, with the exception of fifteen-year-old Lorenzo, fourteen-year-old Olive, and her younger sister Mary Ann, was brutally slain. Lorenzo was left for dead, while the two girls were taken as captives. They were used as slaves and eventually sold to the Mohave Indians. Mary Ann died of starvation, and Olive was later ransomed back into white society and reunited with Lorenzo. In a bizarre twist, she became a celebrity as a result of her ordeal, though her story was largely used as anti–Native American propaganda. The actual site of the killings can only be reached by a four-wheel-drive vehicle. The town of Oatman in western Arizona is named after Olive Oatman.

from the expansive menu. The owner is a Sicily native who attended culinary school in Palermo. The restaurant even received a royal stamp of approval. When England's Prince Harry was in the area for military training in 2011 he stopped by for dinner. After polishing off an entire Meat Lovers pizza, he declared it to the staff to be "the best in the whole world." $$.

Another out of this world experience awaits at the restaurant in the ***Best Western Space Age Lodge*** (401 E. Pima St.; 928-683-2273 or 800-780-7234; bestwestern.com). The food may be standard diner fare but how often do you get to chow down in a place with a spaceship on the roof? The slightly kitschy roadside inn was built in the 1960s during the heady days of preparing to send a man to the moon. The lodge has remained committed to the theme with murals, displays and other small flourishes. $$.

Less than an hour south of Gila Bend on AZ 85 is the tiny town of ***Ajo*** (520-387-7742: ajochamber.com). Though the word *ajo* (ahh-ho) is Spanish for garlic and also is used as a mild expletive, some historians believe the town's name actually originated from a similar-sounding Tohono O'Odham word for paint (ore from this area was used for making pigment). In any case Ajo was the oldest-known mine site in the state, and until the 1980s Phelps Dodge ran a sizable copper-mining operation out of here. The mines originally were made profitable during World War I by John C. Greenway, who also gets the credit for building the town's palm tree–shaded ***Spanish Colonial Plaza*** in Ajo's center. The plaza is a traditional town square created in a Spanish Colonial revival style. In the midst of the plaza is a large, green park and surrounding it are shops, restaurants, and two churches. To the south of the plaza is a Federated church built in 1926. Just north of that structure sits a mission-style Catholic church constructed in 1924.

Ajo began the long slow process of reinventing itself starting in 2000. Led by the International Sonoran Desert Alliance (ISDA) historic buildings have been purchased, restored and reimagined. The once crumbling Curley School dating back to 1919 has been turned into live-work space apartments for a community of artists. The nonprofit ISDA also opened the ***Sonoran Desert Inn and Conference Center*** (55 Orilla Ave.; 520-373-0804; sonorancc.com). The former elementary school now offers airy spacious guest rooms surrounding a courtyard overflowing with lush gardens. $.

Another building that has been restored is now a charming bed-and-breakfast inn. The ***Guest House Inn*** (700 Guest House Rd.; 520-387-6133; guesthouseinn.biz) was built in 1925 by Phelps Dodge Corporation as a guesthouse for its visitors. The inn offers four rooms with private baths. The rooms are furnished in southwestern style, some with Victorian antiques. A hearty breakfast is included, and from the patio you can watch a variety of native birds, including quail and cactus wrens. $.

Thanks to the work of ISDA and other entrepreneurs, Ajo has evolved into one of Arizona's most intriguing small towns and a cultural tourism destination. It also serves as the gateway community to ***Organ Pipe Cactus National Monument*** (520-387-6849, nps.gov/orpi) located 16 miles south off AZ 85. If you were to take a giant octopus, turn it upside down, and plant it in the dirt, you would have a rough idea of what an organ pipe cactus looks like. In color and form these cacti resemble saguaros, but unlike saguaros, they have a half-dozen or more long arms reaching out from a center point. They are quite spectacular, especially during their blooming season. This fantastic show typically occurs at dusk from May through July.

The monument preserves over 500 square miles of pristine Sonoran Desert with over 90 percent of the terrain designated as wilderness. Yet being so far off the beaten path, it's never very crowded. The park features an established campground, primitive and backcountry camping, picnic facilities, hiking trails and two scenic dirt road drives.

Make your first stop the ***Kris Eggle Visitor Center*** for information, maps, and a video presentation. The visitor center honors former park ranger Kris Eggle who was shot and killed by drug smugglers in 2002. Afterward, much of the monument was closed to the public as numerous security measures were implemented. Organ Pipe reopened fully in September 2015. During winter months, guided hikes, van tours, talks, and other programs are offered. While the longer Puerto Blanco Drive requires 4WD in some segments, the popular

Ajo Mountain Drive can be managed in a sedan. This 21-mile loop will take you through the Diablo Mountain Range to Mount Ajo and back to the visitor center. Along the way you'll see many varieties of cacti and desert creatures. In early spring you may see wildflowers, and in the late spring and early summer months, cactus blossoms dot the landscape. Activities include wildlife watching, camping, and hiking. Admission.

After the monument take AZ 86 east toward Tucson. Just past the town of Sells, turn south onto AZ 386. This route will lead you 6,900 feet above sea level to the top of Kitt Peak in the Quinlan Mountains. The view, which takes in the neighboring Baboquivari Mountains and long stretches of Sonoran desert, is not only quite spectacular, but this is the site of ***Kitt Peak National Observatory*** (520-318-8600; noao.edu/kpno). Operated by the National Optical Astronomy Observatory (NOAO), Kitt Peak is home to one of the largest arrays of optical and radio telescopes in the world. Though the climb up a paved road to the observatory is a bit steep, if you're interested in astronomy, it's worth the effort. The visitor center gives one-hour-long guided tours to either the 4-meter or the 2.1-meter telescope as well as the solar telescope. Picnic grounds with barbecue grills also share space on the peak, and many tourists to Kitt Peak bring lunch. The observatory is located on the Tohono O'Odham Reservation, 56 miles southwest of Tucson, and is open daily from 9 a.m. to 3:45 p.m. Tours are held at 10 a.m., 11:30 a.m., and 1:30 p.m. Admission.

Downtown and East Tucson

From Kitt Peak, ***Tucson*** (520-624-1817 or 800-638-8350; visittucson.org) is the next major stop. Known as the Old Pueblo, Tucson was founded in 1775 and is one of the oldest continually inhabited sites in the United States. Archeologists have discovered Hohokam artifacts that date back thousands of years. The community is an eclectic meld of Native American, Mexican, Spanish, Asian, and European cultures. Consider the fact that the town was founded on the site of an ancient Indian settlement by an Irishman serving in the Spanish Army! To learn more, Tucson Visitors Center is located downtown at 811 Euclid Ave.

You'll notice that Tucson is surrounded by mountains. To the west are the Tucson Mountains; to the east, the Rincons. Directly north are the Santa Catalinas, and down south are the Santa Ritas. Some of the peaks are snow-capped in winter, and ***Mount Lemmon*** in the Catalinas is known for being the southernmost skiable peak in the United States. The community of ***Summerhaven*** near the top of the mountain is renowned as a cool summer getaway only an hour's drive from the city. The ***Mount Lemmon Ski Valley*** (520-576-1321; skithelemmon.com) is open and offers a full season of snow sports. In the off-season the ski lift still runs, providing visitors with great views of the Catalinas.

Mountains are very important to Tucsonans. For one thing, they provide landmarks. While you're traveling anywhere on the northwest side of Tucson, glance to the west and you'll notice a small peak with an "A" whitewashed onto the rocks. **Sentinel Peak** ("A" Mountain to locals) is where the community called Chukson ("spring at the foot of the black mountain") began. The "A"—painted every year by University of Arizona freshmen—has been a prominent monument since 1915. There is a narrow, paved road that takes you all the way up Sentinel Peak. The view of the city from the peak, especially as the sun sets and lights begin to twinkle on, is quite spectacular. To reach Sentinel Peak take the Congress Street exit from I-10 and head west toward the peak. There's also a hiking trail leading to the top.

arizonatrivia

Mount Lemmon, in the Santa Catalina Mountains north of Tucson, is the southernmost ski area in the continental United States and is the only mountain in the state named after the first white woman who climbed it—botanist Sara Plummer Lemmon.

From Sentinel Peak you can reach the downtown by simply driving east on Congress Street. Less than two decades ago, downtown Tucson was dead: mortally wounded by new, centrally located shopping malls that forced the downtown department stores to close up. Downtown—roughly bounded by Fourth Avenue on the east, Granada Avenue on the west, Broadway Boulevard on the south, and Sixth Street on the north—became a graveyard that no one wanted to whistle past after dark.

Today the once-silent area, together with neighboring districts such as the university area, is as vibrant and exciting as a jazz sax solo. Downtown has evolved into the cultural hub of Tucson—an eclectic blend of galleries, shops, restaurants, bars, nightclubs and museums crowded together in just a few blocks. It's hard to say what led to the revitalization of downtown but incredible eateries were certainly part of the first wave. The town claims to have the best 23 miles of Mexican food north of the international border, and that would be hard to argue with. Then in December of 2015, Tucson made an international splash among foodies when it became the first city in the United States to be designated a UNESCO City of Gastronomy. The United Nations Educational, Scientific and Cultural Organization (UNESCO) recognized Tucson for its food and agricultural efforts today as well as its cultural farming and food heritage. It's best to visit Tucson with an open mind and an empty stomach.

The innovative Mexican cuisine from *Café Poca Cosa* (110 E. Pennington St.; 520-622-6400; cafepocacosatucson.com) located downtown makes a great welcome to Tucson dinner. The menu changes daily in this cosmopolitan chic eatery but order the Plato Cosa and the chef will select a trio of dishes for you to sample. $$$. Another nearby tasty option is *Maynards Market & Kitchen* (400 Toole Ave.; 520-545-0577; maynardstucson.com), housed in the historic train depot. They're known for inventive but approachable bistro food and award-winning craft cocktails. $$$.

Within walking distance of the downtown galleries is the *Tucson Museum of Art and Historic Block* (140 N. Main Ave.; 520-624-2333; tucsonmuseum ofart.org). The museum, considered to be a mini-Guggenheim in its interior design, houses numerous permanent collections, including a large exhibit of pre-Columbian art. The museum is open Tues through Sun from 10 a.m. to 5 p.m. Admission. The museum offers free admission on the first Thurs of each month from 5 p.m. to 8 p.m. The historic block features five restored properties that offer visitors a look into Tucson's past. Historic buildings are open Wed and Sun only.

As you might suspect of a town located smack-dab in the heart of Old West territory, quite a few rough-and-tumble incidents took place in the downtown area. Life-size sculptures of Wyatt Earp and Doc Holliday outside the train depot commemorate a bloody event following the Gunfight at the O.K. Corral. It was here that Wyatt killed Frank Stillwell, blaming him for the death of his brother Morgan. This marked the beginning of the Earp Vendetta Ride that would claim many lives. At the corner of Church and Pennington Streets, a couple of blocks south of North Main Avenue, a bizarre shooting involving two prominent members of the community occurred in 1891. Dr. John C. Handy, the chief surgeon for the Southern Pacific Railroad (and one-time chancellor for the nascent University of Arizona) attacked Francis J. Heney, the lawyer representing Handy's wife in their divorce. The hotheaded doctor grabbed Heney by the throat, but the attorney drew his pistol and got off a shot, striking Handy in the abdomen. He died soon after the shooting.

A few blocks farther south on Main Avenue and Simpson Street beyond the Convention Center, in the neighborhood known as *Barrio Historico,* stands an adobe wall with a plaque dedicated to *El Tiradito* ("the little castaway"). One version of the story goes that many years ago, a young sheepherder who lived with his wife and his in-laws on a ranch outside of town fell in love with his wife's mother. While meeting in town for an adulterous liaison, they were caught by the sheepherder's father-in-law, who killed the young man and buried him. Because the sheepherder was buried in unconsecrated ground, he was forever doomed as a sinner—a castaway. Today, locals light candles and leave hand-printed prayers at this wishing shrine. It is said that if your candle burns the whole night through, your dream will come true.

Next to El Tiradito is **El Minuto Cafe** (354 S. Main Ave.; 520-882-4145; elminutotucson.com). It's a very popular Mexican restaurant featuring authentic versions of Sonoran cuisine. $$. The café and shrine are both located on the **Turquoise Trail,** a historical walking tour of downtown Tucson that covers 2.5 miles and roughly 2.5 centuries. Designed as a loop and identified by an easy to follow turquoise-colored stripe, the trail begins and ends at the intersection of Church and Washington. This intersection also marks the northeast corner of **Presdio San Agustin del Tucson** (520-837-8119; tucsonpresidio .com), one of the best-kept secrets in

arizonatrivia

A street just north of the Tucson Convention Center is named Calle Carlos Arruza. It may be the only street in the United States named after a bullfighter, one of Mexico's most famous matadors, Carlos Arruza.

town. It was on this site the original fort was built in 1775, establishing the northern edge of the Spanish frontier in Arizona. Reconstructed adobe walls surround a courtyard and acts as an interpretive center and time capsule. Hours vary seasonally. Docent-led tours are offered on Thurs at 11:00 a.m. and Sun at 1 p.m. Living history programs take place on the 2nd and 4th Sat. Admission.

Nearby is **Old Town Artisans** (201 N. Court Ave.; 520-620-1725; oldtown artisanstucson.com). It's a collection of fine art, jewelry, and crafts shops. Two front rooms contain adobe blocks dating back to the 1860s. For a bite to eat, enjoy dining in the cantina or courtyard of **La Cocina** (520-622-0351), which serves up southwestern specialties and American favorites Mon through Sat, starting at 11 a.m. Closing times vary. $.

On Congress Avenue there's lots to see and do. You might want to peruse the many antiques and secondhand shops. At the end of the street is the historic **Hotel Congress** (311 E. Congress St.; 520-622-8848 or 800-722-8848; hotelcongress.com). A funky sort of place, the hotel provides basic accommodations and houses the **Club Congress,** which features live alternative music on weekends. The **Cup Cafe,** where you can get gourmet coffee and a bite to eat, is also within the hotel complex. The club and cafe are considered the "be-seen" hot spots in downtown Tucson.

At 330 S. Scott Ave. is the **Arizona Theatre Company Temple of Music and Art** (520-622-2823 for tickets; arizonatheatre.org), a beautiful complex that includes a cabaret theater, a main auditorium, a cafe, and an art gallery. Performances by the Arizona Theatre Company are held here, as are concerts and other cultural events. The Arizona Theatre Company's season is usually Sept through May. Tickets may be purchased online.

About a three-minute drive east of downtown is **Historic Fourth Avenue** (Merchants Association, 520-624-5004; fourthavenue.org), a lively strip of real estate that has the atmosphere (and the history) of San Francisco's Haight-Ashbury neighborhood. In the 1960s and 1970s, the businesses in this sleepy residential area were dominated by head shops and smoky bars where (nearly) free love and illegal drugs flowed. Today Fourth Avenue has really cleaned up its act. The eclectic mix of shops includes **Bison Witches Bar and Deli** (326 N. Fourth Ave.; 520-740-1541; bisonwitches.com), a restaurant and bar; **Pop Cycle** (422 N. Fourth Ave.; 520-622-3297; popcycleshop.com) selling an eye-catching selection of art made from recycled material; and **Arroyo Design** (224 N. Fourth Ave.; 520-884-1012; arroyo-design.com), a shop featuring custom furniture made from desert wood including mesquite and ironwood. Other shops specialize in antique clothing, books, jewelry, art, candles, records and yes, hookahs and bongs. The more things change, the more they stay the same.

Lots of restaurants to choose from guarantee that you won't go hungry. **Caruso's Italian Restaurant** (434 N. Fourth Ave.; 520-624-5765; carusositalian .com) has been serving Italian food to Tucsonans since it first opened in the 1930s. $$. If your sweet tooth gets the better of you, stop at the corner of Sixth Street and Fourth Avenue to find the **Chocolate Iguana on Fourth Avenue** (431 N. Fourth Ave.; 520-798-1211; chocolateiguanaon4th.com). It sells all sorts of candy, baked goods, and coffee drinks. It also has an interesting selection of greeting cards.

Fourth Avenue is best known locally for its two annual weekend street fairs—one usually runs in early December, and one is in late March. Besides arts, crafts, and food booths (where you can sample some wonderful Tohono O'Odham fry bread), the fairs feature street entertainers and representatives from all sorts of worthy human rights/ animal rights groups. During a typical street fair, Fourth Avenue is blocked off between University Boulevard and Ninth Street, and exhibitors' booths are set up down the center of the avenue.

arizonatrivia

Tucson has thrived under four flags—the Spanish, Mexican, Confederate, and United States.

Additionally, the sidewalks are taken over by people doing face painting and hair weaving and musicians playing everything from folk standards to doo-wop ballads. These events are extremely popular and draw Tucsonans of every background and visitors from every state. Expect to park at least four or five blocks away from Fourth Avenue—and to part with a few bucks for a spot. The fairs usually start Friday afternoon.

To leave Fourth Avenue you can simply drive out of the neighborhood via University Boulevard, or you can take the streetcar. The **Sun Link Streetcar** (520-792-9222; sunlinkstreetcar.com) connects visitors with four business districts, the University of Arizona and many Tucson historic neighborhoods. Running through downtown, along Fourth Avenue and to the college, the streetcar is a fun and convenient way to see the city center. For a nominal fee, you can buy an all-day pass at ticket vending machines at any of the 23 streetcar stops.

Known internationally for its optical sciences department, the **University of Arizona** (520-621-2211; arizona.edu) also has a number of other outstanding programs, including its basketball team, the Wildcats. The school has produced such NBA stars as Sean Elliott, Mike Bibby, Gilbert Arenas, and Steve Kerr. The older part of the campus, just through the main gate on University Boulevard, contains a number of interesting buildings and museums. Among them are **Centennial Hall,** which is a performing arts venue, **Old Main,** which served as the school's first classrooms, and the **Center for Creative Photography** (520-621-7968), which holds an archive of photographs from Ansel Adams and Alfred Steiglitz and features rotating and traveling exhibits. The Center for Creative Photography is open Tues through Fri from 9 a.m. to 4 p.m., and Sat from 1 to 4 p.m.

The University of Arizona Museum of Art (1031 N. Olive Rd.; 520-621-7567; artmuseum.arizona.edu) on the University of Arizona campus has an impressive collection that ranges from pre-Renaissance to twentieth century, including works by Dürer, Rembrandt, Matisse, Picasso, O'Keeffe, and Audubon. The museum is open Tues through Fri from 9 a.m. to 4 p.m., Sat from 9 a.m. to 5 p.m., and Sun from noon to 5 p.m. Call for summer hours. Admission.

Founded in 1893, the **Arizona State Museum** (1013 E. University Blvd.; 520-621-6302; statemuseum.arizona.edu) is also part of the university. It specializes in American Indian cultures of the Southwest and northern Mexico and is recognized as one of the world's finest resources for artifacts (100,000 plus). More than 25,000 ethnographic objects also make up the collection. The museum is open Mon through Sat from 10 a.m. to 5 p.m. Admission.

Just west of campus is the **Arizona History Museum** (949 E. Second St.; 520-628-5774; arizonahistoricalsociety.org). Run by the Arizona Historical Society, this museum features permanent and rotating exhibits on the state's past. There are also user-friendly archives available for those who want to look up any arcane lore about Tucson. The museum is open Mon through Fri from 10 a.m. to 4 p.m., and Sat 11 a.m. to 4 p.m. Admission.

East of campus is the *Arizona Inn* (2200 E. Elm St.; 520-325-1541 or 800-933-1093; arizonainn.com), which is on the National Register of Historic Places. This 1930 hacienda-style hotel not only exudes charm but has the dual advantages of being near the center of town yet isolated enough to provide peace and quiet to its guests. It's a good place to visit in spring and fall just to stroll through the flower-bedecked inner courtyard. The inn is a popular spot for weddings and formal dinners. Visiting celebrities who want to eschew the big resorts often bunk here. $$$.

If you seek not celebrities but celebrated food with a Spanish accent, take a quick trip to *South Tucson,* a separate 1-square-mile city within Tucson's borders. Head south on Tucson Avenue until you can exit onto Twenty-Second Street, and then go west on Twenty-Second Street until you reach South Fourth Avenue and head south.

There are several Mexican restaurants and cafes in this area, including *Guillermo's Double L Restaurant* (1830 S. Fourth Ave.; 520-792-1585). This establishment features Sonoran cuisine, a hybrid created by the indigenous peoples of Northern Mexico using Native American and Spanish influences. If you're bored with bland, fast-food-style tacos, enchiladas, and the like, you'll be pleasantly surprised at the variety of flavors Sonoran cuisine employs. $.

South Tucson is also where the Sonoran hot dog revolution began. In 1993, Daniel Contreras opened a food cart called *El Guero Canelo* (5201 S. 12th St.; 520-295-9005; elguerocanelo.com). The Sonoran is a delicious indulgent dish, a hot dog wrapped in bacon then grilled, tucked into a soft wide bun and smothered with whole pinto beans, diced tomatoes, onions, mustard, mayo and jalapeño sauce. The messy concoction originated in Hermosillo, Sonora, but it exploded on this side of the border in Tucson. In recognition of his work, Contreras received a coveted James Beard Award in 2018. That original location is now a bit more permanent—a walk-up window and picnic tables. The menu has expanded and additional locations have been added. $.

The exhibits may be small but the fun is full-sized at the quirky *Mini Time Machine Museum of Miniatures* (4455 E. Camp Lowell Dr.; 520-881-0606; minitimemachine.org). A striking collection of miniatures are spread throughout themed rooms in this modernistic building. Docent led tours are conducted daily at 1 p.m. Admission.

While there's nothing miniature about *Tohono Chul* (7366 N. Paseo del Norte; 520-742-6455; tohonochulpark.org), it does offer a cozy comfortable corner of wild country. This preserved site of natural Sonoran Desert has an easy-to-follow trail through forty-nine acres that contain about 500 species of plants and animals. Wrens, quails, roadrunners, and other birds frequent the park, and you may see a black-tailed jackrabbit or two. Year-round the park hosts demonstrations on low-water landscaping, lectures on southwestern history, and seasonal events. Tohono Chul also has an art gallery that shows southwestern artists and a tearoom in a hacienda-style home with a plant-filled courtyard. The park is open from 8 a.m. to 5 p.m., with occasional after-hours events. Admission.

Easy access to outdoor activity is a big quality of life factor in Tucson. The east side features a wonderful, hidden arboreal getaway called **Sabino Canyon** (520-749-8700; fs.usda.gov/coronado). Drive east on Tanque Verde Road to Sabino Canyon Road, go north and keep driving, and you'll wind up in the parking lot. Carved from the flanks of the Santa Catalina Mountains, Sabino Canyon is popular with hikers, bikers and picnickers. No private vehicles are allowed. There is a small fee to enter Sabino Canyon. Experienced hikers who visit Sabino Canyon often choose to make the trek to Seven Falls—occasionally quite a spectacular swimming hole, depending on the rain. It's about a 5-mile hike so carry plenty of water.

Incidentally, Tanque Verde Road could probably win an award as one of the strangest-looking streets in Arizona. It has a variety of weird statuary along its route: a life-size Tyrannosaurus rex at the Kolb intersection; an ersatz castle at Golf n' Stuff; a sculpted metal fish jumping out of the dry Tanque Verde wash (river) onto the street; and a wagon sitting on top of boulders at **Trail Dust Town** at 6541 E. Tanque Verde Rd.—an Old West attraction that includes shops, amusement rides, stunt and gunfight shows, a steakhouse and the Museum of the Horse soldier. Not far from the Tanque Verde strip is the **Tanque Verde Ranch** (14301 E. Speedway; 800-234-3833; tanqueverderanch .com). It's an authentic, Old West–style dude ranch that was even used as the location for the Nickelodeon series *Hey Dude*. It has stables, tennis courts, and gourmet dining. Accommodations here are surprisingly luxurious, and the foothills setting is incomparable. $$$.

Tucson is bookended by two segments of a distinctly Arizona national park. The east side of Tucson claims **Saguaro National Park Rincon Mountain District** (520-733-5153; nps.gov/sagu). To reach Saguaro National Park, take Broadway east to Old Spanish Trail and follow the signs. It's nearly 50,000 acres larger than the west side park. Stop at the Saguaro National Park Rincon Mountain District visitor center (open from 9 a.m. to 5 p.m. daily) and ask about the condition and difficulty of the trails before doing any hiking here. There are some easy loop trails, but others are quite difficult. Restrooms and picnic areas are available at both the east side and west side parks. During times of drought when the desert brush is especially dry, you may be asked not to use the barbecue grills. The road is open from 7 a.m. to sunset. Admission fee lasts for seven days.

Tucson's West Side

When driving west on Speedway Boulevard you'll notice that the cacti soon begin to outnumber the houses. Speedway becomes Gates Pass Road, and suddenly you're in the heart of *Saguaro National Park Tucson Mountain District* (928-733-5153; nps.gov/sagu), a terrific place to watch sunsets and take pictures. The park was created to preserve the majestic saguaro cactus, which only grows in the Sonoran Desert. It can take a saguaro ten years to reach an inch in height and fifty-plus years before it grows arms. It's not unusual for a saguaro to be more than one hundred years old, although they're frequently killed off by frost, fire, and bacterial infection. State laws protect these mighty cacti from damage or theft. Several hiking or biking trails run through the park. They range from easy to moderately difficult. Before you start off on any of them, stop by the visitors center and talk to a park ranger. If you've never hiked in the desert before, it presents its own set of challenges. The road is open from 7 a.m. to sunset. Admission fee lasts for seven days.

An interesting attraction on this side of the city is the *Arizona-Sonora Desert Museum* (2021 N. Kinney Rd.; 520-883-2702; desertmuseum.org). It features only plants and animals native to the Sonoran Desert. You can see everything from mountain lions and javelinas to bark scorpions. The museum also has an extensive mineral collection. During summer the museum often holds special evening events so that visitors can look at bats, night-blooming cacti, and other nocturnal phenomena. Museum hours vary; call for information. Admission.

arizonatrivia

The saguaro is the largest cactus growing in the United States.

Tucson is also brimming with entertaining options for experiencing the best of the Old West. Located just down the road from the Arizona-Sonora Desert Museum, *Old Tucson* (520-883-0100; oldtucson.com) was once known as the "Hollywood of the Desert." More than 400 movies have been filmed at this 1880s frontier town set. This working film set also doubles as a place for cowpokes and wannabes to enjoy western-themed buildings, rides and games, set tours, dining, shopping, and shows. Admission.

Santa Cruz County

Heading south from Tucson you'll leave the towering saguaros behind as the landscape takes a more pastoral turn. Rolling grasslands and hillsides sprinkled with mesquite become more prominent. Interstate 19 points almost due south, skirting the edge of the Tohono O'odham Nation.

About 10 miles south is the **Mission San Xavier del Bac** (1950 W. San Xavier Rd.; 520-294-2624; sanxaviermission.org). Father Eusebio Francisco Kino founded the mission in 1692. The current Spanish/Moorish-style church, known as the "White Dove of the Desert" was begun in 1783 and finished in 1797, making it the oldest European structure in Arizona. It remains an active parish so please be respectful. For visitors there is a museum and gift shop on the premises and docent-led tours are offered several times throughout the day, Mon through Sat. Hours vary with the season. You can take a self-guided tour of the church if there isn't a mass or other service going on. Mission is open daily from 7 a.m. to 5 p.m.

Just like many of our lakes, some canyons in Arizona are manmade. Copper ore is excavated from underground tunnels and sometimes, vast yawning open pits. Glean a better understanding of one of Arizona's defining industries at the **ASARCO Mineral Discovery Center** (1421 W. Pima Mine Rd.; 520-625-8233; asarco.com) in Sahuarita. Informative displays and short videos detail the uses of copper, the extraction and refining process. They also offer a tour of the mine starting at the edge of the gorge, two miles long, nearly as wide and a quarter-mile deep. Scenic? Maybe not, but it is impressive. There's no charge to visit the exhibits, theater, gift shop and picnic grounds, but there is a fee for tours. The Discovery Center is open 9 a.m. to 5 p.m. Tues through Sat from Oct through Apr.

Sahuarita is also the site for the **Titan Missile Museum** (520-625-7736; titanmissilemuseum.org), a National Historic Landmark on Duval Mine Road. In the early 1980s, when the Titan II missile silos were deactivated, all but this one were destroyed. Sahuarita's silo is the same today (minus the warhead, of course) as it was when it was part of America's defense program. Guided tours are available of the control room, the crew living quarters, and the missile launch area. The museum contains aircraft and mockups of early space capsules. The museum is open daily. Seasonal hours apply. Admission.

arizonatrivia

In the film *Tin Cup*, Kevin Costner was shown teeing off at the Tubac Golf Resort in southern Arizona.

About 10 miles south on I-19 is Santa Cruz County. Santa Cruz may be Arizona's smallest county but it is rich with history. Indigenous people farmed along the banks of the Santa Cruz River for thousands of years. This was the same waterway that Spanish explorers and missionaries followed as they sought to expand the borders and influence of New Spain.

Another five minutes or so away on I-19 is **Tubac** (520-398-2704; tubacaz
.com), the oldest European settlement in the state—established in 1752 as a
Spanish presidio, or fort, built to protect the nearby mission at Tumacácori. It
has evolved into an artists' colony, a rustic version of Santa Fe, New Mexico.
More than 100 shops are crowded together around the village plaza making
Tubac easy to explore on foot. Shops and art galleries like **K. Newby Gallery & Sculpture Garden** (520-398-9662; newbygallery.com), **Rogoway
Turquoise Tortoise Gallery** (520-398-2041; rogowaygalleries.com), and **Lee
Blackwell Studio** (520-904-2314; leeblackwellstudio.com) offer an eclectic
blend of paintings, sculptures, ceramics, jewelry and crafts items. The commu-
nity has a yearly arts festival in winter and recently added another in the fall,
just in time for holiday shopping. Also in the autumn is a historic re-enactment
of the trek of Juan Bautista de Anza, the Spanish captain of the Tubac Presidio
who set out on a historic expedition in 1775 that led to the founding of San
Francisco. Learn more about Anza and the storied past of the community at the
Tubac Presidio State Historic Park (520-398-2252; azstateparks.com) on
Burruel Street on the east side of town. The crumbling adobe remains of the
original presidio wall are visible in an underground exhibit. Visitors will also
see an impressive museum detailing Spain's influence in the area, Arizona's
first printing press that still works, a furnished 1885 schoolhouse, living history
presentations, colorful courtyard gardens and Otero Hall, filled with epic paintings by renowned artist William Ahrendt capturing the broad sweep of Arizona
history. The park is open daily from 9 a.m. to 5 p.m. Admission.

When hunger pangs strike check out **Elvira's** (2221 E. Frontage Rd.;
520-398-9421; elvirasrestaurant.com). The stylish restaurant is known for its
complex mole sauces. $$. Just south of town in Tumacacori is **Wisdom's Cafe**
(1931 E. Frontage Rd.; 520-398-2397; wisdomscafe.com). This Mexican restau-
rant, established in 1944, is a favorite among visiting celebrities. $.

And if you need a cozy place to rest your head, try the **Tubac Country
Inn** (13 Burruel St.; 520-398-3178; tubaccountryinn.com), a boutique hotel
offering breakfast and located in Tubac's historic area. $$.

Heading south on I-19 takes you to **Tumacácori National Historical
Park** (520-377-5060; nps.gov/tuma). Father Kino established the mission in
1691. Construction began on the church around 1800 and continued for the
next two decades. It was never completed but remains a striking building.
Standing inside the weathered adobe rooms, you can see that the people who
built this mission, which was an integral part of life in the Santa Cruz Valley
during the 1800s, put a tremendous effort into the construction. Behind the
church is a mortuary chapel and cemetery. The visitor center contains an excellent museum. During winter months rangers offer guided tours of two nearby

missions, *San Cayetano de Calabazas and Los Santos Ángeles de Guevavi.* Tours are offered the 2nd and 4th Fri from Jan through Mar. Tumacácori is open daily from 9 a.m. to 5 p.m. Admission. There is an additional fee for tours and reservations can be made through recreation.gov.

Across the road from the mission is the *Santa Cruz Chili & Spice Company* (1868 E. Frontage Rd.; 520-398-2591; santacruzchili.com). It's a great place to liven up your dinner table. The family-owned business is a manufacturer and retailer of chili products, selling gourmet southwestern foods, cookbooks and a selection of herbs and spices.

Another worthwhile stop is *Tumacácori Mesquite Sawmill* (2007 E. Frontage Rd.; 520-398-9356; mesquitedesign.com). The family-run, eco-friendly workshop harvests mesquite trees being removed to restore natural grasslands. Instead of going into burn piles, the wood is turned into unique doors, tables, benches and cabinets. Even the scrap pieces are converted into lovely cutting boards and crosses. They also sell raw lumber to artists and hobbyists.

Another 20 miles down the road and I-19 ends in *Nogales* (520-287-3685; thenogaleschamber.org), Arizona's largest border town. The name Nogales is Spanish for "walnut," an acknowledgement of the walnut trees that once grew here. This is the story of two cities that share not just a name but a heritage, a culture, and strong familial ties. On the American side of the border, it seems like a sleepy bedroom community tucked into rolling hillsides. Architectural buffs will have plenty to explore with styles ranging from Sonoran to Queen Anne Cottage to Pueblo Revival to Bungalow and more. Three self-guided architecture tours feature some of the highlights. Shoppers will want to take a walk on Morley Avenue boasting a wide variety of stores from international merchants. For a look at the border town's history, check out the exhibits at the *Pimería Alta Historical Society & Museum* (136 N. Grand Ave.; 520-287-4621; pimeriaaltamuseum.org), which is housed in the 1914 Old City Hall. In addition to the exhibits, you can see period rooms including the mayor's office, the fire department, and the sheriff's office complete with two holding cells. Hours are Tues through Sat from 11 a.m. to 4 p.m.

It's what's south of the border that some visitors come to see. If you plan to enter Mexico, do your research beforehand about where to go, what areas to avoid, and other safety concerns. A passport is required. Since American auto insurance is not honored in Mexico, you should purchase relatively inexpensive Mexican insurance if you are taking your car across the border. There are a number of clearly marked insurance agencies on the American side where you can buy the necessary policy before taking your vehicle into Mexico. You may also consider parking your vehicle on the American side (you may have to pay a few dollars for a space) and walking across the border.

Instead of heading back to Tucson on 1-19, turn east on AZ 82 to experience an unexpected side of Arizona. This is the **Patagonia-Sonoita Scenic Drive** that crosses ridges, valleys and sweeping plains while skirting mountains, vineyards and hidden lakes. About 12 miles northeast of Nogales you'll spot the turnoff to **Patagonia Lake State Park** (520-287-6965; azstateparks .com). The 265-acre lake fills a lanky valley and offers a campground and cabins, boat rentals, fishing, and swimming. It's a popular birding spot during winter months and jam-packed with water lovers during the summer. The adjacent **Sonoita Creek State Natural Area** (SCSNA) is just that—a natural area preserving the fragile watershed. There are no facilities but hikers will enjoy more than 20 miles of trails and a handful of backcountry campsites. The admission fee to Patagonia Lake allows access to SCSNA.

Continue north into the tree-lined hamlet of **Patagonia** (520-394-7750; patagoniaaz.com), small in size but large on charm. The centerpiece of downtown is a shady park dotted with butterfly gardens, which tells you plenty about Patagonia. A handful of eclectic shops, art galleries and eateries surround the park. If you're hungry, **Gathering Grounds** (319 McKeown Ave.; 520-394-2009; gatheringgroundsaz.com) serves good coffee, light meals and homemade baked goods. $. Or grab a burger or Mexican food at the divey and historic **Wagon Wheel Saloon** (400 W. Naugle Ave.; 520-394-2433). $.

For nature lovers, this area is a delight. Patagonia serves as a gateway community to the Arizona Trail. Also on the edge of town, the Nature Conservancy's **Patagonia-Sonoita Creek Preserve** (520-394-2400; nature.org) is a cottonwood-willow riparian forest with trees as old as 130 years and 100 feet tall. More than 260 species of birds call the preserve home, including the gray hawk, green kingfisher, and violet-crowned hummingbird. There are also whitetail deer, javelina, and coyote. Many species of fish inhabit a perennial stream that runs through the preserve. Hours at the preserve vary seasonally. Guided tours are offered on a regular basis. Admission.

The reason nobody laughs when you say Arizona wines is because of Santa Cruz County, particularly the ranch lands of **Sonoita** and **Elgin** (sonoitaelginchamber.org). Continuing north on AZ 82, you'll reach rolling hills of rich grassy plains. Spanish missionaries planted the first vines in the region during the 1700s. The modern Arizona grape revival also began here when it was discovered the soil and climate were ideally suited for growing grapes. Currently about a dozen vineyards and wine tasting rooms are spread across the hills of the two communities. Sonoita and Elgin comprise Arizona's first federally recognized American Viticulture Area—wine growing regions distinguishable by its unique geographical features. Each vineyard produces vintages reflecting the personality of the owners and terroir of these elegant grasslands.

You'll find restaurants, shops and inns in Sonoita that sit at the crossroads of AZ 82 and 83. Most of the vineyards and tasting rooms are clustered together in Elgin, a few miles to the east. Look for places like **Callaghan Vineyards** (520-455-5322; callaghanvineyards.com), **Flying Leap Vineyards & Distillery** (520-455-5499; flyingleapvineyards.com), **Dos Cabezas WineWorks** (520-455-5141; doscabezas.com), and **Sonoita Vineyards** (520-455-5893; sonoita vineyards.com). Some are open on weekdays but you'll enjoy more spirits on weekends when everyone is pouring.

Continue north from Sonoita on AZ 83. If the landscape looks familiar it's probably because Hollywood also fell in love with the long golden grasslands pressed beneath an endless sky. Dozens of movies have been filmed here, including *Red River*, *The Outlaw Josey Wales*, *David & Bathsheba*, *Tom Horn*, and *Oklahoma!*. For a genuine slice of history, watch for the turnoff to **Empire Ranch** (888-364-2829; empireranchfoundation.org) 6.6 miles north of Sonoita. The working cattle ranch dates back to the 1860s. Many of the historic buildings can be explored by visitors, and free docent-led tours are offered the 2nd and 4th Sat of each month at 11 a.m. (Be sure to call for reservations during summer months.) A short hiking trail winds through a shady grove of cottonwoods along Empire Gulch. Free.

Tombstone Area

Just east of Santa Cruz County is **Cochise County,** a land of legends. This was once the stomping ground of Johnny Ringo, Wyatt Earp, Doc Holliday, Pancho Villa, Cochise, and Geronimo. The town of **Benson** (520-265-8031; benson chamberaz.com) sits along I-10, about 30 miles east of Tucson and serves as an entry point for surrounding communities and some unexpected attractions. Being a transportation center is nothing new for Benson, a former stagecoach stop and railroad hub.

One intriguing getaway can be found in the rolling hills north of Benson. **Gammons Gulch Movie Set & Museum** (520-212-2831; gammonsgulch.com) is a recreated Western town built to serve as a movie set that's also filled with plenty of real history. Buildings constructed from salvaged materials are filled with a collection of artifacts. The town is open for tours from Wed through Sun from Sept to May but because this is a working film set, be sure to call ahead before visiting. Admission.

Bibliophiles may want to take another slight detour to the **Singing Wind Ranch Bookshop** (700 W. Singing Wind Rd.; 520-586-2425), north of I-10 via Ocotillo Road. The bookshop's numerous offerings are grouped helter-skelter within a southwestern ranch house, where hunting for buried treasures is as much fun as finding them. The bookshop is open daily Mon through Sat 10 a.m. to 3 p.m.

You'll find chapters of Benson's past splashed on walls throughout town. More than 30 large murals depict different eras. The visitor center, along with a small museum can be found at 249 E. Fourth St. in a recreated railroad depot. Just across the street is a local favorite, the ***Horseshoe Café & Bakery*** (154 E. Fourth St.; 520-586-2872). Burgers are mouthwatering, and the Mexican fare is good, but they're also known for their giant cinnamon rolls. It's a great spot for watching the trains go by and enjoying some down-home cooking. $.

About 9 miles south of Benson on AZ 90, you'll come to ***Kartchner Caverns State Park*** (520-586-4100; azstateparks.com). These pristine caves are considered to be some of the most beautiful and unusual "living" cave formations in the world. The crystalline underground garden takes shape in an array of unusual formations or "speleothems"—shields, stalactites, stalagmites, columns, cave pearls, soda straws, flowstone, popcorn, rimstone dams, and cave cotton. One of the reasons that Kartchner Caverns is world-renowned is that it is a living cave, where all of the glorious speleothems are still growing. The Throne Room and Rotunda Room, the first rooms open for tours, feature the longest soda straw formation in the United States at 21 feet and 3 inches, and the largest column in the state reaching to an impressive height of 58 feet. The Big Room also has some notable features—the world's most extensive formation of brushite moonmilk, the first reported occurrence of turnip shields, and the first noted occurrence of birdsnest needle formations. The Big Room is also the nursery roost for female cave myotis bats from Apr through Oct, during which time the Big Room is closed in an effort to foster the cave's unique ecosystem. The tours for the Rotunda and Throne Rooms last 90 minutes or more. There's also a Helmet & Headlamp Tour offered on Sat, after the other tours have finished. Reservations are required. The wide smooth trails means Kartchner is one of the few caves accessible by wheelchair. Other activities at the park include wildlife watching, hiking, and camping. Admission.

Heading south from Benson on AZ 80 takes you through more riparian areas to the tucked-away town of ***St. David.*** Like much of southeastern Arizona, this peaceful little village was booming when nearby mines were open. Today, you can visit the ***Holy Trinity Monastery*** (520-720-4642; holytrinity monastery.org). The monastery has a gift shop, library, meditation garden, museum, and other areas that are open to the public.

Tombstone (520-457-9317; tombstonechamber.com), "the town too tough to die," is only a few miles away from St. David on AZ 80. When Indian scout and prospector Ed Schieffelin began searching for ore in the hills east of the San Pedro River, his friends warned he would find only his tombstone. When he discovered a vein of silver in 1877, he wryly named his first mine Tombstone. The town that sprang up became one of the most famous and violent of the Wild West.

Driving into town, high on a hill to your left, you'll see the infamous **Boothill Graveyard** (520-457-3300; tombstoneboothillgiftshop.com), where the victims of the Gunfight at the O.K. Corral were buried, along with many other notorious residents. You can take a self-guided tour of the cemetery, photograph the sometimes comical markers (HERE LIES LESTER MOORE / FOUR SHOTS FROM A .44 / NO LES, NO MORE), and shop in the gift shop. The cemetery is open from 8 a.m. to 6 p.m. Admission.

The community of Tombstone is rightfully proud of its place in American history. As much as $85 million in various ores was removed from the mines in its environs before they ceased operation. Even in the wild and woolly 1880s, such wealth created a level of culture not found in most western communities, including literary societies, theater, and musical groups. Important mine-related events that occurred here were reported all over the country. When the mines ceased operations, Tombstone struggled to hang on. Novels, movies and television shows detailing—and often exaggerating—the exploits of Wyatt Earp eventually generated renewed interest.

arizonatrivia

The San Pedro River in southeastern Arizona's Cochise County actually flows northward into the United States from Mexico.

Despite the touristy trappings of today's Tombstone, it's still a powerful experience for anyone with a fascination of the Old West to visit. All through town small signs are posted listing the numerous gunfights and killings that took place on that site. You soon realize that you're walking in the footsteps of history.

Tombstone's downtown is closed to traffic—at least of the vehicular kind. Stagecoaches still clip-clop up and down the streets. Climb aboard (for a small fee) and take a short narrated tour. The coaches load on Allen Street, the heart of the historic district.

One must-stop is the **Bird Cage Theatre** (535 E. Allen St.; 520-457-3421; tombstonebirdcage.com), a legendary gambling hall, saloon, and cathouse that operated from 1881 until 1889. This was the site of the longest poker game in history, running non-stop for eight years, five months and three days. The atmosphere was so wild in here that 140 bullet holes decorate the walls from gun battles and general high spirits of the miners and cowboys. The Bird Cage Theatre is open daily for tours, and it's worth seeing as a good example of the type of place where frontier men entertained themselves. Hours are from 9 a.m.

to 6 p.m. They also offer ghost tours in the evenings, which is appropriate since the Bird Cage is said to be one of the most haunted buildings in Arizona. Legend has it that 26 men died on these wooden floors. Admission.

Body counts were so high during the mining town's rowdy heyday, it was said "Tombstone had a man for breakfast every morning." The most famous spasm of violence took place on October 26, 1881 when a long-simmering feud came to a head in a vacant lot near the back entrance of the O.K. Corral. City Marshal Virgil Earp deputized his brothers Wyatt and Morgan, and dentist turned gambler Doc Holliday. Wearing black frock coats the four lawmen strode through the streets to face a group of ranchers and rustlers that included Ike and Billy Clanton, Frank and Tom McLaury and Billy Claiborne. Heated words were exchanged and no one knows which side drew first. Ike Clanton and Billy Claiborne fled as the fight commenced. The shooting lasted for 30 seconds and when it was over the McLaury brothers and Billy Clanton lay dead in the street. Virgil, Morgan and Holliday suffered wounds. Wyatt was the only participant who emerged unscathed. Today the **O.K. Corral** (326 E. Allen St.; 520-457-3456; ok-corral.com) preserves the most famous shootout of the American West. Reenactments are staged several times a day with each show providing the context of the times and the escalating tensions between the factions before the roar of gunfire unfolds. Arrive early enough so you can tour the other exhibits, including a working blacksmith shop, stables, C. S. Fly's Photo Gallery, a cowboy bunkhouse and a prostitute's crib. The complex also includes the actual gunfight site with life-size statues representing where the participants stood when the shooting began. Admission.

Take a look at the reason the town exists at all with a tour of the ***Goodenough Mine*** (501 Toughnut St.; 520-457-3333; goodenoughsilvermine.com). Knowledgeable guides lead visitors into the underground tunnels below the streets of Tombstone. The mine dates back to 1878, with excavation beginning the following year. Learn how the tunnels were dug and shored up, how the miners worked, how the veins of ore were followed and more. The mine is open from 10 a.m. to 4 p.m. and tours last about an hour. Admission.

Another anchor of the community is ***Tombstone Courthouse Historic State Park*** (223 Toughnut St.; 520-457-3311; azstateparks.com). Construction was completed in 1882 on the two-story Victorian courthouse that once held the offices of the sheriff, recorder, and treasurer, courtrooms, and jail. The graceful old building has been restored and features high ceilings, arched entryways and a spiral staircase. The recreated gallows out back marks the spot where seven men met their demise at the end of a noose. Exhibits cover all aspects of Tombstone's rich history, which ranges far beyond a single gunfight. It is open from 9 a.m. to 5 p.m. Admission.

On a happier note, Tombstone is also home to the ***world's largest rose tree*** (planted in 1885), located at the ***Rose Tree Museum*** (118 S. Fourth St.; 520-457-3326; tombstonerosetree.com). The Lady Banksia rose tree is in the courtyard of a home that once belonged to Amelia Adamson, grown from a shoot given to her by the wife of a Scottish immigrant. The roses bloom from mid-Mar to mid-Apr, and even when the bush is dormant, you can enjoy the museum displays within the converted home. The displays recount life in early Tombstone. The museum is open daily from 11 a.m. to 5 p.m. Admission.

You haven't really visited Tombstone if you don't push through a saloon's swinging doors. The ***Crystal Palace Saloon*** (436 E. Allen St.; 520-457-3611; crystalpalacesaloon.com) is long famous for serving "good whisky and tolerable water." They've also added a slate of tasty burgers, steaks, ribs and pizza. $$. ***Big Nose Kate's*** (417 E. Allen St.; 520-457-3107; bignosekates.info) is packed with western décor and features live music at lunchtime and in the evenings. The wide-ranging menu offers something for everyone. $$.

If you decide to stay in Tombstone, try the ***Larian Motel*** (410 E. Fremont St.; 520-457-2272; tombstonemotels.com) sitting right at the edge of the historic district. This classic motor court offers spotlessly clean comfortable rooms and a friendly atmosphere. $. Likewise, the ***Tombstone Bordello Bed & Breakfast*** (107 W. Allen St.; 520-457-2394; tombstonebordello.com) is close to the action. The historic adobe home features nine tastefully decorated rooms, a home-cooked breakfast and a lush desert garden. $$.

Bisbee, Douglas, and Sierra Vista

Continuing south on AZ 80 takes you to one of Arizona's most intriguing towns: **Bisbee** (520-432-3554; discoverbisbee.com). Formerly a mining town—the primary ore being excavated was copper—Bisbee is now best known as a free-spirited artists' community. Set in the Mule Mountains, the older section of Bisbee (which can easily be covered on foot but is not particularly accessible for wheelchairs) may remind you a bit of a retro San Francisco. The wooden Victorian buildings that dot the hillside and line the narrow main street have maintained their quaint charm. Many buildings and neighborhoods can only be reached by stairs. Bisbee is the southernmost mile-high city in the US and since 1929 has served as county seat for Cochise County. Stop by the visitor center, located in the Queen Mine Tour building at 478 Dart Rd. to gather any information you might need. While there you may want to take the underground tour of the **Queen Mine** (520-432-2071 or 866-432-2071; queenminetour.com). Tour guides take visitors deep into the defunct mine aboard original miniature train cars and describe the dangers and techniques of hard rock mining. Please call for current tour times. Admission.

Next, you may want to wander into the ***Bisbee Mining and Histori-cal Museum*** (5 Copper Queen Plz.; 520-432-7071; bisbeemuseum.org) (just look for the train out front). The museum, situated in the 1897 Copper Queen Consolidated Mining Offices, details Bisbee's mining history and has displays of minerals that were found in and around the Mule Mountains. It also offers a glimpse into the town's past by describing its transition from boom to bust. The museum, part of the Smithsonian Affiliations Program, is open daily from 10 a.m. to 4 p.m. Admission.

Be sure to stop by the grand ***Copper Queen Hotel*** (11 Howell Ave.; 520-432-2216; copperqueen.com), the longest continuously operated hotel in Arizona. Rumor has it that a few friendly spirits inhabit the rooms of this classic hotel. The most famous ghost is Julia Lowell, a prostitute who fell in love with one of her clients and killed herself when he did not share her attraction. Her room, 315, is much in demand. Ghost Tours are also conducted on the 1st and 3rd Thurs of each month for interested guests. $$.

Visitors looking for one-of-a-kind treasures will find Bisbee's winding streets a virtual paradise. Galleries, boutiques, gem shops, and antiques stores are plentiful, offering everything from locally mined Bisbee Blue turquoise to original art—much of it is created by local artisans.

Established in the early '90s, ***55 Main Gallery*** (55 Main St.; 520-432-4694) displays original art, clothing, and handcrafted jewelry. ***Óptimo Custom Hat-works*** (47 Main St.; 520-432-4544; optimohatworks.com) sells Panama straw and felt hats. While walking the main drag, you might want to stop and sample the eclectic mix of honey products at ***The Killer Bee Guy*** (20 Main St.; 520-227-5429; killerbeeguy.com). In addition to the fabulous array of honey butters, you'll also find the spicy "Smooth Horseradish Honey Mustard," which won the 2005 Napa Valley World Mustard Competition bronze award and the 2008 bronze award for their "Smooth Original Honey Mustard."

Dining is equally eclectic in this historic hillside burg. What started out as a simple hot dog stand has evolved into one of Bisbee's most popular eater-ies. ***Jimmy's*** (938 W. AZ 92; 520-432-5911; jimmysbisbee.com) starts with pre-mium ingredients and careful preparation, and features a variety of heaping, reasonably-priced sandwiches, burgers, dogs, and specialty items. $. You can't go wrong at ***High Desert Market and Cafe*** (520-432-6775; highdesertmarket .net) for a snack or a meal. Located at 203 Tombstone Canyon, they prepare a full café menu including gourmet salads, pizzas, and quiches to go with their fresh baked goods. $. ***Cafe Roka*** (35 Main St.; 520-432-5153; caferoka.com) is known as the destination restaurant of southeastern Arizona. The menu changes with the seasons but every dinner is a four-course feast that can be paired with their extensive collection of local wines. Reservations are recommended. $$.

Besides the aforementioned Copper Queen, there are several comfortable, unique places to stay in town. ***Copper City Inn*** (99 Main St.; 520-432-1418; coppercityinn.com) offers three beautifully appointed rooms, each with a balcony overlooking the town. Attention to detail is impeccable including a complementary bottle of wine awaiting your arrival. $$. The ***School House Inn Bed and Breakfast*** (818 Tombstone Canyon Rd.; 520-432-2996; schoolhouseinnbb.com) is, as the name implies, a former schoolhouse. It has airy yet cozy rooms with private bathrooms. $$.

For nostalgia fanatics perhaps the only logical lodging choice would be ***The Shady Dell*** (1 Douglas Rd.; 520-432-3567; theshadydell.com). This cluster of restored vintage Airstream trailers ranges from a 1949 Airstream to a 1951 Royal Mansion. Each RV is furnished with period artifacts, chenille bedspreads, and radios tuned to swing music. Also part of the swinging scene is a Chris-Craft yacht and a Tiki Bus, both from 1947. $$.

From Bisbee you can either continue along AZ 80 to Douglas, on the Mexican border, or you can backtrack north on AZ 80 and take AZ 90 west to Sierra Vista.

Let's consider ***Douglas*** (520-364-2477; greaterdouglaschamber.com) first, which sits across the border from Agua Prieta (*ah-wah pree-etta,* meaning "dark water"), Mexico.

History buffs can take a detour on the Geronimo Trail, a well-graded dirt road, to the restored ***Slaughter Ranch*** (520-678-7935; slaughterranch.com), about 15 miles east of Douglas—and truly off the beaten path! John Slaughter, a former Texas Ranger, was the sheriff of Cochise County during the late 1880s. He is credited with running a lot of the riffraff out of the area. The ***Slaughter Ranch*** includes several historic buildings, walking paths, and lovely grounds overlooking Mexico. It is open Wed through Sun from 9:30 a.m. to 3:30 p.m. but it's always a good idea to call first. Admission.

If comfort and a certain early twentieth-century elegance are what you're looking for in lodgings, check into ***The Gadsden Hotel*** (1046 G Ave.; 520-364-4481; thegadsdenhotel.com). The Gadsden was built in 1907 as a grand hotel for cattle barons and other well-heeled travelers, including Wilford Brimley, Paul Newman, Eleanor Roosevelt, Amelia Earhart, Johnny Depp, Faye Dunaway, Lee Marvin, and Jerry Lewis. It, too, is rumored to be inhabited by a few friendly ghosts and has been featured on several paranormal television programs! It boasts a spacious lobby with an Italian marble staircase and four marble columns decorated in fourteen-karat gold leaf. Legend has it that a chip in the marble staircase was made by Pancho Villa riding his horse up the steps. This hotel, listed on the National Register of Historic Places, is being restored to its former glory. $$.

Once you've seen Douglas, you can either head west to Sierra Vista or north to Willcox.

The city of *Sierra Vista* (520-417-6960 or 800-288-3861; visitsierravista .com) can be reached by taking I-10 east from Tucson to AZ 90, or by taking AZ 80 west to AZ 90. Nestled along the San Pedro River and flanked by the towering Huachuca Mountains, Sierra Vista is known to birders around the world. A good starting point is the *San Pedro Riparian National Conservation Area* (520-258-7200; blm.gov/az). This area protects 40 miles of riparian habitat of the San Pedro River, which supports more than 350 species of birds. *The San Pedro House* (9800 AZ 90; 520-508-4445; sanpedroriver.org/wpfspr) serves as visitor center and educational hub for the preserve. The historic ranch house includes a bookstore and gift shop, and is the starting point for guided bird and river walks. It's open daily from 9:30 a.m. to 4:30 p.m. The riparian area is open from dawn till dusk.

Another excellent birding spot is *Ramsey Canyon Preserve* (520-335-8740; nature.org), which is protected by the Nature Conservancy. A languid hiking trail traces spring-fed Ramsey Creek as it flows down from the mountains. This shady canyon bristles with hummingbirds and is just one of the many reasons Sierra Vista is known as the "Hummingbird Capital of the World." This proliferation of tiny winged wonders (fourteen species) is the cornerstone of the annual *Southwest Wings* (sabo.org) birding festival that takes place every August in Sierra Vista and surrounding habitats. Ramsey Canyon is open Thurs through Mon year round; hours vary slightly by season. Admission.

At the preserve's entrance, the *Ramsey Canyon Inn Bed and Breakfast* (520-378-3010; ramseycanyoninn.com) has modern accommodations and freshly baked pies. Space in this facility books fast! $$.

Just outside the preserve is the nonprofit *Arizona Folklore Preserve* (520-378-6165; arizonafolklore.com). There Arizona's Official State Balladeer, Dolan Ellis, entertains visitors with the songs, legends, and poetry of the Old West, accompanied by stunning photographic images he has collected. The Arizona Folklore Preserve is open on weekends for performances by Ellis (a former member of the New Christy Minstrels) and other folk artists and is dedicated to the collection, presentation, and preservation of Arizona folklore.

arizonatrivia

Dueling deities: **Church Square** in the city of Douglas is believed to be the only place in the world with four churches on four corners in the same block.

Fort Huachuca is just a few minutes west of Sierra Vista. An army base that today serves as headquarters for the US Army's Intelligence Center and Information Systems Command, the fort's history stretches back to the 1870s, when it was established as a camp to protect settlers against Apache raiders. It has had an interesting history as a base for the soldiers who tracked down Geronimo and the troops who battled Pancho Villa, as well as home for the African-American cavalry units that came to be known as the Buffalo Soldiers. The fort had its ups and downs after World War II. It even closed for a while. In 1954 it was turned into the army's electronic proving ground.

Modern accommodations and charming bed-and-breakfast inns are plentiful in Sierra Vista, with nearly 900 rooms available. The nicest full-service hotel is the 148-room ***Windemere Hotel & Conference Center*** (2047 S. AZ 92; 520-459-5900; windemerehotel.com), located a few miles from the turnoff for Ramsey Canyon. $.

Willcox and Chiricahua National Monument

From Sierra Vista, travel north on AZ 90 back through Benson and then east on I-10. In 14 miles you pass through scenic ***Texas Canyon,*** which is known for its strange and spectacular rock formations. There's a rest area there if you're looking for a photo op. If you want to explore the canyon by foot or on horseback, you may want to take exit 318 and follow Dragoon Rd a quarter mile to check into the ***Triangle T Guest Ranch*** (520-586-7533; azretreatcenter .com). The ranch offers your choice of casitas and also a restaurant and saloon. Activities include horseback riding and jeep tours. $$.

Day-trippers will enjoy a visit to the nearby ***Amerind Museum*** (520-586-3666; amerind.org), which sits on property that was once part of the Triangle T. Native American artifacts are on display in a stunning collection, including prehistoric items recovered from Texas Canyon. An impressive gallery of western art stands next to the museum. The grounds also include walking paths and picnic tables set amid the boulder fields. Open Tues through Sun from 10 a.m. to 4 p.m. Admission.

Just four miles further east, at exit 322 resides a throwback roadside attraction, the infamous ***Thing.*** This "Thing" isn't the hand from *The Addams Family* series or the creature from either the John Carpenter or the Howard Hawks science fiction films. It's the *other* thing. The one advertised on the giant yellow billboards you can't help but see unless you drive through southeastern Arizona with your eyes closed. The "museum" (for want of a better description) housing "The Thing?? Mysteries of the Ages" is a barnlike building that for about three-and-a-half decades also has contained a variety of antiques. Its proud centerpiece is a mummy-like figure encased in glass. No one knows for certain if this is a genuine mummy. (It's possible: Some cliff-dwelling Native American tribes tucked their dead away in places out of reach of scavengers, and more than a few of these bodies have been recovered.) In any case, you can get in for a buck or so, and I recommend the museum to Stephen King aficionados, lovers of roadside Americana, and anyone who grew up in the 1950s or 1960s who read EC or Warren horror comics ("Look, Johnny—that thing is moving! EEYYYIII!").

The next town you reach is **Willcox** (520-384-2272; willcoxchamber.com), located in the Sulphur Springs Valley, an agricultural paradise. Family farms and orchards thrive here, along with ranches. Cattle still graze here but they do so at the edge of vineyards. This is the center of Arizona's burgeoning wine industry, producing 74 percent of the wine grapes growing in the state. In 2016, Willcox was granted AVA (American Viticultural Area) status. Tasting rooms are open in downtown, or visitors can tour the wineries where they can overlook rows of vines framed by rising mountains. **Wines of Willcox** (willcoxwines .com) provides information, maps and a list of vino-related events.

For a historic look at the area, stop by the **Chiricahua Regional Museum** (127 E. Maley St.; 520-384-3971), which chronicles the area's rich history and agriculture-based economy. The museum is open Mon through Sat from 10 a.m. to 5 p.m. Admission.

You'll find that the scenery around Willcox is quite lovely. In places this high-desert community barely resembles the Southwest. Nowhere is this more apparent than on the marsh-like **Willcox Playa Wildlife Refuge,** just south of town. Bird-watchers may want to plan a visit to occur between late Oct and mid-Feb to catch a glimpse of the sandhill cranes that nest in the playa. Sandhill

Cowboy Singer Rex Allen

Willcox's favorite son unquestionably is cowboy singer Rex Allen, whose film, television, and recording career is celebrated at the **Rex Allen "Arizona Cowboy" Museum & Willcox Cowboy Hall of Fame** (150 N. Railroad Ave.; 520-384-4583; rexallenmuseum.org). The museum also contains exhibits about frontier settlers and the cowboy way of life. The museum is open Mon from 10 a.m. to 1 p.m. when it usually features live music, a fun jam session with local musicians. It's also open Tues through Sat from 11 a.m. to 3 p.m., but minus the tunes. Admission.

Willcox hosts an annual **Rex Allen Days** (rexallendays.org) festival the first weekend in October. Featured events include a rodeo, a parade, and stage shows.

cranes are believed to be one of the oldest living species of birds. Standing 4 feet tall with a 5- to 7-foot wingspan, they are quite spectacular. Each Jan, Willcox stages a major celebration of the cranes' arrival (by the thousands) during the ***Wings over Willcox*** event (520-384-2272; wingsoverwillcox.com).

You can reach historic sites like the Chiricahua National Monument and the adobe ruins of Fort Bowie by taking AZ 186 southeast. It's 32 miles to the turn-off (on AZ 181) to ***Chiricahua National Monument*** (520-824-3560; nps.gov/chir). Here you'll find some of the most unusual and spectacular scenery in the state. Yet it's far enough off the beaten path that crowds are never a problem. The mountains rise from the desert grasslands and are crowned by an array of stone columns, towers, spires, pinnacles and balanced rocks, fringed by forest. Take the Bonita Canyon Drive through the monument, and you'll reach the top of Massai Point. You can park here and get a terrific view of the Chiricahua Mountain range, known as the "Wonderland of Rocks." Picnic tables, camping sites, and restrooms are available at marked areas within the monument. Miles of hiking trails provide a closer look at the fanciful formations. The ***Faraway Ranch Historic District*** preserves several buildings dating back to frontier times. Tours of the ranch house are offered on Sat and Sun when staffing permits. The visitor center is open daily from 8 a.m. to 4:30 p.m. Free.

Just north of the monument is ***Fort Bowie National Historic Site*** (520-847-2500; nps.gov/fobo), located a few miles down unpaved Apache Pass Road. But be prepared for a hike. The fort was established in 1862 to protect travelers from Apache raids. Today all that remains are crumbling adobe walls. A museum on the grounds displays exhibits illustrating the fort's history. An easy 1.5-mile walk from the parking lot to the fort travels past the ruins of a Butterfield Stage Coach Station and a cemetery where the son of Apache leader Geronimo is buried. The visitor center is open daily from 8:30 a.m. to 4:00 p.m. The Ruins Trail is open from sunrise to sunset.

The Chiricahua Mountains may be the most striking of Arizona's "sky island" mountains, but the range to their west is not far behind. The ***Dragoon Mountains*** are a long narrow line of mountains, stretching for 25 miles from south to north and topped with clusters of granite boulders, and oak and pine woodlands. This rough fortress once provided refuge to Apache chief, Cochise. Here in the mountains, Cochise and his followers could find food, water and medicine. They also had a commanding view of the valleys below making a surprise attack virtually impossible. After 11 years of bloody warfare, Cochise, for whom the county is named, signed the Broken Arrow Peace Treaty in 1872 at Council Rocks on the western flank of the Dragoons. When he died of natural causes two years later, his body was buried amid the granite outcroppings in an area now known as ***Cochise Stronghold*** (520-364-3468; fs.usda

.gov/coronado). The Stronghold can be reached via the Cochise Trail, a scenic hiking path climbing up and over the rocky ridgelines. The trail starts from the Cochise Stonghold Campground, located at the end of Ironwood Rd (unpaved for several miles) off US 191 in Sunsites.

Places to Stay in Southern Arizona

PATAGONIA

The Duquesne House Inn & Gardens
357 Duquesne Ave.
(520) 394-2732
theduquesnehouse.com
A former boarding house for miners reimagined as a lovely inn. Private patios are surrounded by lush gardens. $$.

TUBAC

Tubac Golf Resort and Spa
One Ave. De Otero
(520) 398-2211
tubacgolfresort.com
This resort is part of Historic Hotels of America and features structures dating back more than a century. Each hotel room is uniquely designed and features plush beds with updated bathrooms.
The resort is adjacent to 27-holes of golf and three gourmet restaurants. $$$.

TUCSON

El Presidio Bed and Breakfast Inn
297 N. Main Ave.
(800) 349-6151
elpresidiobbinn.com
The historic inn, an exquisite example of American Territorial, is tucked away amid lavish gardens in downtown. $$.

The Hilton Tucson East
7600 E. Broadway Blvd.
(520) 721-5600
This full-service atrium hotel has spacious rooms with mountain views. $$.

Westin La Paloma Resort & Spa
3800 E. Sunrise Dr.
(520) 742-6000
westinlapalomaresort.com
This vast property in north Tucson has 487 rooms, a spa, a pool with a waterslide, four restaurants, and stunning views. $$$.

YUMA

Hilton Garden Inn Yuma Pivot Point
310 N. Madison Ave.
(928) 783-1500
hiltongardeninn3.hilton.com
This lovely property sits on the banks of Colorado River just steps from downtown. Grab a room on the backside of the 4th floor for the best views. $$.

Places to Eat in Southern Arizona

BISBEE

Bisbee's Table
#2 Copper Queen Plz.
(520) 432-6788
bisbeetable.com
This dining room has a reputation for having the best burgers in town. Other menu items include salads, sandwiches, Mexican specialties, pasta, salmon, and steaks. Reservations are recommended. $$.

Cafe Cornucopia
14 Main St.
(520) 432-4820
This local favorite serves homemade soups, salads, and sandwiches in a casual setting. $.

FOR MORE INFORMATION ABOUT SOUTHERN ARIZONA

Arizona Department of Tourism
visitarizona.com

Benson-San Pedro Valley Chamber of Commerce
bensonchamberaz.com

Bisbee Tourism
discoverbisbee.com

Greater Sierra Vista Area Tourism
sierravista.org

Green Valley–Sahuarita Chamber of Commerce
greenvalleychamber.com

Metropolitan Tucson Convention & Visitors Bureau
visittucson.org

Nogales-Santa Cruz Chamber of Commerce
thenogaleschamber.org

Patagonia Area Business Association
patagoniaaz.com

Tombstone Chamber of Commerce
tombstonechamber.com

Tubac Chamber of Commerce
tubacaz.com

Yuma Convention and Visitors Bureau
visityuma.com

SIERRA VISTA

Indochine Family Restaurant
1299 E. Fry Blvd.
(520) 459-2805
indochinesv.com
Tucked away in a strip mall, this place is known for authentic Vietnamese cuisine with an occasional twist. $$.

SONOITA

Vineyard Café
3252 AZ 82
(520) 455-4779
vineyardcafesonoita.com
The Vineyard serves a creative menu of breakfast and lunch dishes using fresh ingredients. $$.

TOMBSTONE

Longhorn Restaurant
501 E. Allen St.
(520) 457-3405
bignosekates.info/longhorn
The oldest continuously operated restaurant in Tombstone is housed in a historic building and is known for steaks, ribs, Mexican food and more. $$.

TUBAC

Melio's Trattoria
2261 E. Frontage Rd.
(520) 398-8494
meliosristorante.com
Italian food created in the Roman tradition. $$.

Stables Ranch Grille & Patios
One Ave de Otero
(520) 398-2211
tubacgolfresort.com
The restaurant in the Tubac Golf Resort and Spa features savory steak and fish entrees with artistic desserts and excellent service. Diners can enjoy the summer nights under the starry sky. Live music on the weekends. $$.

TUCSON

Blue Willow Restaurant
2616 N. Campbell Ave.
(520) 327-7577
bluewillowtucson.com
Family owned for more than thirty years, Blue Willow is rated as one

of Tucson's "Best for Breakfast and Outdoor Dining." The menu features simple, fresh food day and evening. $$.

El Charro Mexican Cafe
311 N. Court Ave.
(520) 622-1922
elcharrocafe.com
Oldest family-operated Mexican restaurant in the United States, with a long tradition of spicing things up! There are multiple locations but the original is downtown and claims to be where the chimichanga originated. $$.

Sweet Tomatoes
(two locations)
6202 E. Broadway Blvd.
(520) 747-3864
4420 N. Stone Ave.
(520) 293-3343
All you care to eat from a buffet of fresh salads, from-scratch soups, and hot muffins. $.

YUMA

The Crossing Grill & Bar
2690 S. Fourth Ave.
(928) 726-5551
Talk about selection! From steak and prime rib to burgers, seafood, and pasta, The Crossing

has a little something for everyone at prices that won't break the bank. $$.

River City Grill
600 W. Third St.
(928) 782-7988
rivercitygrill.com
This delightful restaurant serves Caribbean, Mediterranean, Pacific Rim and Indian cuisine with a focus on trendy fish dishes. $$.

Takos & Beer
2701 S. Fourth Ave.
(928) 783-0099
This cozy eatery puts a gourmet spin on tacos in a casual modern setting. $.

Index